The Ultimate Plant Based Cookbook for Beginners

600 Quick & Easy Plant-Based RECIPES for Healthy Homemade Meals

Julia Criswell

Copyright © 2020 by Julia Criswell

All Right Reserved.

Under no circumstances, no part of this publication may be reproduced, distributed, or transmitted in any form or by any means, including photocopying, recording, or other electronic or mechanical methods, or by any information storage and retrieval system without the prior written permission of the copyright holder.

The information in this book is accurate and complete, however, the author and the publisher do not warrant the accuracy of the information, text and graphics contained within the book due to the rapidly changing nature of science, research, known and unknown facts and internet. The author and the publisher do not hold any responsibility for errors, omissions or contrary interpretation of the subject matter herein. This book is presented solely for motivational and informational purposes only.

CONTENTS

INTRODUCTION 9

BASIC INGREDIENTS FOR PLANT-BASED RECIPES 11

1. Simple Vegetable Broth 11
2. Parsley Veggie Broth 11
3. Turnip & Parsnip Broth 11
4. Plant-Based Cashew Cheese 11
5. Plant-Based Cheddar Cheese 12
6. Plant-Based Mozzarella Cheese 12
7. Plant-Based Parmesan Cheese 12
8. Cashew Cream Cheese 12
9. Tofu Mayonnaise 12

BREAKFAST & SMOOTHIES 13

10. Coconut Porridge with Strawberries 13
11. Broccoli Hash Browns 13
12. No-Bread Avocado Sandwich 13
13. Mexican Tofu Scramble 13
14. Lemon-Almond Waffles 14
15. Almond Flour English Muffins 14
16. Pesto Bread Twists 14
17. Classic French Toasts 14
18. Creamy Sesame Bread 15
19. Mixed Seeds Bread 15
20. Breakfast Naan Bread 15
21. Mushroom & Spinach Chickpea Omelet 16
22. Coconut & Raspberry Pancakes 16
23. Blueberry Chia Pudding 16
24. Potato & Cauliflower Hash Browns 16
25. Pumpkin Cake with Pistachios 17
26. Scrambled Tofu with Bell Pepper 17
27. Veggie Panini 17
28. Cheddar Grits with Soy Chorizo 17
29. Vanilla Crepes with Berry Cream Compote Topping 18
30. Morning Naan Bread with Mango Jam 18
31. Crispy Corn Cakes 18
32. Coconut Chia Pudding 19
33. Chocolate & Carrot Bread with Raisins 19
34. Tropical French Toasts 19
35. Mushroom Crepes 19
36. Banana French Toast with Strawberry Syrup 20
37. Cashew Cheese Pimiento Biscuits 20
38. Orange-Glazed Raspberry Muffins 20
39. Strawberry & Pecan Breakfast 20
40. Orange Granola with Hazelnuts 21
41. Sweet Orange Crepes 21
42. Coconut Oat Bread 21
43. Spicy Quinoa Bowl with Black Beans 21
44. Almond & Raisin Granola 22
45. Pecan & Pumpkin Seed Oat Jars 22
46. Simple Apple Muffins 22
47. Almond Yogurt with Berries & Walnuts 22
48. Blueberry Muesli Breakfast 22
49. Chocolate-Mango Quinoa Bowl 23
50. Orange-Carrot Muffins with Cherries 23
51. Lemony Quinoa Muffins 23
52. Almond Oatmeal Porridge 23
53. Morning Pecan & Pear Farro 24
54. Blackberry Waffles 24
55. Classic Walnut Waffles with Maple Syrup 24
56. Orange-Bran Cups with Dates 24
57. Apple-Date Couscous with Macadamia Nuts 24
58. Coconut Blueberry Muffins 25
59. Scrambled Tofu with Swiss Chard 25
60. Tangerine Banana Toast 25
61. Maple Banana Oats 25
62. Thyme Pumpkin Stir-Fry 25
63. Raspberry Almond Smoothie 26
64. Sweet Kiwi Oatmeal Bars 26
65. Spicy Apple Pancakes 26
66. Almond & Coconut Granola with Cherries 26
67. Cinnamon Buckwheat with Almonds 26
68. Amazing Yellow Smoothie 27
69. Hearty Smoothie 27
70. Carrot-Strawberry Smoothie 27
71. Power Green Smoothie 27
72. Maple Blueberry Smoothie 27
73. Energy Chia-Peach Smoothie 27
74. Morning Green Smoothie 28
75. Apple Chocolate Smoothie 28
76. Mango Rice Pudding 28
77. Tropical Smoothie Bowl 28
78. Coconut Fruit Smoothie 28
79. Cranberry Oat Cookies 28
80. Delicious Matcha Smoothie 29
81. Simple Pear Oatmeal 29
82. Fresh Peach Smoothie 29
83. Choco-Berry Smoothie 29
84. Banana-Strawberry Smoothie 29
85. Berry Quinoa Bowl 29

SOUPS & STEWS 30

86. Spinach & Kale Soup with Fried Collards 30
87. Tofu Goulash Soup 30
88. Coconut Cream Pumpkin Soup 30
89. Celery & Potato Soup 30
90. Medley of Mushroom Soup 31
91. Cauliflower Dill Soup 31
92. Broccoli Fennel Soup 31
93. Asian-Style Bean Soup 31
94. Mexican Tortilla Soup 32
95. Spicy Bean Soup 32
96. Rice Wine Mushroom Soup 32
97. Tangy Bean Tomato Soup 32
98. Spinach & Potato Soup 32
99. Turmeric Bean Soup 33
100. Arugula Coconut Soup 33
101. Roasted Basil & Tomato Soup 33
102. Pressure Cooker Green Onion & Potato Soup 33
103. Bell Pepper & Mushroom Soup 34
104. Cayenne Pumpkin Soup 34
105. Cream Soup of Zucchini with Walnuts 34
106. Homemade Ramen Soup 34
107. Black-Eyed Pea Soup 34
108. Cauliflower Soup with Leeks 35
109. Lime Lentil Soup 35
110. Spinach, Rice & Bean Soup 35
111. Ginger Broccoli Soup 35
112. Rice Noodle Soup with Beans 35
113. Vegetable & Rice Soup 36
114. Daikon & Sweet Potato Soup 36
115. Chickpea & Vegetable Soup 36
116. Italian Bean Soup 36
117. Brussels Sprouts & Tofu Soup 36
118. Rosemary White Bean Soup 37
119. Mushroom & Tofu Soup 37
120. Butternut Squash Coconut Cream Soup 37
121. Coconut Mushroom Soup 37
122. Pomodoro Cream Soup 37
123. Pasta & Tomato Soup 38
124. Mustard Green & Potato Soup 38
125. Sunday Soup 38
126. Pumpkin Soup with Apples 38
127. Potato Soup with Kale 38
128. Mediterranean Soup 39
129. Hot Bean & Corn Soup 39
130. Vegetable Soup with Vermicelli 39
131. Mushroom Curry Soup 39
132. Garlicky Broccoli Soup 39
133. Vegetable & Black Bean Soup 40
134. Basil Coconut Soup 40
135. Habanero Bean Soup with Brown Rice 40
136. Green Onion Corn & Bean Soup 40
137. Celery Butternut Squash Soup 40
138. Coconut & Tofu Soup 41
139. Garlic Veggie Bisque 41
140. Ginger Squash Soup 41
141. Easy Garbanzo Soup 41
142. Noodle Soup 42
143. Hot Lentil Soup with Zucchini 42
144. Coconut Artichoke Soup with Almonds 42
145. Classic Minestrone Soup 42
146. Turnip & Rutabaga Soup 42
147. Mushroom Rice Soup 43
148. Cold Vegetable Soup 43
149. Shallot Lentil Soup with Walnuts 43
150. Lime Pumpkin Soup 43
151. Brown Rice & Bean Chili 43
152. Spicy Potato Soup 44
153. Sweet African Soup 44
154. Spinach Soup with Gnocchi 44
155. Celery & Potato Rice Soup 44
156. Rotini & Tomato Soup 44
157. Rosemary Tomato Soup with Parmesan Croutons 45
158. Butternut Squash Soup 45
159. Green Bean & Rice Soup 45
160. Pumpkin & Garbanzo Chili with Kale 45
161. Spanish Gazpacho 46
162. Green Bean & Zucchini Velouté 46
163. Cabbage & Red Bean Chili 46
164. Vegetable Chili 46
165. Chili Gazpacho 46
166. Carrot & Mushroom Broth 47
167. Fennel & Corn Chowder 47
168. Fennel & Parsnip Bisque 47
169. Pearl Barley & Vegetable Stew 47
170. Kale & Potato Stew 47
171. Mushroom, Chickpea & Eggplant Stew 48
172. Caribbean Lentil Stew 48
173. Tomato Lentil Stew 48
174. Homemade Succotash Stew 48
175. Sudanese Veggie Stew 48
176. Balsamic Veggie & Rice Stew 49
177. Chicago-Style Vegetable Stew 49
178. Moroccan Bean Stew 49
179. Mushroom & Bean Stew 49
180. Asian Veggie Stew 50
181. Mediterranean Vegetable Stew 50
182. Chili Cannellini Bean Stew 50
183. Fall Medley Stew 50

SALADS & ENTRÉES 51

184. Greek Salad 51
185. Squash Salad 51
186. Beet Tofu Salad 51
187. Mango Rice Salad with Lime Dressing 51

#	Title	Page
188.	Savory Pasta Salad with Cannellini Beans	51
189.	Bean & Farro Salad	52
190.	Orange & Kale Salad	52
191.	African Zucchini Salad	52
192.	Tangy Nutty Brussel Sprout Salad	52
193.	Warm Collard Salad	52
194.	Roasted Mushrooms and Green Beans Salad	53
195.	Bean & Couscous Salad	53
196.	Seitan & Spinach Salad a la Puttanesca	53
197.	Tomato & Avocado Lettuce Salad	53
198.	Fried Broccoli Salad with Tempeh & Cranberries	54
199.	Balsamic Lentil Salad	54
200.	Warm Green Bean & Potato Salad	54
201.	Millet Salad with Olives & Cherries	54
202.	Daikon Salad with Caramelized Onion	54
203.	Quick Fresh Salad	55
204.	Radish & Tomato Salad	55
205.	Carrot & Cabbage Salad with Avocado & Capers	55
206.	Chickpea & Celery Salad	55
207.	Mexican Bean Salad	55
208.	Traditional Lebanese Salad	55
209.	Cucumber, Lettuce & Tomato Salad	56
210.	Tropical Salad	56
211.	Mediterranean Pasta Salad	56
212.	Zucchini & Bell Pepper Salad with Beans	56
213.	Bulgur & Kale Salad	56
214.	Cashew & Raisin Salad with & Haricots Verts	57
215.	Lettuce & Tomato Salad with Quinoa	57
216.	Minty Eggplant Salad	57
217.	Potato & Green Bean Salad	57
218.	Artichoke & Potato Salad	58
219.	Italian Vegetable Relish	58
220.	Colorful Quinoa Salad	58
221.	Radish & Cabbage Ginger Salad	58
222.	Coleslaw & Spinach Salad with Grapefruit	58
223.	Lemon Potato Salad with Kalamata Olives	59
224.	Beet & Cucumber Salad with Balsamic Dressing	59
225.	Chinese-Style Cabbage Salad	59
226.	Radicchio & Cabbage Coleslaw	59
227.	Avocado Salad with Sesame Seeds	59
228.	Cilantro Chickpea & Corn Salad	60
229.	Easy Pineapple & Jicama Salad	60
230.	Broccoli & Mango Rice Salad	60
231.	Mom´s Caesar Salad	60
232.	Baked Potato & Black-Eyed Pea Salad	60
233.	Fantastic Green Salad	61
234.	Chickpea & Quinoa Salad with Capers	61
235.	Apple & Spinach Salad with Walnut Crunch	61
236.	Dijon Potato Salad	61
237.	Apple & Arugula Salad with Walnuts	61
238.	Bean & Roasted Parsnip Salad	62
239.	Christmas Potato Salad	62
240.	Apple & Kale Salad with Raspberry Vinaigrette	62
241.	Carrot Salad with Cherries & Pecans	62
242.	Beet Slaw with Apples	62
243.	Spinach Salad with Blackberries & Pecans	62
244.	Festive Nicoise Salad Potato Salad	63
245.	Cowboy Salad	63
246.	Bell Pepper & Quinoa Salad	63
247.	Dijon Potato & Carrot Salad	63
248.	Tomato Bean & Bulgur Salad	63
249.	Cucumber & Pear Rice Salad	64
250.	Lemony Ditalini Salad with Chickpeas	64
251.	Apple & Spinach Salad with Nuts & Cranberries	64
252.	Chickpea & Faro Entrée	64
253.	Corn & Bean Quesadillas	64

LUNCH 65

#	Title	Page
254.	Tofu Cabbage Stir-Fry	65
255.	Smoked Tempeh with Broccoli Fritters	65
256.	Cheesy Cauliflower Casserole	65
257.	Spicy Veggie Steaks with Green Salad	65
258.	Mushroom Curry Pie	66
259.	Tofu & Spinach Lasagna with Red Sauce	66
260.	Curried Tofu with Buttery Cabbage	66
261.	Avocado Coconut Pie	67
262.	Green Avocado Carbonara	67
263.	Mushroom & Green Bean Biryani	67
264.	Baked Cheesy Spaghetti Squash	68
265.	Kale & Mushroom Pierogis	68
266.	Vegan Mushroom Pizza	68
267.	Grilled Zucchini with Spinach Avocado Pesto	68
268.	Eggplant Fries with Chili Aioli & Beet Salad	69
269.	Tofu Skewers with Salsa Verde & Squash Mash	69
270.	Mushroom Lettuce Wraps	69
271.	Chili Bean & Brown Rice Tortillas	70
272.	Cashew Buttered Quesadillas with Leafy Greens	70
273.	Asparagus with Creamy Puree	70
274.	Kale Mushroom Galette	70
275.	White Pizza with Mixed Mushrooms	71
276.	Seitan Cakes with Broccoli Mash	71
277.	Spicy Cheese with Tofu Balls	71
278.	Quinoa & Veggie Burgers	72
279.	Baked Tofu with Roasted Peppers	72
280.	Zoodle Bolognese	72
281.	Zucchini Boats with Vegan Cheese	72
282.	Roasted Butternut Squash with Chimichurri	73
283.	Sweet and Spicy Brussel Sprout Stir-Fry	73
284.	Black Bean Burgers with BBQ Sauce	73
285.	Creamy Brussels Sprouts Bake	73
286.	Basil Pesto Seitan Panini	74
287.	Jalapeño Quinoa Bowl with Lima Beans	74
288.	Caprese Casserole	74
289.	Tempeh Garam Masala Bake	74
290.	American-Style Tempeh Bake with Garden Peas	75
291.	Seitan Cauliflower Gratin	75

#	Item	Page
292.	Tomato Artichoke Pizza	75
293.	Zesty Rice Bowls with Tempeh	76
294.	Vegan Cordon Bleu Casserole	76
295.	Tempeh Coconut Curry Bake	76
296.	Savoy Cabbage Rolls with Tofu & Buckwheat	76
297.	Tofu Loaf with Nuts	77
298.	Mexican-Style Soy Chorizo & Rice Bowls	77
299.	Pesto Mushroom Pizza	77
300.	Tomato & Alfredo Fettuccine	77
301.	Green Beans & Grilled Tempeh	78
302.	Pea & Basil Fettuccine	78
303.	Scallion Sweet Potatoes with Chili Corn Salad	78
304.	Plant-Based Cheddar Broccoli Gratin	78
305.	Stuffed Zucchini Rolls with Tempeh & Tofu	78
306.	Hot Seitan with Rice	79
307.	Oat & Chickpea Burgers with Avocado Dip	79
308.	Bell Pepper & Tempeh Balls with Asparagus	79
309.	Bean & Spinach Casserole	80
310.	Chickpea & Bean Patties	80
311.	Vegetable & Hummus Pizza	80
312.	Black Olive & Chickpea Lunch	80
313.	Basil & Tofu Stuffed Portobello Mushrooms	81
314.	Kale Pizza with Grilled Zucchini	81
315.	Amazing Tofu Burgers	81
316.	Bean Gyros	81
317.	Saucy Seitan with Sesame Seeds	82
318.	Gingery Pea & Potato Skillet	82
319.	Broccoli Stuffed Cremini Mushrooms	82
320.	Tempeh & Vegetable Stir-Fry	82
321.	Watercress & Mushroom Spaghetti	82
322.	Rice with Green Lentil & Celery	83
323.	Spinach & Chickpea Pizza with Avocado	83
324.	Herby Quinoa with Walnuts	83
325.	Pasta Primavera with Cherry Tomatoes	83
326.	Cherry & Quinoa Tacos	84
327.	Quinoa a la Puttanesca	84
328.	Acorn Squash Stuffed with Beans & Spinach	84
329.	Cabbage & Bean Stir-Fry	84
330.	Hot Paprika Lentils	84
331.	Lemony Green Bean Risotto	85
332.	Chipotle Kidney Bean Chili	85
333.	Carrot & Black Bean Chili	85
334.	Special Butternut Squash Chili	85
335.	Mediterranean Chickpeas with Vegetables	85
336.	Southern Bean Salad	86
337.	Hot Coconut Beans with Vegetables	86
338.	Seitan & Lentil Chili	86
339.	White Salad with Walnut Pesto	86
340.	Hot Lentil Tacos with Guacamole	86
341.	Curried Indian Rolls	87
342.	Dijon Faro & Walnut Salad	87
343.	Awesome Barley Jambalaya	87
344.	Baked Mustard Beans	87
345.	Hot Bean Salad	88
346.	Rice, Lentil & Spinach Pilaf	88
347.	Parsley Bean & Olives Salad	88
348.	Habanero Pinto Beans with Bell Pepper Pot	88
349.	Cucumber & Carrot Pizza with Pesto	88

DINNER 89

#	Item	Page
350.	Black-Eyed Pea Oat Bake	89
351.	Paprika Fava Bean Patties	89
352.	Walnut Lentil Burgers	89
353.	Couscous & Quinoa Burgers	89
354.	Bean & Pecan Sandwiches	90
355.	Homemade Kitchari	90
356.	Picante Green Rice	90
357.	Asian Quinoa Sauté	90
358.	Faro & Black Bean Loaf	91
359.	Cuban-Style Millet	91
360.	Traditional Cilantro Pilaf	91
361.	Oriental Bulgur & White Beans	91
362.	One-Pot Red Lentils with Mushrooms	91
363.	Sherry Shallot Beans	92
364.	Celery Buckwheat Croquettes	92
365.	Oregano Chickpeas	92
366.	Matcha-Infused Tofu Rice	92
367.	Chinese Fried Rice	92
368.	Savory Seitan & Bell Pepper Rice	93
369.	Asparagus & Mushrooms with Mashed Potatoes	93
370.	Green Pea & Lemon Couscous	93
371.	Chimichurri Fusili with Navy Beans	93
372.	Quinoa & Chickpea Pot	93
373.	Buckwheat Pilaf with Pine Nuts	94
374.	Italian Holiday Stuffing	94
375.	Pressure Cooker Green Lentils	94
376.	Cherry & Pistachio Bulgur	94
377.	Mushroom Fried Rice	94
378.	Bean & Brown Rice with Artichokes	95
379.	Pressure Cooker Celery & Spinach Chickpeas	95
380.	Veggie Paella with Lentils	95
381.	Curry Bean with Artichokes	95
382.	Endive Slaw with Olives	95
383.	Paprika Cauliflower Tacos	96
384.	Simple Pesto Millet	96
385.	Peppered Pinto Beans	96
386.	Black-Eyed Peas with Sun-Dried Tomatoes	96
387.	Vegetarian Quinoa Curry	96
388.	Alfredo Rice with Green Beans	97
389.	Korean-Style Millet	97
390.	Lemony Chickpeas with Kale	97
391.	Dinner Rice & Lentils	97
392.	Sesame Kale Slaw	97
393.	Spicy Steamed Broccoli	97
394.	Garlic Roasted Carrots	98
395.	Eggplant & Hummus Pizza	98

396.	Miso Green Cabbage	98	423.	Sautéed Veggies with Rice ... 104
397.	Steamed Broccoli with Hazelnuts	98	424.	French Vegetable Byaldi ... 104
398.	Cilantro Okra	98	425.	Roasted Sweet Potato Porridge ... 104
399.	Citrus Asparagus	99	426.	Balsamic Artichoke Hearts ... 104
400.	Japanese-Style Tofu with Haricots Vert	99	427.	Melon & Cucumber Gazpacho ... 105
401.	Raisin & Orzo Stuffed Tomatoes	99	428.	Artichoke & Tomato Tart with Peanuts ... 105
402.	Rosemary Baked Potatoes with Cherry Tomatoes	99	429.	Chili Broccoli & Beans with Almonds ... 105
403.	Parsley Carrots & Parsnips	99	430.	Dilly Potatoes ... 105
404.	Sesame Roasted Broccoli with Brown Rice	100	431.	Orange Kale Stir-Fry ... 105
405.	Date Caramelized Vegetables	100	432.	Parsley Faro & Bean Casserole ... 106
406.	Squash & Zucchini Stir-Fry	100	433.	Sicilian Spaghetti Squash ... 106
407.	Sweet Potatoes with Curry Glaze	100	434.	Sesame Tempeh Sauté ... 106
408.	Spaghetti Squash in Tahini Sauce	100	435.	Bell Pepper & Spinach with Walnuts ... 106
409.	Cumin Red & White Cabbage with Apples	101	436.	Creamy Bell Pepper Goulash ... 107
410.	Basil Beet Pasta	101	437.	Thyme Black Bean Loaf with Artichokes ... 107
411.	Sherry Eggplants with Cherry Tomatoes	101	438.	Pomegranate Bell Peppers & Eggplants ... 107
412.	Tofu Eggplant Pizza	101	439.	Lemony Arugula with Pine Nuts ... 107
413.	Maple Green Cabbage Hash	101	440.	Leek & Mushroom Stroganoff ... 108
414.	Raisin & Pine Nut Zucchini Rolls	102	441.	Couscous & Lentil Curry ... 108
415.	Almond & Chickpea Patties	102	442.	Lentil & Sweet Potato Tortillas ... 108
416.	Korean-Style Buckwheat	102	443.	Cayenne Kale ... 108
417.	Basil Bell Pepper & Mushroom Medley	102	444.	Cinnamon-Brandy Acorn Squash ... 108
418.	Peanut Quinoa & Chickpea Pilaf	102	445.	Mustard Tofu & Cauliflower ... 109
419.	Spicy Vegetable Paella	103	446.	Eggplant with Tofu ... 109
420.	Baked Potatoes & Asparagus & Pine Nuts	103	447.	Lentil Stuffed Avocados ... 109
421.	Italian Potato & Swiss Chard Au Gratin	103	448.	Spicy Broccoli in Pecan Pesto ... 109
422.	Bean & Pecan Stuffed Mushrooms	103	449.	Bulgur & Bean Bowls with Tortilla Chips ... 109

SNAKS & SIDES ... 110

450.	Kentucky Cauliflower with Mashed Parsnips	110	475.	Carrot Nori Rolls ... 116
451.	Spinach Chips with Guacamole Hummus	110	476.	Cinnamon-Maple Popcorn ... 116
452.	Buttered Carrot Noodles with Kale	110	477.	Mediterranean Tahini Beans ... 116
453.	Parsley Pumpkin Noodles	110	478.	Hot Crunchy Nuts ... 116
454.	Curry Cauli Rice with Mushrooms	111	479.	Beet & Carrot Stir-Fry ... 116
455.	Mixed Seed Crackers	111	480.	Mustard Tofu-Avocado Wraps ... 117
456.	Grilled Tofu Mayo Sandwiches	111	481.	Maple-Glazed Butternut Squash ... 117
457.	Mushroom Broccoli Faux Risotto	111	482.	Tofu & Tomato Sandwiches ... 117
458.	Baked Spicy Eggplant	112	483.	Parmesan Baby Potatoes ... 117
459.	Mashed Broccoli with Roasted Garlic	112	484.	Guacamole with Daikon ... 117
460.	Spicy Pistachio Dip	112	485.	Tofu Stuffed Peppers ... 118
461.	Paprika Roasted Nuts	112	486.	Crispy Squash Nacho Chips ... 118
462.	Mixed Vegetables with Basil	112	487.	Pepita Cheese Tomato Chips ... 118
463.	Onion Rings & Kale Dip	113	488.	Baked Brussels Sprouts with Cranberries ... 118
464.	Soy Chorizo Stuffed Cabbage Rolls	113	489.	Four-Seed Crackers ... 118
465.	Sesame Cabbage Sauté	113	490.	Pecan Tempeh Cakes ... 119
466.	Tomatoes Stuffed with Chickpeas & Quinoa	114	491.	Lemon-Maple Glazed Carrots ... 119
467.	Herbed Vegetable Traybake	114	492.	Walnut & Tempeh Ball ... 119
468.	Louisiana-Style Sweet Potato Chips	114	493.	Yummy Vegetarian Burritos ... 119
469.	Bell Pepper & Seitan Balls	114	494.	Roman Balsamic Tomato Bruschetta ... 119
470.	Parmesan Broccoli Tots	114	495.	Spicy Nut Burgers ... 120
471.	Chocolate Bars with Walnuts	115	496.	Soy Chorizo & Avocado Tacos ... 120
472.	Dijon Roasted Asparagus	115	497.	Hazelnut Snack ... 120
473.	Paprika Tofu & Zucchini Skewers	115	498.	Curry Mango-Tofu Pitas ... 120
474.	Strawberries Stuffed with Banana Cream	115	499.	Homemade Seedy Bars ... 120

500.	Crispy Mushroom Wontons 121	514.	Paprika Baked Beans 124
501.	French Mushroom Tarts 121	515.	Middle Eastern Onion Phyllo 124
502.	Chickpea & Pecan Balls 121	516.	Arugula & Hummus Pitas 124
503.	Maple-Pumpkin Cookies 121	517.	Authentic Guacamole 124
504.	Vegetable & Rice Vermicelli Lettuce Rolls 122	518.	Cucumber Stuffed Tomatoes 124
505.	Garbanzo Quesadillas with Salsa 122	519.	Minty Berry Cocktail 125
506.	Coconut & Parsley Wraps 122	520.	Swiss Chard & Pecan Stuffed Mushrooms 125
507.	Tarragon Potato Chips 122	521.	Green Salsa 125
508.	Tamari Lentil Dip 122	522.	Primavera Lettuce Rolls 125
509.	Chili Roasted Hazelnuts 123	523.	Citrus-Parsley Mushrooms 125
510.	Balsamic Roasted Red Pepper & Pecan Crostini 123	524.	Mustard Mac & Cheese 126
511.	Paprika Hummus with Mushrooms 123	525.	Grilled Vegetables with Romesco Dip 126
512.	Bell Peppers Stuffed with Spinach & Tofu 123	526.	Cacao Nut Bites 126
513.	Kale & Hummus Pinwheels 123	527.	Berries, Nuts & Cream Bowl 126

DESSERTS & SWEET TREATS 127

528.	Vanilla Brownies 127	565.	Easy Maple Rice Pudding 135
529.	Vegan Cheesecake with Blueberries 127	566.	Vanilla Cookies with Poppy Seeds 136
530.	Lime Avocado Ice Cream 127	567.	Kiwi & Peanut Bars 136
531.	Walnut Chocolate Squares 127	568.	Tropical Cheesecake 136
532.	Vanilla White Chocolate Pudding 128	569.	Raisin Oatmeal Biscuits 136
533.	Aunt´s Apricot Tarte Tatin 128	570.	Coconut & Chocolate Brownies 136
534.	Southern Apple Cobbler with Raspberries 128	571.	Cashew & Plum Cheesecake 137
535.	Chocolate Peppermint Mousse 129	572.	Peanut Chocolate Brownies 137
536.	Raspberries Turmeric Panna Cotta 129	573.	Chocolate Campanelle with Hazelnuts 137
537.	Summer Banana Pudding 129	574.	Poppy-Granola Balls with Chocolate 137
538.	Baked Apples Filled with Nuts 129	575.	Coconut Chia Pudding 138
539.	Mint Ice Cream 129	576.	Homemade Goji Berry Chocolate Granita 138
540.	Cardamom Coconut Fat Bombs 130	577.	Maple Fruit Crumble 138
541.	Cinnamon Faux Rice Pudding 130	578.	Sherry-Lime Mango Dessert 138
542.	White Chocolate Fudge 130	579.	Almond & Chia Bites with Cherries 138
543.	Macedonia Salad with Coconut & Pecans 130	580.	Glazed Chili Chocolate Cake 138
544.	Berry Hazelnut Trifle 130	581.	Vanilla Cranberry & Almond Balls 139
545.	Avocado Truffles with Chocolate Coating 130	582.	Pressure Cooker Apple Cupcakes 139
546.	Vanilla Berry Tarts 131	583.	Roasted Apples Stuffed with Pecans & Dates ... 139
547.	Chocolate Fudge with Nuts 131	584.	Caribbean Pudding 139
548.	Chocolate & Peanut Butter Cookies 131	585.	Mango Chocolate Fudge 140
549.	Mixed Berry Yogurt Ice Pops 131	586.	Coconut & Chocolate Macaroons 140
550.	Holiday Pecan Tart 132	587.	Melon Chocolate Pudding 140
551.	Coconut Chocolate Barks 132	588.	Sicilian Papaya Sorbet 140
552.	Nutty Date Cake 132	589.	Hazelnut Topped Coconut Caramelized Bananas 140
553.	Berry Cupcakes with Cashew Cheese Icing 132	590.	Apple & Cashew Quiche 140
554.	Coconut & Chocolate Cake 133	591.	Tofu & Almond Pancakes 141
555.	Berry Macedonia with Mint 133	592.	Almond Berry Cream 141
556.	Cinnamon Pumpkin Pie 133	593.	Blueberry Lime Granizado 141
557.	Party Matcha & Hazelnut Cheesecake 134	594.	Coconut Bars with Chocolate Chips 141
558.	Pistachios & Chocolate Popsicles 134	595.	Lemon Blackberry Cake 141
559.	Oatmeal Cookies with Hazelnuts 134	596.	Cinnamon Tropical Cobbler 142
560.	Coconut Chocolate Truffles 134	597.	Balsamic-Glazed Caramelized Quinces 142
561.	Layered Raspberry & Tofu Cups 134	598.	Pumpkin Brownie 142
562.	Cashew & Cranberry Truffles 135	599.	Coconut & Date Truffles with Walnuts 142
563.	Coconut Peach Tart 135	600.	Pumpkin & Mango Lemon Cake 142
564.	Mango Muffins with Chocolate Chips 135		

RECIPE INDEX 143

INTRODUCTION

When I was growing up, I had to learn fast the rules for keeping my body in the best shape and excellent health, and going on a plant-based lifestyle was my secret.

I have been dieting primarily on plant-based foods for the last couple of years, and I feel happy, energetic, and full of life. That's why I take this opportunity to share my experiences with you through this cookbook.

This Plant-Based Cookbook is one stemmed from a deep place of passion and lessons where I guide regular dieters and beginners who want to make the switch to the plant-based lifestyle on its importance in the current age. It takes into consideration a trendy style of eating, busy schedules, and tasty ideas to ensure that each recipe produced isn't boring but delicious enough to enjoy cooking and eating.

My suggestion for you is to give the recipes a straight dive in and enjoy all the scrumptious goodness that awaits you.

What is the Plant-Based Diet?

While the plant-based diet may seem to be torn between the vegetarian and vegan diet, it is not any of them. In fact, it's not a diet but a healthy lifestyle.

It is no surprise that there is a vast argument claiming that the plant-based diet is either a vegan one (which is plant-focused) or vegetarian (which accommodates some amount of animal foods). Both cases are still incorrect. The plant-based diet uses food from plants, and it strongly rejects processed foods like white rice and added sugars. On the other hand, vegan and vegetarian diets allow some processed foods.

In this book, my goal is to present you with plant-based recipes in its most wholesome forms. The cookbook seeks to guide you. Especially the beginners on the plant-based diet, to appreciate the essentials of whole-based plant foods, giving you flexible options and various cooking combinations.

Benefits of the Plant-Based diet

Plant foods are an excellent source for many nutrients that boost the body's metabolism in many ways. They are easy to digest thanks to their rich content of antioxidants.

- **Reduced Risk of Heart Diseases**

Processed and animal foods are culprits for many heart diseases. Whole foods plant-based diet is better at nourishing the body with essential nutrients while improving the heart's function to produce and transport blood to and from the various body parts.

- **Prevents and Heals Diabetes**

Plant-based foods are excellent at reducing high blood sugars. Many studies comparing a vegetarian and vegan diet to a regular meat-filled diet proved that dieting with more plant foods reduced the risk of diabetes by 50%.

- **Improved Cognitive Incline**

Fruits and vegetables are excellent for cleansing and boosting metabolism. They release high numbers of plant compounds and antioxidants that slow or prevent cognitive decline. On a plant-based diet, the brain is boosted with sustainable energy, which promotes sharp memory, language, thinking, and judgment abilities.

- **Quick Weight Loss**

A high animal food diet is known to drive weight gain. Switching to a plant-based diet helps the body shed fat walls easily, which quickly drives weight loss.

What to eat on the Plant-Based lifestyle and PB Swaps

- **Fruits** - consume a wide range of fruits, either fresh, dried, boiled, pureed, etc.
- **Vegetables** - all vegetables are permissible on the plant-based diet, and they also provide lots of essential vitamins and minerals for the body.
- **Legumes** are an excellent source for plant-based protein and fiber. Fiber is one nutrient that many people lack, and it's important to boost its content in the body.
- **Whole Grains** provide nutrients like selenium, copper, and magnesium to the body. Meanwhile, they are rich in fiber when consumed in their whole forms. Avoid processed flours, rice, pasta, and bread on the plant-based diet but consume brown rice, whole-wheat pasta, whole-grain bread, oats, barley, buckwheat, rye, quinoa, spelt.
- **Nuts and Nut Butters** - Nuts are an essential source of selenium, vitamin E, and plant-based protein. They are excellent additions to desserts, smoothies, and snacks.
- **Seeds** are rich in calcium, vitamins, and healthy fats. Consume chia seeds, hemp seeds, flaxseeds, pumpkin seeds, sunflower seeds, sesame seeds, etc.
- **Healthy Oils and Fats** - Plants offer some sweet-smelling, healthy oils and fats options, which are perfect for baking, frying, sautéing, etc. They serve as an excellent dairy replacement and are rich in omega-3 fatty acids. Use olive oil, avocados, canola oil, walnuts, peanuts, hemp seeds, flaxseeds, chia seeds, cashew nuts, coconut oil.
- **Plant-Based Milk, Cream, and Cheeses** - going plant-based doesn't mean staying away from creamy, milky, cheesy foods. You can enjoy plant-based alternatives using almond milk, soy milk, rice milk, cashew milk, coconut milk, coconut cream, cashew cream, hemp milk, oats milk.
- **Plant-Based Meats** - Have tofu, tempeh, seitan.
- **Spices, Herbs, and Condiments** - all spices, herbs, and plant-based condiments are permissible on the plant-based diet. Use basil, parsley, turmeric, curry, black pepper, rosemary, oregano, thyme, sage, marjoram, salt, salsa, soy sauce, nutritional yeast, vinegar, homemade BBQ sauce, a homemade plant-based mayonnaise, etc.
- **Beverages** - You can drink coffee, sparkling water, tea, smoothies, etc.

BASIC INGREDIENTS FOR PLANT-BASED RECIPES

Simple Vegetable Broth

Ingredients for 4 servings

- 3 tbsp olive oil
- 2 onions, quartered
- 2 carrots, chopped
- 1 cup celeriac, chopped
- 2 garlic cloves, unpeeled and crushed
- 6 cups water
- 2 tsp soy sauce
- ⅓ cup chopped fresh cilantro
- 1 bay leaf
- Salt to taste
- ½ tsp black peppercorns

Directions and Total Time: 45 minutes

Warm the oil in a pot over medium heat. Place in onions, carrots, celeriac, and garlic. Cook for 5 minutes until softened. Pour in water, soy sauce, cilantro, bay leaf, and peppercorns. Bring to a boil, lower the heat and simmer uncovered for 30 minutes.

Let cool for a few minutes, then pour over a strainer into a pot. Divide between glass mason jars and allow cooling completely. Seal and store in the fridge up to 5 days or 1 month in the freezer.

Parsley Veggie Broth

Ingredients for 4 servings

- 1 onion, sliced
- 1 parsnip, chopped
- 1 celery stalk, chopped
- 1 potato, unpeeled and chopped
- 3 garlic cloves, minced
- 2 tbsp olive oil
- Salt and black pepper to taste
- 6 cups water
- ⅓ cup chopped fresh parsley

Directions and Total Time: 1 hour 25 minutes

Preheat oven to 425 F. Grease a baking dish with cooking spray. Put in the onion, parsnip, celery, potato, and garlic and spread them in a single layer. Sprinkle with oil, salt, and pepper. Roast the veggies for 30 minutes, turning once by half. Let cool for 10 minutes.

Transfer the vegetables to a pot over medium heat. Add in water, parsley, and salt. Bring to a boil, then lower the heat and simmer uncovered for 45 minutes until the broth has reduced slightly.

Let cool for a few minutes, then pour over a strainer into a pot. Divide between glass mason jars and allow cooling completely. Seal and store in the fridge for up to 5 days or 1 month in the freezer.

Turnip & Parsnip Broth

Ingredients for 4 servings

- 1 tbsp olive oil
- 1 onion, chopped
- 2 carrots, chopped
- 2 parsnips, coarsely chopped
- 1 turnip, coarsely chopped
- 6 cups water
- 1 beet, quartered
- 3 garlic cloves, sliced
- ¾ cup chives, chopped
- 2 bay leaves
- Salt and black pepper to taste

Directions and Total Time: 1 hour 45 minutes

Warm oil in a pot and place onion, carrots, parsnips, and turnip. Cook for 10 minutes. Pour in water, beet, garlic, chives, bay leaves, salt, and pepper. Bring to a boil, then lower the heat and simmer for 1 ½ hours. Let cool for a few minutes, then pour over a strainer into a pot. Divide between glass mason jars and allow cooling completely. Seal and store in the fridge up to 5 days.

Plant-Based Cashew Cheese

Ingredients for 4 servings

- 1 cup raw cashew nuts
- 2 tbsp freshly squeezed lemon juice
- 2 tablespoons nutritional yeast
- ¼ tsp garlic powder
- Salt and black pepper to taste
- ¼ cup water or as needed

Directions and Total Time: 10 minutes

In a blender, process the cashew nuts, lemon juice, nutritional yeast, garlic powder, salt, black pepper, and water until smooth. Adjust the taste with more lemon juice, salt, and black pepper as desired and blend again. Pour the mixture into an airtight container and use it as the recipe desires.

Plant-Based Cheddar Cheese

Ingredients for 4 servings

1 cup raw cashew nuts	2 tbsp coconut oil	1 tbsp Dijon mustard
1 red bell pepper, chopped	1 tsp garlic powder	¼ cup nutritional yeast
¼ cup tahini	2 tsp onion powder	½ tsp smoked paprika
1 tbsp tamarind sauce	1 tbsp tomato paste	1/8 tsp cayenne pepper
1 lemon, juiced	2 tsp apple cider vinegar	1 tbsp xanthan gum

Directions and Total Time: 10 minutes + chilling time

Grease a round dish with cooking spray and set aside. Pour 1 cup of water into a pot and mix in xanthan gum. Bring to a boil for 1 minute with continuous stirring. Pour the mixture into a food processor.

Add in cashew nuts, red bell pepper, salt, 1/3 cup of water, tahini, tamarind sauce, lemon juice, coconut oil, garlic powder, onion powder, tomato paste, apple cider vinegar, Dijon mustard, nutritional yeast, smoked paprika, and cayenne pepper and blend the ingredients until smooth. Quickly pour the mixture into the round dish and spread around well. Place in the fridge to set, 45 minutes to 1 hour. Remove the bowl from the fridge and invert the cheese onto a plate.

Plant-Based Mozzarella Cheese

Ingredients for 4 servings

1 cup raw cashew nuts	1 ½ tbsp freshly juiced lemon	½ cup unsweetened almond milk
¼ cup plant-based yogurt	2 tbsp nutritional yeast	4 tbsp tapioca starch

Directions and Total Time: 10 minutes + chilling time

Soak the cashews in hot water for 1 hour or overnight. Drain well. Pour the cashews into a food processor and add the yogurt, lemon juice, salt, nutritional yeast, almond milk, tapioca, and process until smooth and creamy while scraping the sides into the mixture.

Adjust the taste as needed with more salt for saltiness, nutritional yeast for cheesiness, yogurt for creaminess, and lemon juice for acidity. The texture should be smooth, creamy, and pourable.

Add the mix to a medium skillet and cook over medium heat while whisking until thickened and ball-like shape forms, 4-5 minutes. Reduce the heat to low, then use a wooden spoon to mix the mixture until loose ball forms. Transfer the mixture to a small mixing bowl. Cover the bowl with plastic wrap, refrigerate for 1 hour, and then scoop 1 tbsp pieces and form into mozzarella-like balls. Use as the recipe requires.

Plant-Based Parmesan Cheese

Ingredients for 4 servings

1 cup of raw cashews	1 tbsp Italian seasoning	½ cup nutritional yeast

Directions and Total Time: 5 minutes

In a blender, pour in the cashew nuts, Italian seasoning, nutritional yeast, and salt. Process the ingredients until smooth. Use as the recipe requires.

Cashew Cream Cheese

Ingredients for 4 servings

1 cup cashew nuts, soaked	½ cup water	¼ tsp salt

Directions and Total Time: 5 minutes

Blend the cashew nuts, water, and salt in a blender until smooth. To lighten the cream, add some water until your desired thickness is achieved.

Tofu Mayonnaise

Ingredients for 4 servings

8 oz silken tofu, cubed	1 tsp distilled white vinegar	¼ tsp Dijon mustard
1 tsp freshly squeezed lemon juice	½ tsp nutritional yeast	¼ tsp pure maple syrup

Directions and Total Time: 5 minutes

In a blender, process tofu, lemon juice, white vinegar, nutritional yeast, Dijon mustard, salt, and maple syrup until smooth.

BREAKFAST & SMOOTHIES

Coconut Porridge with Strawberries

Ingredients for 2 servings

1 tbsp flax seed powder	1 tbsp coconut flour	5 tbsp coconut cream
1 oz olive oil	1 pinch ground chia seeds	Thawed frozen strawberries

Directions and Total Time: 12 minutes

In a small bowl, mix the flax seed powder with the 3 tbsp water, and allow soaking for 5 minutes.

Place a non-stick saucepan over low heat and pour in the olive oil, vegan "flax egg," coconut flour, chia seeds, and coconut cream. Cook the mixture while stirring continuously until your desired consistency is achieved. Turn the heat off and spoon the porridge into serving bowls. Top with 4 to 6 strawberries and serve immediately.

Broccoli Hash Browns

Ingredients for 4 servings

3 tbsp flax seed powder	½ white onion, grated	1 tbsp freshly ground black pepper
1 head broccoli, cut into florets	1 tsp salt	5 tbsp plant butter, for frying

Directions and Total Time: 35 minutes

In a small bowl, mix the flax seed powder with 9 tbsp water, and allow soaking for 5 minutes. Pour the broccoli into a food processor and pulse a few times until smoothly grated.

Transfer the broccoli into a bowl, add the vegan "flax egg," white onion, salt, and black pepper. Use a spoon to mix the ingredients evenly and set aside 5 to 10 minutes to firm up a bit. Place a large non-stick skillet over medium heat and drop 1/3 of the plant butter to melt until no longer shimmering.

Ladle scoops of the broccoli mixture into the skillet (about 3 to 4 hash browns per batch). Flatten the pancakes to measure 3 to 4 inches in diameter, and fry until golden brown on one side, 4 minutes. Turn the pancakes with a spatula and cook the other side to brown too, another 5 minutes.

Transfer the hash browns to a serving plate and repeat the frying process for the remaining broccoli mixture. Serve the hash browns warm with green salad.

No-Bread Avocado Sandwich

Ingredients for 2 servings

1 avocado, sliced	2 oz little gem lettuce	1 oz tofu, sliced
1 large red tomato, sliced	½ oz plant butter	Freshly chopped parsley to garnish

Directions and Total Time: 10 minutes

Put the avocado on a plate and place the tomato slices by the avocado. Arrange the lettuce (with the inner side facing you) on a flat plate to serve as the base of the sandwich.

To assemble the sandwich, smear each leave with plant butter, and arrange some tofu slices in the leaves. Then, share the avocado and tomato slices on each cheese. Garnish with parsley and serve.

Mexican Tofu Scramble

Ingredients for 4 servings

8 oz water-packed extra firm tofu	1 tomato, finely chopped	1 tsp Mexican-style chili powder
2 tbsp plant butter, for frying	2 tbsp freshly chopped scallions	3 oz grated plant-based Parmesan
1 green bell pepper, finely chopped	Salt and black pepper to taste	

Directions and Total Time: 46 minutes

Place the tofu in between two parchment papers to drain liquid for about 30 minutes.

Melt the plant butter in a large non-stick skillet until no longer foaming. Crumble the tofu into the plant butter and fry until golden brown, stirring occasionally, making sure not to break the tofu into tiny pieces. The goal is to have the tofu like scrambled eggs, about 4 to 6 minutes.

Stir in the bell pepper, tomato, scallions, and cook until the vegetables are soft, about 4 minutes. Then, season with salt, black pepper, chili powder, and stir in the cheese to incorporate and melt about 2 minutes. Spoon the scramble into a serving platter and serve warm.

Lemon-Almond Waffles

Ingredients for 4 servings

2 tbsp flax seed powder	A pinch salt	1 cup fresh almond butter
2/3 cup almond flour	1 ½ cups almond milk	2 tbsp pure maple syrup
2 ½ tsp baking powder	2 tbsp plant butter	1 tsp fresh lemon juice

Directions and Total Time: 20 minutes

In a medium bowl, mix the flaxseed powder with 6 tbsp water and allow soaking for 5 minutes. Add the almond flour, baking powder, salt, and almond milk. Mix until well combined. Preheat a waffle iron and brush with some plant butter. Pour in a quarter cup of the batter, close the iron and cook until the waffles are golden and crisp, 2-3 minutes.

Transfer the waffles to a plate and make more waffles using the same process and ingredient proportions. In a bowl, mix the almond butter with the maple syrup and lemon juice. Spread the top with the almond-lemon mixture and serve.

Almond Flour English Muffins

Ingredients for 4 servings

2 tbsp flax seed powder	½ tsp baking powder	3 tbsp plant butter
2 tbsp almond flour	1 pinch of salt	

Directions and Total Time: 20 minutes

In a small bowl, mix the flax seed with 6 tbsp water until evenly combined and leave to soak for 5 minutes. In another bowl, evenly combine the almond flour, baking powder, and salt. Then, pour in the vegan "flax egg" and whisk again. Let the batter sit for 5 minutes to set.

Melt plant butter in a frying pan and add the mixture in four dollops. Fry until golden brown on one side, then flip the bread with a spatula and fry further until golden brown. Serve.

Pesto Bread Twists

Ingredients for 6 servings

1 ½ cups grated plant-based mozzarella cheese		
1 tbsp flax seed powder	½ tsp salt	2 oz pesto
4 tbsp coconut flour	1 tsp baking powder	Olive oil for brushing
½ cup almond flour	5 tbsp plant butter	

Directions and Total Time: 35 minutes

First, mix the flax seed powder with 3 tbsp water in a bowl, and set aside to soak for 5 minutes.

Preheat oven to 350 F and line a baking sheet with parchment paper. In a bowl, evenly combine the coconut flour, almond flour, salt, and baking powder. Melt the plant butter and cheese in a deep skillet over medium heat and stir in the vegan "flax egg." Mix in the flour mixture until a firm dough forms.

Turn the heat off, transfer the mixture in between two parchment papers, and then use a rolling pin to flatten out the dough of about an inch's thickness.

Remove the parchment paper on top and spread the pesto all over the dough. Now, use a knife to cut the dough into strips, twist each piece, and place it on the baking sheet.

Brush with olive oil and bake for 15 to 20 minutes until golden brown.

Remove the bread twist; allow cooling for a few minutes, and serve with warm almond milk.

Classic French Toasts

Ingredients for 2 servings

4 tbsp flaxseed	1 ½ tsp baking powder	½ tsp cinnamon powder
1 tsp plant butter	A pinch of salt	2 tbsp plant butter
2 tbsp coconut flour	2 tbsp coconut cream	
2 tbsp almond flour	2 tbsp coconut milk whipping cream	

Directions and Total Time: 16 minutes

For the vegan "flax egg," whisk flax seed powder and 12 tbsp water in two separate bowls and leave to soak for 5 minutes.

Grease a glass dish (for the microwave) with 1 tsp plant butter. In another bowl, mix coconut flour, almond flour, baking powder, and salt.

When the flaxseed egg is ready, whisk one portion with the coconut cream and add the mixture to the dry ingredients. Continue whisking until the mixture is smooth with no lumps. Pour the dough into the glass dish and microwave for 2 minutes or until the bread's middle part is done. Take out and allow the bread to cool. Remove the bread and slice in half. Return to the glass dish.

Whisk the remaining vegan "flax egg" with the coconut milk whipping cream until well combined. Pour the mixture over the bread slices and leave to soak. Turn the bread a few times to soak in as much of the batter. Melt 2 tbsp of the plant butter in a frying pan and fry the bread slices on both sides. Transfer to a serving plate, sprinkle with cinnamon powder, and serve.

Creamy Sesame Bread

Ingredients for 6 servings

4 tbsp flax seed powder	1 cup coconut flour	1 tsp baking powder
2/3 cup cashew cream cheese	2 tbsp psyllium husk powder	1 tbsp sesame seeds
4 tbsp sesame oil + for brushing	1 tsp salt	

Directions and Total Time: 40 minutes

In a bowl, mix the flax seed powder with 1 ½ cups water until smoothly combined and set aside to soak for 5 minutes. Preheat oven to 400 F. When the vegan "flax egg" is ready, beat in the cream cheese and sesame oil until well mixed.

Whisk in the coconut flour, psyllium husk powder, salt, and baking powder until adequately blended.

Grease a 9 x 5 inches baking tray with cooking spray, and spread the dough in the tray. Allow the mixture to stand for 5 minutes and then brush with some sesame oil.

Sprinkle with the sesame seeds and bake the dough for 30 minutes or until golden brown on top and set within. Take out the bread and allow cooling for a few minutes. Slice and serve.

Mixed Seeds Bread

Ingredients for 6 servings

3 tbsp ground flax seeds	½ cup chia seeds	2/3 cup cashew cream cheese
¾ cup coconut flour	1 tsp ground caraway seeds	½ cup melted coconut oil
1 cup almond flour	1 tsp hemp seeds	¾ cup coconut cream
3 tsp baking powder	¼ cup psyllium husk powder	1 tbsp poppy seeds
5 tbsp sesame seeds	1 tsp salt	

Directions and Total Time: 55 minutes

Preheat oven to 350 F and line a loaf pan with parchment paper.

For the vegan "flax egg," whisk flax seed powder with ½ cup water, and let the mixture sit to soak for 5 minutes. In a bowl, evenly combine the coconut flour, almond flour, baking powder, sesame seeds, chia seeds, ground caraway seeds, hemp seeds, psyllium husk powder, and salt.

In another bowl, use an electric hand mixer to whisk the cream cheese, coconut oil, coconut whipping cream, and vegan "flax egg." Pour the liquid ingredients into the dry ingredients, and continue whisking with the hand mixer until a dough forms. Transfer the dough to the loaf pan, sprinkle with poppy seeds, and bake in the oven for 45 minutes or until a knife inserted into the bread comes out clean. Remove the parchment paper with the bread, and allow cooling on a rack.

Breakfast Naan Bread

Ingredients for 6 servings

¾ cup almond flour	½ tsp baking powder	4 oz plant butter
2 tbsp psyllium husk powder	1/3 cup olive oil	2 garlic cloves, minced
½ tsp salt	Plant butter for frying	

Directions and Total Time: 25 minutes

In a bowl, mix the almond flour, psyllium husk powder, salt, and baking powder.

Mix in some olive oil and 2 cups of boiling water to combine the ingredients, like a thick porridge. Stir thoroughly and allow the dough to rise for 5 minutes.

Divide the dough into 6 to 8 pieces and mold into balls. Place the balls on a parchment paper and flatten with your hands.

Melt the plant butter in a frying pan and fry the naan on both sides to have a beautiful, golden color. Transfer the naan to a plate and keep warm in the oven. For the garlic butter, add the remaining plant butter to the frying pan and sauté the garlic until fragrant, about 3 minutes. Pour the garlic butter into a bowl and serve as a dip along with the naan.

Mushroom & Spinach Chickpea Omelet

Ingredients for 4 servings

1 cup chickpea flour	1/3 cup nutritional yeast	1 cup sautéed button mushrooms
½ tsp onion powder	½ tsp baking soda	½ cup chopped fresh spinach
½ tsp garlic powder	1 green bell pepper, chopped	1 cup halved cherry tomatoes
¼ tsp white pepper	3 scallions, chopped	1 tbsp fresh parsley leaves

Directions and Total Time: 25 minutes

In a medium bowl, mix the chickpea flour, onion powder, garlic powder, white pepper, nutritional yeast, and baking soda until well combined. Heat a medium skillet over medium heat and add a quarter of the batter. Swirl the pan to spread the batter across the pan. Scatter a quarter each of the bell pepper, scallions, mushrooms, and spinach on top and cook until the bottom part of the omelet sets, 1-2 minutes.

Carefully flip the omelet and cook the other side until set and golden brown. Transfer the omelet to a plate and make the remaining omelets. Serve the omelet with the tomatoes and garnish with the parsley leaves.

Coconut & Raspberry Pancakes

Ingredients for 4 servings

2 tbsp flax seed powder	1 tsp baking soda	½ tsp cinnamon powder
½ cup coconut milk	A pinch salt	2 tbsp unsweetened coconut flakes
¼ cup fresh raspberries, mashed	1 tbsp coconut sugar	2 tsp plant butter
½ cup oat flour	2 tbsp pure date syrup	Fresh raspberries for garnishing

Directions and Total Time: 25 minutes

In a medium bowl, mix the flax seed powder with the 6 tbsp water and allow thicken for 5 minutes. Mix in coconut milk and raspberries. Add the oat flour, baking soda, salt, coconut sugar, date syrup, and cinnamon powder. Fold in the coconut flakes until well combined.

Working in batches, melt a quarter of the butter in a non-stick skillet and add ¼ cup of the batter. Cook until set beneath and golden brown, 2 minutes. Flip the pancake and cook on the other side until set and golden brown, 2 minutes. Transfer to a plate and make the remaining pancakes using the rest of the ingredients in the same proportions. Garnish the pancakes with some raspberries and serve warm!

Blueberry Chia Pudding

Ingredients for 2 servings

¾ cup coconut milk	½ cup blueberries	Chopped walnuts to garnish
½ tsp vanilla extract	2 tbsp chia seeds	

Directions and Total Time: 5 minutes + chilling time

In a blender, pour the coconut milk, vanilla extract, and half of the blueberries. Process the ingredients at high speed until the blueberries have incorporated into the liquid. Open the blender and mix in the chia seeds. Share the mixture into two breakfast jars, cover, and refrigerate for 4 hours to allow the mixture gel. Garnish the pudding with the remaining blueberries and walnuts. Serve immediately.

Potato & Cauliflower Hash Browns

Ingredients for 4 servings

3 tbsp flax seed powder	1 big head cauliflower, riced	Salt and black pepper to taste
2 large potatoes, shredded	½ white onion, grated	4 tbsp plant butter

Directions and Total Time: 35 minutes

In a medium bowl, mix the flaxseed powder and 9 tbsp water. Allow thicken for 5 minutes for the vegan "flax egg." Add the potatoes, cauliflower, onion, salt, and black pepper to the vegan "flax egg" and mix until well combined. Allow sitting for 5 minutes to thicken.

Working in batches, melt 1 tbsp of plant butter in a non-stick skillet and add 4 scoops of the hashbrown mixture to the skillet. Make sure to have 1 to 2-inch intervals between each scoop.

Use the spoon to flatten the batter and cook until compacted and golden brown on the bottom part, 2 minutes. Flip the hashbrowns and cook further for 2 minutes or until the vegetable cook and is golden brown. Transfer to a paper-towel-lined plate to drain grease. Make the remaining hashbrowns using the remaining ingredients. Serve warm.

Pumpkin Cake with Pistachios

Ingredients for 4 servings

- 2 tbsp flaxseed powder
- 3 tbsp vegetable oil
- ¾ cup canned pumpkin puree
- ½ cup pure corn syrup
- 3 tbsp pure date sugar
- 1 ½ cups whole-wheat flour
- ½ tsp cinnamon powder
- ½ tsp baking powder
- ¼ tsp cloves powder
- ½ tsp allspice powder
- ½ tsp nutmeg powder
- 2 tbsp chopped pistachios

Directions and Total Time: 70 minutes

Preheat the oven to 350 F and lightly coat an 8 x 4-inch loaf pan with cooking spray. In a bowl, mix the flax seed powder with 6 tbsp water and allow thicken for 5 minutes to make the vegan "flax egg."

In a bowl, whisk the vegetable oil, pumpkin puree, corn syrup, date sugar, and vegan "flax egg." In another bowl, mix the flour, cinnamon powder, baking powder, cloves powder, allspice powder, and nutmeg powder. Add this mixture to the wet batter and mix until well combined. Pour the batter into the loaf pan, sprinkle the pistachios on top, and gently press the nuts onto the batter to stick.

Bake in the oven for 50-55 minutes or until a toothpick inserted into the cake comes out clean. Remove the cake onto a wire rack, allow cooling, slice, and serve.

Scrambled Tofu with Bell Pepper

Ingredients for 4 servings

- 2 tbsp plant butter, for frying
- 1 (14 oz) pack firm tofu, crumbled
- 1 red bell pepper, chopped
- 1 green bell pepper, chopped
- 1 tomato, finely chopped
- 2 tbsp chopped fresh green onions
- Salt and black pepper to taste
- 1 tsp turmeric powder
- 1 tsp Creole seasoning
- ½ cup chopped baby kale
- ¼ cup grated plant-based Parmesan

Directions and Total Time: 20 minutes

Melt the plant butter in a skillet over medium heat and add the tofu. Cook with occasional stirring until the tofu is light golden brown while, making sure not to break the tofu into tiny bits but to have scrambled egg resemblance, 5 minutes.

Stir in the bell peppers, tomato, green onions, salt, black pepper, turmeric powder, and Creole seasoning. Sauté until the vegetables soften, 5 minutes. Mix in the kale to wilt, 3 minutes and then half of the plant-based Parmesan cheese. Allow melting for 1 to 2 minutes and then turn the heat off. Top with the remaining cheese and serve warm.

Veggie Panini

Ingredients for 4 servings

- 1 tbsp olive oil
- 1 cup sliced button mushrooms
- Salt and black pepper to taste
- 1 ripe avocado, sliced
- 2 tbsp freshly squeezed lemon juice
- 1 tbsp chopped parsley
- ½ tsp pure maple syrup
- 8 slices whole-wheat ciabatta
- 4 oz sliced plant-based Parmesan

Directions and Total Time: 30 minutes

Heat the olive oil in a medium skillet over medium heat and sauté the mushrooms until softened, 5 minutes. Season with salt and black pepper. Turn the heat off.

Preheat a panini press to medium heat, 3 to 5 minutes. Mash the avocado in a medium bowl and mix in the lemon juice, parsley, and maple syrup. Spread the mixture on 4 bread slices, divide the mushrooms and plant-based Parmesan cheese on top. Cover with the other bread slices and brush the top with olive oil. Grill the sandwiches one after another in the heated press until golden brown, and the cheese is melted. Serve.

Cheddar Grits with Soy Chorizo

Ingredients for 6 servings

- 1 cup quick-cooking grits
- ½ cup grated plant-based cheddar
- 2 tbsp peanut butter
- 1 cup soy chorizo, chopped
- 1 cup corn kernels
- 2 cups vegetable broth

Directions and Total Time: 25 minutes

Preheat oven to 380 F.

Pour the broth in a pot and bring to a boil over medium heat. Stir in salt and grits. Lower the heat and cook until the grits are thickened, stirring often. Turn the heat off, put in the plant-based cheddar cheese, peanut butter, soy chorizo, and corn, and mix well. Spread the mixture into a greased baking dish and bake for 45 minutes until slightly puffed and golden brown. Serve right away.

Vanilla Crepes with Berry Cream Compote Topping

Ingredients for 4 servings

For the berry cream:

2 tbsp plant butter	1 tsp vanilla extract	½ cup fresh raspberries
2 tbsp pure date sugar	½ cup fresh blueberries	½ cup whipped coconut cream

For the crepes:

2 tbsp flax seed powder	¼ tsp salt	1 ½ cups water
1 tsp vanilla extract	2 cups almond flour	3 tbsp plant butter for frying
1 tsp pure date sugar	1 ½ cups almond milk	

Directions and Total Time: 35 minutes

Melt butter in a pot over low heat and mix in the date sugar, and vanilla. Cook until the sugar melts and then toss in berries. Allow softening for 2-3 minutes. Set aside to cool.

In a medium bowl, mix the flax seed powder with 6 tbsp water and allow thicken for 5 minutes to make the vegan "flax egg." Whisk in vanilla, date sugar, and salt. Pour in a quarter cup of almond flour and whisk, then a quarter cup of almond milk, and mix until no lumps remain. Repeat the mixing process with the remaining almond flour and almond milk in the same quantities until exhausted.

Mix in 1 cup of water until the mixture is runny like that of pancakes and add the remaining water until it is lighter. Brush a large non-stick skillet with some butter and place over medium heat to melt. Pour 1 tablespoon of the batter in the pan and swirl the skillet quickly and all around to coat the pan with the batter. Cook until the batter is dry and golden brown beneath, about 30 seconds.

Use a spatula to carefully flip the crepe and cook the other side until golden brown too. Fold the crepe onto a plate and set aside. Repeat making more crepes with the remaining batter until exhausted. Plate the crepes, top with the whipped coconut cream and the berry compote. Serve immediately.

Morning Naan Bread with Mango Jam

Ingredients for 4 servings

¾ cup almond flour	2 cups boiling water	1 lemon, juiced
1 tsp salt + extra for sprinkling	2 tbsp plant butter for frying	A pinch saffron powder
1 tsp baking powder	4 cups heaped chopped mangoes	1 tsp cardamom powder
1/3 cup olive oil	1 cup pure maple syrup	

Directions and Total Time: 40 minutes

In a large bowl, mix the almond flour, salt, and baking powder. Mix in the olive oil and boiling water until smooth, thick batter forms. Allow the dough to rise for 5 minutes. Form balls out of the dough, place each on a baking paper, and use your hands to flatten the dough.

Working in batches, melt the plant butter in a large skillet and fry the dough on both sides until set and golden brown on each side, 4 minutes per bread. Transfer to a plate and set aside for serving.

Add mangoes, maple syrup, lemon juice, and 3 tbsp water in a pot and cook until boiling, 5 minutes. Mix in saffron and cardamom powders and cook further over low heat until the mangoes soften. Mash the mangoes with the back of the spoon until relatively smooth with little chunks of mangoes in a jam. Cool completely. Spoon the jam into sterilized jars and serve with the naan bread.

Crispy Corn Cakes

Ingredients for 4 servings

1 tbsp flaxseed powder	1 tsp salt	4 tbsp olive oil
2 cups yellow cornmeal	2 tsp baking powder	1 cup tofu mayonnaise for serving

Directions and Total Time: 35 minutes

In a bowl, mix the flax seed powder with 3 tbsp water and allow thicken for 5 minutes to form the vegan "flax egg." Mix in 1 cup of water and then whisk in the cornmeal, salt, and baking powder until soup texture forms but not watery.

Heat a quarter of the olive oil in a griddle pan and pour in a quarter of the batter. Cook until set and golden brown beneath, 3 minutes. Flip the cake and cook the other side until set and golden brown too. Plate the cake and make three more with the remaining oil and batter. Top the cakes with some tofu mayonnaise before serving.

Coconut Chia Pudding

Ingredients for 4 servings

- 1 cup coconut milk
- ½ tsp vanilla extract
- 3 tbsp chia seeds
- ½ cup granola
- 2/3 cup chopped sweet nectarine

Directions and Total Time: 5 minutes+ cooling time

In a medium bowl, mix the coconut milk, vanilla, and chia seeds until well combined. Divide the mixture between 4 breakfast cups and refrigerate for at least 4 hours to allow the mixture to gel. Top with the granola and nectarine. Serve.

Chocolate & Carrot Bread with Raisins

Ingredients for 4 servings

- 1 ½ cup whole-wheat flour
- ¼ cup almond flour
- ¼ tsp salt
- ¼ tsp cloves powder
- ¼ tsp cayenne pepper
- 1 tbsp cinnamon powder
- ½ tsp nutmeg powder
- 1 ½ tsp baking powder
- 2 tbsp flax seed powder
- ½ cup pure date sugar
- ¼ cup pure maple syrup
- ¾ tsp almond extract
- 1 tbsp grated lemon zest
- ½ cup unsweetened applesauce
- ¼ cup olive oil
- 4 carrots, shredded
- 3 tbsp unsweetened chocolate chips
- 2/3 cup black raisins

Directions and Total Time: 75 minutes

Preheat oven to 375 F and line a loaf tin with baking paper. In a bowl, mix all the flours, salt, cloves powder, cayenne pepper, cinnamon powder, nutmeg powder, and baking powder.

In another bowl, mix the flax seed powder, 6 tbsp water, and allow thicken for 5 minutes. Mix in the date sugar, maple syrup, almond extract, lemon zest, applesauce, and olive oil. Combine both mixtures until smooth and fold in the carrots, chocolate chips, and raisins.

Pour the mixture into a loaf pan and bake in the oven until golden brown on top or a toothpick inserted into the bread comes out clean, 45-50 minutes. Remove from the oven, transfer the bread onto a wire rack to cool, slice, and serve.

Tropical French Toasts

Ingredients for 4 servings

- 2 tbsp flax seed powder
- 1 ½ cups unsweetened almond milk
- ½ cup almond flour
- 2 tbsp maple syrup + extra for drizzling
- 2 pinches of salt
- ½ tbsp cinnamon powder
- ½ tsp fresh lemon zest
- 1 tbsp fresh pineapple juice
- 8 whole-grain bread slices

Directions and Total Time: 55 minutes

Preheat the oven to 400 F and lightly grease a roasting rack with olive oil. Set aside.

In a medium bowl, mix the flax seed powder with 6 tbsp water and allow thicken for 5 to 10 minutes. Whisk in the almond milk, almond flour, maple syrup, salt, cinnamon powder, lemon zest, and pineapple juice. Soak the bread on both sides in the almond milk mixture and allow sitting on a plate for 2 to 3 minutes.

Heat a large skillet over medium heat and place the bread in the pan. Cook until golden brown on the bottom side. Flip the bread and cook further until golden brown on the other side, 4 minutes in total. Transfer to a plate, drizzle some maple syrup on top and serve immediately.

Mushroom Crepes

Ingredients for 4 servings

- 1 cup whole-wheat flour
- 1 tsp onion powder
- ½ tsp baking soda
- ¼ tsp salt
- 1 cup pressed, crumbled tofu
- ⅓ cup plant-based milk
- ¼ cup lemon juice
- 2 tbsp extra-virgin olive oil
- ½ cup finely chopped mushrooms
- ½ cup finely chopped onion
- 2 cups collard greens

Directions and Total Time: 25 minutes

Combine the flour, onion powder, baking soda, and salt in a bowl. Blitz the tofu, milk, lemon juice, and oil in a food processor over high speed for 30 seconds. Pour over the flour mixture and mix to combine well. Add in the mushrooms, onion, and collard greens.

Heat a skillet and grease with cooking spray. Lower the heat and spread a ladleful of the batter across the surface of the skillet. Cook for 4 minutes on both sides or until set. Remove to a plate. Repeat the process until no batter is left, greasing with a little more oil, if needed. Serve.

Banana French Toast with Strawberry Syrup

Ingredients for 8 servings

1 banana, mashed
1 cup coconut milk
1 tsp pure vanilla extract
¼ tsp ground nutmeg
½ tsp ground cinnamon
1 ½ tsp arrowroot powder
A pinch of salt
8 slices whole-grain bread
1 cup strawberries
2 tbsp water
2 tbsp maple syrup

Directions and Total Time: 40 minutes

Preheat oven to 350 F.

In a bowl, stir banana, coconut milk, vanilla, nutmeg, cinnamon, arrowroot, and salt. Dip each bread slice in the banana mixture and arrange on a baking tray. Spread the remaining banana mixture over the top. Bake for 30 minutes, until the tops are lightly browned. In a pot over medium heat, put the strawberries, water, and maple syrup. Simmer for 15-10 minutes, until the berries breaking up and the liquid has reduced. Serve topped with the strawberry syrup.

Cashew Cheese Pimiento Biscuits

Ingredients for 4 servings

2 cups whole-wheat flour
2 tsp baking powder
1 tsp salt
½ tsp baking soda
½ tsp garlic powder
¼ tsp black pepper
¼ cup plant butter, cold and cubed
¾ cup coconut milk
1 cup shredded cashew cheese
1 (4 oz) jar chopped pimientos,
1 tbsp melted unsalted plant butter

Directions and Total Time: 30 minutes

Preheat the oven to 450 F and line a baking sheet with parchment paper. Set aside. In a medium bowl, mix the flour, baking powder, salt, baking soda, garlic powder, and black pepper. Add the cold butter using a hand mixer until mixture is the size of small peas. Pour in ¾ of the coconut milk and continue whisking. Continue adding the remaining coconut milk, a tablespoonful at a time, until dough forms.

Mix in the cashew cheese and pimientos. (If the dough is too wet to handle, mix in a little bit more of flour until it is manageable). Place the dough on a lightly floured surface and flatten the dough into ½-inch thickness.

Use a 2 ½-inch round cutter to cut out biscuits' pieces from the dough. Gather, re-roll the dough once and continue cutting out biscuits. Arrange the biscuits on the prepared pan and brush the tops with the melted butter. Bake for 12-14 minutes, or until the biscuits are golden brown. Cool and serve.

Orange-Glazed Raspberry Muffins

Ingredients for 4 servings

2 tbsp flax seed powder
2 cups whole-wheat flour
1 ½ tsp baking powder
A pinch salt
½ cup plant butter, softened
2 cups pure date sugar
½ cup oat milk
2 tsp vanilla extract
1 lemon, zested
1 cup dried raspberries
2 tbsp orange juice

Directions and Total Time: 40 minutes

Preheat oven to 400 F and grease 6 muffin cups with cooking spray. In a small bowl, mix the flax seed powder with 6 tbsp water and allow thicken for 5 minutes to make the vegan "flax egg." In a medium bowl, mix the flour, baking powder, and salt. In another bowl, cream the plant butter, half of the date sugar, and vegan "flax egg." Mix in the oat milk, vanilla, and lemon zest.

Combine both mixtures, fold in raspberries, and fill muffin cups two-thirds way up with the batter. Bake for 20-25 minutes. In a medium bowl, whisk orange juice and remaining date sugar until smooth. Remove the muffins when ready and transfer to a wire rack to cool. Drizzle the glaze on top to serve.

Strawberry & Pecan Breakfast

Ingredients for 2 servings

1 (14-oz) can coconut milk, refrigerated overnight
1 cup granola
½ cup pecans, chopped
1 cup sliced strawberries

Directions and Total Time: 15 minutes

Drain the coconut milk liquid. Layer the coconut milk solids, granola, and strawberries in small glasses. Top with chopped pecans and serve right away.

Orange Granola with Hazelnuts

Ingredients for 5 servings

2 cups rolled oats
¾ cup whole-wheat flour
1 tbsp ground cinnamon
1 tsp ground ginger

½ cup sunflower seeds
½ cup hazelnuts, chopped
½ cup pumpkin seeds
½ cup shredded coconut

1 ¼ cups orange juice
½ cup dried cherries
½ cup goji berries

Directions and Total Time: 50 minutes

Preheat oven to 350 F.

In a bowl, combine the oats, flour, cinnamon, ginger, sunflower seeds, hazelnuts, pumpkin seeds, and coconut. Pour in the orange juice, toss to mix well.

Transfer to a baking sheet and bake for 15 minutes. Turn the granola and continue baking until it is crunchy, about 30 minutes. Stir in the cherries and goji berries and store in the fridge for up to 14 days.

Sweet Orange Crepes

Ingredients for 4 servings

2 tbsp flax seed powder
1 tsp vanilla extract
1 tsp pure date sugar

¼ tsp salt
2 cups almond flour
1 ½ cups oat milk

½ cup melted plant butter
3 tbsp fresh orange juice
3 tbsp plant butter for frying

Directions and Total Time: 30 minutes

In a medium bowl, mix the flax seed powder with 6 tbsp water and allow thicken for 5 minutes to make the vegan "flax egg." Whisk in the vanilla, date sugar, and salt.

Pour in a quarter cup of almond flour and whisk, then a quarter cup of oat milk, and mix until no lumps remain. Repeat the mixing process with the remaining almond flour and almond milk in the same quantities until exhausted.

Mix in the plant butter, orange juice, and half of the water until the mixture is runny like pancakes. Add the remaining water until the mixture is lighter. Brush a non-stick skillet with some butter and place over medium heat to melt.

Pour 1 tablespoon of the batter in the pan and swirl the skillet quickly and all around to coat the pan with the batter. Cook until the batter is dry and golden brown beneath, about 30 seconds.

Use a spatula to flip the crepe and cook the other side until golden brown too. Fold the crepe onto a plate and set aside. Repeat making more crepes with the remaining batter until exhausted. Drizzle some maple syrup on the crepes and serve.

Coconut Oat Bread

Ingredients for 4 servings

4 cups whole-wheat flour
¼ tsp salt

½ cup rolled oats
1 tsp baking soda

1 ¾ cups coconut milk, thick
2 tbsp pure maple syrup

Directions and Total Time: 50 minutes

Preheat the oven to 400 F.

In a bowl, mix flour, salt, oats, and baking soda. Add in coconut milk and maple syrup and whisk until dough forms. Dust your hands with some flour and knead the dough into a ball. Shape the dough into a circle and place on a baking sheet.

Cut a deep cross on the dough and bake in the oven for 15 minutes at 450 F. Then, reduce the temperature to 400 F and bake further for 20 to 25 minutes or until a hollow sound is made when the bottom of the bread is tapped. Slice and serve.

Spicy Quinoa Bowl with Black Beans

Ingredients for 4 servings

1 cup brown quinoa, rinsed
3 tbsp plant-based yogurt
½ lime, juiced

2 tbsp chopped fresh cilantro
1 (5 oz) can black beans, drained
3 tbsp tomato salsa

¼ avocado, sliced
2 radishes, shredded
1 tbsp pepitas (pumpkin seeds)

Directions and Total Time: 25 minutes

Cook the quinoa with 2 cups of slightly salted water in a medium pot over medium heat or until the liquid absorbs, 15 minutes. Spoon the quinoa into serving bowls and fluff with a fork.

In a small bowl, mix the yogurt, lime juice, cilantro, and salt. Divide this mixture on the quinoa and top with the beans, salsa, avocado, radishes, and pepitas. Serve immediately.

Almond & Raisin Granola

Ingredients for 8 servings

5 ½ cups old-fashioned oats	1 cup golden raisins	½ tsp ground cinnamon
1 ½ cups chopped walnuts	1 cup shaved almonds	¼ tsp ground allspice
½ cup shelled sunflower seeds	1 cup pure maple syrup	A pinch of salt

Directions and Total Time: 20 minutes

Preheat oven to 325 F. In a baking dish, place the oats, walnuts, and sunflower seeds. Bake for 10 minutes. Lower the heat from the oven to 300 F. Stir in the raisins, almonds, maple syrup, cinnamon, allspice, and salt. Bake for an additional 15 minutes. Allow cooling before serving.

Pecan & Pumpkin Seed Oat Jars

Ingredients for 5 servings

2 ½ cups old-fashioned rolled oats	5 cups unsweetened soy milk	1 tsp ground cardamom
5 tbsp pumpkin seeds	2 ½ tsp agave syrup	1 tsp ground ginger
5 tbsp chopped pecans	Salt to taste	

Directions and Total Time: 10 minutes + chilling time

In a bowl, put oats, pumpkin seeds, pecans, soy milk, agave syrup, salt, cardamom, and ginger and toss to combine. Divide the mixture between mason jars. Seal the lids and transfer to the fridge to soak for 10-12 hours.

Simple Apple Muffins

Ingredients for 4 servings

For the muffins:

1 flax seed powder + 3 tbsp water	2 tsp baking powder	1/3 cup melted plant butter
1 ½ cups whole-wheat flour	¼ tsp salt	1/3 cup flax milk
¾ cup pure date sugar	1 tsp cinnamon powder	2 apples, chopped

For topping:

1/3 cup whole-wheat flour	½ cup cold plant butter, cubed
½ cup pure date sugar	1 ½ tsp cinnamon powder

Directions and Total Time: 40 minutes

Preheat oven to 400 F and grease 6 muffin cups with cooking spray. In a bowl, mix the flax seed powder with water and allow thicken for 5 minutes to make the vegan "flax egg."

In a bowl, mix flour, date sugar, baking powder, salt, and cinnamon powder. Whisk in the butter, vegan "flax egg," flax milk, and fold in the apples. Fill the muffin cups two-thirds way up with the batter.

In a bowl, mix remaining flour, date sugar, cold butter, and cinnamon powder. Sprinkle the mixture on the muffin batter. Bake for 20 minutes. Remove the muffins onto a wire rack, allow cooling, and serve.

Almond Yogurt with Berries & Walnuts

Ingredients for 4 servings

4 cups almond milk	2 tbsp pure malt syrup	¼ cup chopped toasted walnuts
Dairy-Free yogurt, cold	2 cups mixed berries, chopped	

Directions and Total Time: 10 minutes

In a medium bowl, mix the yogurt and malt syrup until well-combined. Divide the mixture into 4 breakfast bowls. Top with the berries and walnuts. Enjoy immediately.

Blueberry Muesli Breakfast

Ingredients for 5 servings

2 cups spelt flakes	¼ cup raisins	¼ cup non-dairy chocolate chips
2 cups puffed cereal	¼ cup dried cranberries	3 tsp ground cinnamon
¼ cup sunflower seeds	¼ cup chopped dried figs	½ cup coconut milk
¼ cup almonds	¼ cup shredded coconut	½ cup blueberries

Directions and Total Time: 10 minutes

In a bowl, combine the spelt flakes, puffed cereal, sunflower seeds, almonds, raisins, cranberries, figs, coconut, chocolate chips, and cinnamon. Toss to mix well. Pour in the coconut milk. Let sit for 1 hour and serve topped with blueberries.

Chocolate-Mango Quinoa Bowl

Ingredients for 2 servings

- 1 cup quinoa
- 1 tsp ground cinnamon
- 1 cup non-dairy milk
- 1 large mango, chopped
- 3 tbsp unsweetened cocoa powder
- 2 tbsp almond butter
- 1 tbsp hemp seeds
- 1 tbsp walnuts
- ¼ cup raspberries

Directions and Total Time: 35 minutes

In a pot combine the quinoa, cinnamon, milk, and 1 cup water over medium heat. Bring to a boil, low heat, and simmer covered for 25-30 minutes. In a bowl, mash the mango and mix cocoa powder, almond butter, and hemp seeds. In a serving bowl, place cooked quinoa and mango mixture. Top with walnuts and raspberries. Serve immediately.

Orange-Carrot Muffins with Cherries

Ingredients for 6 servings

- 1 tsp vegetable oil
- 2 tbsp almond butter
- ¼ cup non-dairy milk
- 1 orange, peeled
- 1 carrot, coarsely chopped
- 2 tbsp chopped dried cherries
- 3 tbsp molasses
- 2 tbsp ground flaxseed
- 1 tsp apple cider vinegar
- 1 tsp pure vanilla extract
- ½ tsp ground cinnamon
- ½ tsp ground ginger
- ¼ tsp ground nutmeg
- ¼ tsp allspice
- ¾ cup whole-wheat flour *oats?*
- 1 tsp baking powder
- ½ tsp baking soda
- ½ cup rolled oats
- 2 tbsp raisins
- 2 tbsp sunflower seeds

Directions and Total Time: 45 minutes

Preheat oven to 350 F. Grease 6 muffin cups with vegetable oil.

In a food processor, add the almond butter, milk, orange, carrot, cherries, molasses, flaxseed, vinegar, vanilla, cinnamon, ginger, nutmeg, and allspice and blend until smooth.

In a bowl, combine the flour, baking powder, and baking soda. Fold in the wet mixture and gently stir to combine. Mix in the oats, raisins, and sunflower seeds. Divide the batter between muffin cups. Put in a baking tray and bake for 30 minutes.

Lemony Quinoa Muffins

Ingredients for 5 servings

- 2 tbsp coconut oil melted, plus more for coating the muffin tin
- ¼ cup ground flaxseed
- 2 cups unsweetened lemon curd
- ½ cup pure date sugar
- 1 tsp apple cider vinegar
- 2 ½ cups whole-wheat flour
- 1 ½ cups cooked quinoa
- 2 tsp baking soda
- A pinch of salt
- ½ cup raisins

Directions and Total Time: 25 minutes

Preheat oven to 400 F.

In a bowl, combine the flaxseed and ½ cup water. Stir in the lemon curd, sugar, coconut oil, and vinegar. Add in flour, quinoa, baking soda, and salt. Put in the raisins, be careful not to fluffy.

Divide the batter between greased with coconut oil cups of the tin and bake for 20 minutes until golden and set. Allow cooling slightly before removing from the tin. Serve.

Almond Oatmeal Porridge

Ingredients for 4 servings

- 2 ½ cups vegetable broth
- 2 ½ cups almond milk
- ½ cup steel-cut oats
- 1 tbsp pearl barley
- ½ cup slivered almonds
- ¼ cup nutritional yeast
- 2 cups old-fashioned rolled oats

Directions and Total Time: 25 minutes

Pour the broth and almond milk in a pot over medium heat and bring to a boil. Stir in oats, pearl barley, almond slivers, and nutritional yeast. Reduce the heat and simmer for 20 minutes. Add in the rolled oats, cook for an additional 5 minutes, until creamy. Allow cooling before serving.

Morning Pecan & Pear Farro

Ingredients for 4 servings

2 cups water	1 cup farro	2 pears, peeled, cored, and chopped
½ tsp salt	1 tbsp plant butter	¼ cup chopped pecans

Directions and Total Time: 20 minutes

Bring water to a boil in a pot over high heat. Stir in salt and farro. Lower the heat, cover, and simmer for 15 minutes until the farro is tender and the liquid has absorbed. Turn the heat off and add in the butter, pears, and pecans. Cover and rest for 12-15 minutes. Serve immediately.

Blackberry Waffles

Ingredients for 4 servings

1 ½ cups whole-heat flour	½ tsp salt	1 tsp lemon zest
½ cup old-fashioned oats	1 tsp ground cinnamon	¼ cup plant butter, melted
¼ cup date sugar	2 cups soy milk	½ cup fresh blackberries
3 tsp baking powder	1 tbsp fresh lemon juice	

Directions and Total Time: 15 minutes

Preheat the waffle iron.

In a bowl, mix flour, oats, sugar, baking powder, salt, and cinnamon. Set aside. In another bowl, combine milk, lemon juice, lemon zest, and butter. Pour into the wet ingredients and whisk to combine. Add the batter to the hot greased waffle iron, using approximately a ladleful for each waffle. Cook for 3-5 minutes, until golden brown. Repeat the process until no batter is left. Serve topped with blackberries.

Classic Walnut Waffles with Maple Syrup

Ingredients for 4 servings

1 ¾ cups whole-wheat flour	1 tbsp baking powder	3 tbsp pure maple syrup
⅓ cup coarsely ground walnuts	1 ½p cups soy milk	3 tbsp plant butter, melted

Directions and Total Time: 15 minutes

Preheat the waffle iron and grease with oil. Combine the flour, walnuts, baking powder, and salt in a bowl. Set aside. In another bowl, mix the milk and butter. Pour into the walnut mixture and whisk until well combined. Spoon a ladleful of the batter onto the waffle iron. Cook for 3-5 minutes, until golden brown. Repeat the process until no batter is left. Top with maple syrup to serve.

Orange-Bran Cups with Dates

Ingredients for 12 servings

1 tsp vegetable oil	½ cup dates, chopped	½ tsp salt
3 cups bran flakes cereal	3 tsp baking powder	⅓ cup brown sugar
1 ½ cups whole-wheat flour	½ tsp ground cinnamon	¾ cup fresh orange juice

Directions and Total Time: 30 minutes

Preheat oven to 400 F. Grease a 12-cup muffin tin with oil.

Mix the bran flakes, flour, dates, baking powder, cinnamon, and salt in a bowl. In another bowl, combine the sugar and orange juice until blended. Pour into the dry mixture and whisk. Divide the mixture between the cups of the muffin tin. Bake for 20 minutes or until golden brown and set. Cool for a few minutes before removing from the tin and serve.

Apple-Date Couscous with Macadamia Nuts

Ingredients for 4 servings

3 cups apple juice	1 tsp ground cinnamon	½ cup dried dates
1 ½ cups couscous	¼ tsp ground cloves	½ cup chopped macadamia nuts

Directions and Total Time: 20 minutes

Pour the apple juice in a pot over medium heat and bring to a boil. Stir in couscous, cinnamon, and cloves. Turn the heat off and cover. Let sit for 5 minutes, until the liquid is absorbed. Using a fork, fluff the couscous and add the dates and macadamia nuts, stir to combine. Serve warm.

Coconut Blueberry Muffins

Ingredients for 12 servings

1 tbsp coconut oil melted
1 cup quick-cooking oats
1 cup boiling water
½ cup almond milk
¼ cup ground flaxseed
1 tsp almond extract
1 tsp apple cider vinegar
1 ½ cups whole-wheat flour
½ cup pure date sugar
2 tsp baking soda
A pinch of salt
1 cup blueberries

Directions and Total Time: 30 minutes

Preheat oven to 400 F.

In a bowl, stir in the oats with boiling water until they are softened. Pour in the coconut oil, milk, flaxseed, almond extract, and vinegar. Add in the flour, sugar, baking soda, and salt. Gently stir in blueberries.

Divide the batter between a greased with coconut oil muffin tin. Bake for 20 minutes until lightly brown. Allow cooling for 10 minutes. Using a spatula, run the sides of the muffins to take out. Serve.

Scrambled Tofu with Swiss Chard

Ingredients for 5 servings

1 (14-oz) package tofu, crumbled
2 tsp olive oil
1 onion, chopped
3 cloves minced garlic
1 celery stalk, chopped
2 large carrots, chopped
1 tsp chili powder
½ tsp ground cumin
½ tsp ground turmeric
Salt and black pepper to taste
5 cups Swiss chard

Directions and Total Time: 35 minutes

Heat the oil in a skillet over medium heat. Add in the onion, garlic, celery, and carrots. Sauté for 5 minutes. Stir in tofu, chili powder, cumin, turmeric, salt, and pepper, cook for 7-8 minutes more. Mix in the Swiss chard and cook until wilted, about 3 minutes. Allow cooling and seal and serve.

Tangerine Banana Toast

Ingredients for 4 servings

3 bananas
1 cup almond milk
Zest and juice of 1 tangerine
1 tsp ground cinnamon
¼ tsp grated nutmeg
4 slices bread
1 tbsp olive oil

Directions and Total Time: 25 minutes

Blend the bananas, almond milk, tangerine juice, tangerine zest, cinnamon, and nutmeg until smooth in a food processor. Spread into a baking dish. Submerge the bread slices in the mixture for 3-4 minutes. Heat the oil in a skillet over medium heat. Fry the bread for 5 minutes until golden brown. Serve hot.

Maple Banana Oats

Ingredients for 4 servings

3 cups water
1 cup steel-cut oats
2 bananas, mashed
¼ cup pumpkin seeds
2 tbsp maple syrup
A pinch of salt

Directions and Total Time: 35 minutes

Bring water to a boil in a pot, add in oats, and lower the heat. Cook for 20-30 minutes. Put in the mashed bananas, cook for 3-5 minutes more. Stir in maple syrup, pumpkin seeds, and salt. Serve.

Thyme Pumpkin Stir-Fry

Ingredients for 2 servings

1 cup pumpkin, shredded
1 tbsp olive oil
½ onion, chopped
1 carrot, peeled and chopped
2 garlic cloves, minced
½ tsp dried thyme
1 cup chopped kale
Salt and black pepper to taste

Directions and Total Time: 25 minutes

Heat the oil in a skillet over medium heat. Sauté onion and carrot for 5 minutes. Add in garlic and thyme, cook for 30 seconds until the garlic is fragrant. Place in pumpkin, cook for 10 minutes until tender. Stir in kale, cook for 4 minutes until the kale wilts. Season with salt and pepper. Serve hot.

Raspberry Almond Smoothie

Ingredients for 4 servings

1 ½ cups almond milk
½ cup raspberries
Juice from half lemon
½ tsp almond extract

Directions and Total Time: 5 minutes

In a blender or smoothie maker, pour the almond milk, raspberries, lemon juice, and almond extract. Puree the ingredients on high speed until the raspberries have blended almost entirely into the liquid. Pour the smoothie into serving glasses. Stick in some straws and serve immediately.

Sweet Kiwi Oatmeal Bars

Ingredients for 12 servings

2 cups uncooked rolled oats
2 cups all-purpose flour
1 ½ cups pure date sugar
1 ½ tsp baking soda
½ tsp ground cinnamon
1 cup plant butter, melted
4 cups kiwi, chopped
¼ cup organic cane sugar
2 tbsp cornstarch

Directions and Total Time: 50 minutes

Preheat oven to 380 F. Grease a baking dish.

In a bowl, mix the oats, flour, date sugar, baking soda, salt, and cinnamon. Put in butter and whisk to combine. In another bowl, combine the kiwis, cane sugar, and cornstarch until the kiwis are coated. Spread 3 cups of oatmeal mixture on a greased baking dish and top with kiwi mixture and finally put the remaining oatmeal mixture on top. Bake for 40 minutes. Allow cooling and slice into bars.

Spicy Apple Pancakes

Ingredients for 4 servings

2 cups almond milk
1 tsp apple cider vinegar
2 ½ cups whole-wheat flour
2 tbsp baking powder
½ tsp baking soda
1 tsp sea salt
½ tsp ground cinnamon
¼ tsp grated nutmeg
¼ tsp ground allspice
½ cup applesauce
1 cup water
1 tbsp coconut oil

Directions and Total Time: 30 minutes

Whisk the almond milk and apple cider vinegar in a bowl and set aside. In another bowl, combine the flour, baking powder, baking soda, salt, cinnamon, nutmeg, and allspice. Transfer the almond mixture to another bowl and beat with the applesauce and water.

Pour in the dry ingredients and stir. Melt some coconut oil in a skillet over medium heat. Pour a ladle of the batter and cook for 5 minutes, flipping once until golden. Repeat the process until the batter is exhausted. Serve warm.

Almond & Coconut Granola with Cherries

Ingredients for 6 servings

½ cup coconut oil, melted
½ cup maple syrup
1 tsp vanilla extract
3 tsp pumpkin pie spice
4 cups rolled oats
⅓ cup whole-wheat flour
¼ cup ground flaxseed
½ cup sunflower seeds
½ cup slivered almonds
½ cup shredded coconut
½ cup dried cherries
½ cup dried apricots, chopped

Directions and Total Time: 45 minutes

Preheat oven to 350 F.

In a bowl, combine the coconut oil, maple syrup, and vanilla. Add in the pumpkin pie spice. Put oats, flour, flaxseed, sunflower seeds, almonds, and coconut in a baking sheet and toss to combine. Coat with the oil mixture. Spread the granola out evenly. Bake for 25 minutes. Once ready, break the granola into chunks and stir in the cherries and apricots. Bake another 5 minutes. Allow cooling and serve.

Cinnamon Buckwheat with Almonds

Ingredients for 4 servings

1 cup almond milk
1 cup water
1 cup buckwheat groats, rinsed
1 tsp cinnamon
¼ cup chopped almonds
2 tbsp pure date syrup

Directions and Total Time: 20 minutes

Place almond milk, water, and buckwheat in a pot over medium heat and bring to a boil. Lower the heat and simmer covered for 15 minutes. Allow sitting covered for 5 minutes. Mix in the cinnamon, almonds, and date syrup. Serve warm.

Amazing Yellow Smoothie

Ingredients for 4 servings

1 banana	1 cup chopped apricots	1 carrot, peeled and chopped
1 cup chopped mango	1 cup strawberries	1 cup water

Directions and Total Time: 5 minutes

Put the banana, mango, apricots, strawberries, carrot, and water in a food processor. Pulse until smooth, add more water if needed. Divide between glasses and serve.

Hearty Smoothie

Ingredients for 3 servings

1 banana	1 cup broccoli sprouts	¼ tsp ground cinnamon
½ cup coconut milk	2 cherries, pitted	¼ tsp ground cardamom
1 cup water	1 tbsp hemp hearts	1 tbsp grated fresh ginger

Directions and Total Time: 5 minutes

In a food processor, place banana, coconut milk, water, broccoli, cherries, hemp hearts, cinnamon, cardamom, and ginger. Blitz until smooth. Divide between glasses and serve.

Carrot-Strawberry Smoothie

Ingredients for 2 servings

1 cup peeled and diced carrots	1 apple, chopped	2 cups unsweetened almond milk
1 cup strawberries	2 tbsp maple syrup	

Directions and Total Time: 5 minutes

Place in a food processor all the ingredients. Blitz until smooth. Pour in glasses and serve.

Power Green Smoothie

Ingredients for 2 servings

1 banana, sliced	1 cup sliced kiwi	1 cup unsweetened coconut milk
2 cups kale	1 orange, cut into segments	

Directions and Total Time: 10 minutes

In a food processor, put the banana, kale, kiwi, orange, and coconut milk. Pulse until smooth. Serve right away in glasses.

Maple Blueberry Smoothie

Ingredients for 4 servings

4 cups chopped arugula	4 cups unsweetened almond milk	4 tbsp maple syrup
2 cups frozen blueberries	Juice of 2 limes	

Directions and Total Time: 5 minutes

In a food processor, blitz the arugula, blueberries, almond milk, lime juice, and maple syrup until smooth. Serve.

Energy Chia-Peach Smoothie

Ingredients for 2 servings

1 banana, sliced	1 cup almond milk	1 tbsp chia seeds
1 peach, chopped	1 scoop plant-based protein powder	1 cucumber, chopped

Directions and Total Time: 5 minutes

Purée the banana, peach, almond milk, protein powder, chia seeds, and cucumber for 50 seconds until smooth in a food processor. Serve immediately in glasses.

Morning Green Smoothie

Ingredients for 2 servings

1 avocado
1 cup chopped cucumber
2 cups curly endive

2 apples, peeled and cored
2 tbsp lime juice
2 cups soy milk

½-inch piece peeled fresh ginger
2 tbsp chia seeds
1 cup unsweetened coconut yogurt

Directions and Total Time: 5 minutes

Put in a food processor the avocado, cucumber, curly endive, apple, lime juice, soy milk, ginger, chia seeds, and coconut yogurt. Blend until smooth. Serve.

Apple Chocolate Smoothie

Ingredients for 4 servings

1 cup applesauce
2 tbsp plant protein powder
1 tbsp flaxseed
1 tbsp unsweetened cacao powder

1 tbsp peanut butter
1 tbsp maple syrup
1 cup spinach, chopped
½ cup non-dairy milk

1 cup water
1 tsp matcha powder
1 tsp cocoa nibs

Directions and Total Time: 5 minutes

Put in a food processor the applesauce, protein powder, flaxseed, cacao powder, peanut butter, maple syrup, spinach, milk, water, matcha powder, and cocoa nibs. Pulse until smooth. Divide between glasses and serve.

Mango Rice Pudding

Ingredients for 4 servings

1 cup brown rice
1 ½ cups non-dairy milk

3 tbsp pure date sugar
2 tsp pumpkin pie spice

1 mango, chopped
2 tbsp chopped walnuts

Directions and Total Time: 55 minutes

In a pot over medium heat, add the rice, 2 cups water, milk, sugar, and pumpkin pie spice. Bring to a boil, lower the heat and simmer for 50 minutes, until the rice is soft and the liquid is absorbed. Put in the mango and stir to combine. Top with walnuts to serve.

Tropical Smoothie Bowl

Ingredients for 4 servings

4 bananas, sliced
1 cup papaya

1 cup baked granola, crushed
2 cups fresh raspberries

½ cup slivered almonds
4 cups plant-based milk

Directions and Total Time: 10 minutes

Put bananas, raspberries, and milk in a food processor and pulse until smooth. Transfer to a bowl and stir in granola. Top with almonds and serve.

Coconut Fruit Smoothie

Ingredients for 3 servings

1 cup strawberries
1 cup chopped watermelon
1 cup cranberries

1 tbsp chia seeds
½ cup coconut milk
1 cup water

1 tsp goji berries
2 tbsp fresh mint, chopped

Directions and Total Time: 5 minutes

In a food processor, put the strawberries, watermelon, cranberries, chia seeds, coconut milk, water, goji berries, and mint. Pulse until smooth, adding more water or milk if needed. Divide between 3 glasses and serve.

Cranberry Oat Cookies

Ingredients for 2 servings

½ cup rolled oats
1 tbsp whole-wheat flour

½ tsp baking powder
2 tbsp pure date sugar

¼ cup applesauce
2 tbsp dried cranberries

Directions and Total Time: 20 minutes

Combine the oats, flour, baking powder, and sugar in a bowl. Add in applesauce and cranberries. Stir until well combined. Form 2 cookies out of the mixture and microwave for 1 ½ minutes. Allow cooling before serving.

Delicious Matcha Smoothie

Ingredients for 4 servings

1 cup chopped pineapple	1 cup chopped spinach	½ cup almond milk
1 cup chopped mango	½ avocado	1 tsp matcha green tea powder

Directions and Total Time: 5 minutes

Purée everything in a blender until smooth, adding 1 cup water if needed. In a food processor, place the pineapple, mango, spinach, avocado, almond milk, water, and matcha powder. Blitz until smooth. Divide between 4 glasses and serve.

Simple Pear Oatmeal

Ingredients for 2 servings

1 ¼ cups apple cider	⅔ cup rolled oats	1 tbsp pure date syrup
1 pear, peeled, cored, and chopped	1 tsp ground cinnamon	

Directions and Total Time: 20 minutes

Pour the apple cider in a pot over medium heat and bring to a boil. Add in the pear, oats, and cinnamon. Lower the heat and simmer for 3-4 minutes, until the oatmeal thickens. Divide between bowls and drizzle with date syrup. Serve immediately.

Fresh Peach Smoothie

Ingredients for 2 servings

1 avocado	1 cup peach chunks	Juice of 1 lime
2 cups baby spinach	2 cups unsweetened almond milk	2 tbsp maple syrup

Directions and Total Time: 5 minutes

In a food processor, combine the avocado, spinach, pear, milk, lime, and maple syrup. Purée until smooth and serve.

Choco-Berry Smoothie

Ingredients for 2 servings

1 tbsp poppy seeds	2 cups blackberries	2 tbsp cocoa powder
2 cups unsweetened soy milk	2 tbsp pure agave syrup	

Directions and Total Time: 10 minutes

Submerge poppy seeds in soy milk and let sit for 5 minutes. Transfer to a food processor and add in the soy milk, blackberries, agave syrup, and cocoa powder. Blitz until smooth. Serve right away in glasses.

Banana-Strawberry Smoothie

Ingredients for 4 servings

4 bananas, sliced	4 cups kale
4 cups strawberries	4 cups plant-based milk

Directions and Total Time: 5 minutes

In a food processor, add in bananas, strawberries, kale, and milk and blitz until smooth. Divide between glasses and serve.

Berry Quinoa Bowl

Ingredients for 4 servings

3 cups cooked quinoa	2 bananas, sliced	½ cup chopped raw hazelnuts
1 ⅓ cups unsweetened almond milk	2 cups berries	¼ cup agave syrup

Directions and Total Time: 5 minutes

In a large bowl, combine the quinoa, milk, banana, raspberries, blueberries, and hazelnuts. Divide between serving bowls and top with agave syrup to serve.

SOUPS & STEWS

Spinach & Kale Soup with Fried Collards

Ingredients for 4 servings

4 tbsp plant butter
1 cup fresh spinach, chopped
1 cup fresh kale, chopped
1 large avocado

3 ½ cups coconut cream
4 cups vegetable broth
3 tbsp chopped fresh mint leaves
Salt and black pepper to taste

Juice from 1 lime
1 cup collard greens, chopped
2 garlic cloves, minced
1 pinch of green cardamom powder

Directions and Total Time: 16 minutes

Melt 2 tbsp of plant butter in a saucepan over medium heat and sauté spinach and kale for 5 minutes. Turn the heat off. Add the avocado, coconut cream, vegetable broth, salt, and pepper. Puree the ingredients with an immersion blender until smooth. Pour in the lime juice and set aside.

Melt the remaining plant butter in a pan and add the collard greens, garlic, and cardamom; sauté until the garlic is fragrant and has achieved a golden brown color, about 4 minutes. Fetch the soup into serving bowls and garnish with fried collards and mint. Serve warm.

Tofu Goulash Soup

Ingredients for 4 servings

1 ½ cups extra-firm tofu, crumbled
3 tbsp plant butter
1 white onion
2 garlic cloves
8 oz chopped butternut squash

1 red bell pepper
1 tbsp paprika powder
¼ tsp red chili flakes
1 tbsp dried basil
½ tbsp crushed cardamom seeds

Salt and black pepper to taste
1 ½ cups crushed tomatoes
4 cups vegetable broth
1 ½ tsp red wine vinegar
Chopped cilantro to serve

Directions and Total Time: 25 minutes

Melt plant butter in a pot over medium heat and sauté onion and garlic for 3 minutes. Stir in tofu and cook for 3 minutes; add the butternut squash, bell pepper, paprika, red chili flakes, basil, cardamom seeds, salt, and pepper. Cook for 2 minutes. Pour in tomatoes and vegetable broth. Bring to a boil, reduce the heat and simmer for 10 minutes. Mix in red wine vinegar. Garnish with cilantro and serve.

Coconut Cream Pumpkin Soup

Ingredients for 4 servings

2 small red onions, cut into wedges
2 garlic cloves, skinned
10 oz pumpkin, cubed

10 oz butternut squash
2 tbsp olive oil
4 tbsp plant butter

Juice of 1 lime
¾ cup tofu mayonnaise
Toasted pumpkin seeds for garnish

Directions and Total Time: 55 minutes

Preheat oven to 400 F.

Place onions, garlic, and pumpkin in a baking sheet and drizzle with olive oil. Season with salt and pepper. Roast for 30 minutes or until the vegetables are golden brown and fragrant. Remove the vegetables from the oven and transfer to a pot. Add 2 cups of water, bring the ingredients to boil over medium heat for 15 minutes. Turn the heat off. Add in plant butter and puree until smooth. Stir in lime juice and tofu mayonnaise. Spoon into serving bowls and garnish with pumpkin seeds to serve.

Celery & Potato Soup

Ingredients for 6 servings

2 tbsp olive oil
1 onion, chopped
1 carrot, chopped
1 celery stalk, chopped

2 garlic cloves, minced
1 golden beet, peeled and diced
1 yellow bell pepper, chopped
1 Yukon Gold potato, diced

6 cups vegetable broth
1 tsp dried thyme
Salt and black pepper to taste
1 tbsp lemon juice

Directions and Total Time: 55 minutes

Heat the oil in a pot over medium heat. Place the onion, carrot, celery, and garlic. Cook for 5 minutes or until softened. Stir in beet, bell pepper, and potato, cook uncovered for 1 minute. Pour in the broth and thyme. Season with salt and pepper. Cook for 45 minutes until the vegetables are tender. Serve sprinkled with lemon juice.

Medley of Mushroom Soup

Ingredients for 4 servings

- 4 oz unsalted plant butter
- 1 small onion, finely chopped
- 1 clove garlic, minced
- 5 oz button mushrooms, chopped
- 5 oz cremini mushrooms, chopped
- 5 oz shiitake mushrooms, chopped
- ½ lb celery root, chopped
- ½ tsp dried rosemary
- 1 vegetable stock cube, crushed
- 1 tbsp plain vinegar
- 1 cup coconut cream
- 4 – 6 leaves basil, chopped

Directions and Total Time: 40 minutes

Place a saucepan over medium-high heat, add the plant butter to melt, then sauté the onion, garlic, mushrooms, and celery root in the butter until golden brown and fragrant, about 6 minutes. Fetch out some mushrooms and reserve for garnishing. Add the rosemary, 3 cups of water, stock cube, and vinegar. Stir the mixture and bring it to a boil for 6 minutes. After, reduce the heat and simmer the soup for 15 minutes or until the celery is soft.

Mix in the coconut cream and puree the ingredients using an immersion blender. Simmer for 2 minutes. Spoon the soup into serving bowls, garnish with the reserved mushrooms and basil. Serve.

Cauliflower Dill Soup

Ingredients for 4 servings

- 2 tbsp coconut oil
- ½ lb celery root, trimmed
- 1 garlic clove
- 1 medium white onion
- ¼ cup fresh dill, roughly chopped
- 1 tsp cumin powder
- ¼ tsp nutmeg powder
- 1 head cauliflower, cut into florets
- 3 ½ cups seasoned vegetable stock
- 5 oz plant butter
- Juice from 1 lemon
- ¼ cup coconut whipping cream

Directions and Total Time: 26 minutes

Set a pot over medium heat, add the coconut oil and allow heating until no longer shimmering.

Add the celery root, garlic clove, and onion; sauté the vegetables until fragrant and soft, about 5 minutes. Stir in the dill, cumin, and nutmeg, and fry further for 1 minute. Mix in the cauli florets and vegetable stock. Bring the soup to a boil for 12 to 15 minutes or until the cauliflower is soft. Turn the heat off. Add the plant butter and lemon juice. Puree the ingredients with an immersion blender until smooth. Mix in coconut whipping cream and season the soup with salt and black pepper. Serve warm.

Broccoli Fennel Soup

Ingredients for 4 servings

- 1 fennel bulb, chopped
- 10 oz broccoli, cut into florets
- 3 cups vegetable stock
- Salt and black pepper to taste
- 1 garlic clove
- 1 cup cashew cream cheese
- 3 oz plant butter
- ½ cup chopped fresh oregano

Directions and Total Time: 25 minutes

Put the fennel and broccoli into a pot, and cover with the vegetable stock. Bring the ingredients to a boil over medium heat until the vegetables are soft, about 10 minutes. Season the liquid with salt and black pepper, and drop in the garlic. Simmer the soup for 5 to 7 minutes and turn the heat off.

Pour the cream cheese, plant butter, and oregano into the soup; puree the ingredients with an immersion blender until completely smooth. Adjust the taste with salt and black pepper. Spoon the soup into serving bowls and serve.

Asian-Style Bean Soup

Ingredients for 4 servings

- 1 cup canned cannellini beans
- 2 tsp curry powder
- 2 tsp olive oil
- 1 red onion, diced
- 1 tbsp minced fresh ginger
- 2 cubed sweet potatoes
- 1 cup sliced zucchini
- Salt and black pepper to taste
- 4 cups vegetable stock
- 1 bunch spinach, chopped
- Toasted sesame seeds

Directions and Total Time: 55 minutes

Mix the beans with 1 tsp of curry powder until well combined. Warm the oil in a pot over medium heat. Place the onion and ginger and cook for 5 minutes until soft. Add in sweet potatoes and cook for 10 minutes. Put in zucchini and cook for 5 minutes. Season with the remaining curry, pepper, and salt.

Pour in the stock and bring to a boil. Lower the heat and simmer for 25 minutes. Stir in beans and spinach. Cook until the spinach wilts and remove from the heat. Garnish with sesame seeds to serve.

Mexican Tortilla Soup

Ingredients for 4 servings

- 1 (14.5-oz) can diced tomatoes
- 1 (4-oz) can green chiles, chopped
- 2 tbsp olive oil
- 1 cup canned sweet corn
- 1 red onion, chopped
- 2 garlic cloves, minced
- 2 jalapeño peppers, sliced
- 4 cups vegetable broth
- 8 oz seitan, cut into ¼-inch strips
- Salt and black pepper to taste
- ¼ cup chopped fresh cilantro
- 3 tbsp fresh lime juice
- 4 corn tortillas, cut into strips
- 1 ripe avocado, chopped

Directions and Total Time: 40 minutes

Preheat oven to 350 F. Heat the oil in a pot over medium heat. Place sweet corn, garlic, jalapeño, and onion and cook for 5 minutes. Stir in broth, seitan, tomatoes, canned chiles, salt, and pepper. Bring to a boil, then lower the heat and simmer for 20 minutes. Put in the cilantro and lime juice, stir. Adjust the seasoning.

Meanwhile, arrange the tortilla strips on a baking sheet and bake for 8 minutes until crisp. Serve the soup into bowls and top with tortilla strips and avocado.

Spicy Bean Soup

Ingredients for 4 servings

- 2 tbsp olive oil
- 1 medium onion, chopped
- 2 large garlic cloves, minced
- 1 carrot, chopped
- 1 (15.5-oz) can cannellini beans, drained
- 5 cups vegetable broth
- ¼ tsp crushed red pepper
- Salt and black pepper to taste
- 3 cups chopped baby spinach

Directions and Total Time: 40 minutes

Heat oil in a pot over medium heat. Place in carrot, onion, and garlic and cook for 3 minutes. Put in beans, broth, red pepper, salt, and black pepper and stir. Bring to a boil, then lower the heat and simmer for 25 minutes. Stir in baby spinach and cook for 5 minutes until the spinach wilts. Serve warm.

Rice Wine Mushroom Soup

Ingredients for 4 servings

- 2 tbsp olive oil
- 4 green onions, chopped
- 1 carrot, chopped
- 8 oz shiitake mushrooms, sliced
- 3 tbsp rice wine
- 2 tbsp soy sauce
- 4 cups vegetable broth
- Salt and black pepper to taste
- 2 tbsp parsley, chopped

Directions and Total Time: 25 minutes

Heat the oil in a pot over medium heat. Place the green onions and carrot and cook for 5 minutes.

Stir in mushrooms, rice wine, soy sauce, broth, salt, and pepper. Bring to a boil, then lower the heat and simmer for 15 minutes. Top with parsley and serve warm.

Tangy Bean Tomato Soup

Ingredients for 5 servings

- 2 tsp olive oil
- 1 onion, chopped
- 2 garlic cloves, minced
- 1 cup mushrooms, chopped
- Sea salt to taste
- 1 tbsp dried basil
- ½ tbsp dried oregano
- 1 (19-oz) can diced tomatoes
- 1 (14-oz) can kidney beans, drained
- 5 cups water
- 2 cups chopped mustard greens

Directions and Total Time: 30 minutes

Heat the oil in a pot over medium heat. Place in the onion, garlic, mushrooms, and salt and cook for 5 minutes. Stir in basil and oregano, tomatoes, and beans. Pour in water and stir. Simmer for 20 minutes and add in mustard greens; cook for 5 minutes until greens soften. Serve immediately.

Spinach & Potato Soup

Ingredients for 4 servings

- 2 tbsp olive oil
- 1 onion, chopped
- 2 garlic cloves, minced
- 4 cups vegetable broth
- 2 russet potatoes, cubed
- ½ tsp dried oregano
- ¼ tsp crushed red pepper
- 1 bay leaf
- Salt to taste
- 4 cups chopped spinach
- 1 cup green lentils, rinsed

Directions and Total Time: 55 minutes

Warm the oil in a pot over medium heat. Place the onion and garlic and cook covered for 5 minutes. Stir in broth, potatoes, oregano, red pepper, bay leaf, lentils, and salt. Bring to a boil, then lower the heat and simmer uncovered for 30 minutes. Add in spinach and cook for another 5 minutes. Discard the bay leaf and serve immediately.

Turmeric Bean Soup

Ingredients for 6 servings

- 3 tbsp olive oil
- 1 onion, chopped
- 2 carrots, chopped
- 1 sweet potato, chopped
- 1 yellow bell pepper, chopped
- 2 garlic cloves, minced
- 4 tomatoes, chopped
- 6 cups vegetable broth
- 1 bay leaf
- Salt to taste
- 1 tsp ground cayenne pepper
- 1 (15.5-oz) can white beans, drained
- ⅓ cup whole-wheat pasta
- ¼ tsp turmeric

Directions and Total Time: 50 minutes

Heat the oil in a pot over medium heat. Place onion, carrots, sweet potato, bell pepper, and garlic. Cook for 5 minutes. Add in tomatoes, broth, bay leaf, salt, and cayenne pepper. Stir and bring to a boil. Lower the heat and simmer for 10 minutes. Put in white beans and simmer for 15 more minutes.

Cook the pasta in a pot with boiling salted water and turmeric for 8-10 minutes, until pasta is al dente. Strain and transfer to the soup. Discard the bay leaf. Spoon into a bowl and serve.

Arugula Coconut Soup

Ingredients for 4 servings

- 1 tsp coconut oil
- 1 onion, diced
- 2 cups green beans
- 4 cups water
- 1 cup arugula, chopped
- 1 tbsp fresh mint, chopped
- Sea salt and black pepper to taste
- ¾ cup coconut milk

Directions and Total Time: 30 minutes

Place a pot over medium heat and heat the coconut oil. Add in the onion and sauté for 5 minutes. Pour in green beans and water. Bring to a boil, lower the heat and stir in arugula, mint, salt, and pepper. Simmer for 10 minutes. Stir in coconut milk. Transfer to a food processor and blitz the soup until smooth. Serve.

Roasted Basil & Tomato Soup

Ingredients for 4 servings

- 2 lb tomatoes, halved
- 2 tsp garlic powder
- 3 tbsp olive oil
- 1 tbsp balsamic vinegar
- Salt and black pepper to taste
- 4 shallots, chopped
- 2 cups vegetable broth
- ½ cup basil leaves, chopped

Directions and Total Time: 60 minutes

Preheat oven to 450 F.

In a bowl, mix tomatoes, garlic, 2 tbsp of oil, vinegar, salt, and pepper. Arrange the tomatoes onto a baking dish. Sprinkle with some olive oil, garlic powder, balsamic vinegar, salt, and pepper. Bake for 30 minutes until the tomatoes get dark brown color. Take out from the oven; reserve.

Heat the remaining oil in a pot over medium heat. Place the shallots and cook for 3 minutes, stirring often. Add in roasted tomatoes and broth. Bring to a boil, then lower the heat and simmer for 10 minutes. Transfer to a food processor and blitz the soup until smooth. Serve topped with basil.

Pressure Cooker Green Onion & Potato Soup

Ingredients for 5 servings

- 3 green onions, chopped
- 4 garlic cloves, minced
- 1 tbsp olive oil
- 6 russet potatoes, chopped
- ½ (13.5-oz) can coconut milk
- 5 cups vegetable broth
- Salt and black pepper to taste

Directions and Total Time: 25 minutes

Set your IP to Sauté. Place in green onions, garlic, and olive oil. Cook for 3 minutes until softened. Add in potatoes, coconut milk, broth, and salt. Lock the lid in place, set time to 6 minutes on High. Once ready, perform a natural pressure release for 10 minutes. Allow cooling for a few minutes. Using an immersion blender, blitz the soup until smooth. Serve.

Bell Pepper & Mushroom Soup

Ingredients for 6 servings

3 tbsp olive oil
1 onion, chopped
1 large carrot, chopped
1 lb mixed bell peppers, chopped

1 cup cremini mushrooms, quartered
1 cup white mushrooms, quartered
6 cups vegetable broth
¼ cup chopped fresh parsley

1 tsp minced fresh thyme
Salt and black pepper to taste

Directions and Total Time: 45 minutes

Heat the oil in a pot over medium heat. Place onion, carrot, and celery and cook for 5 minutes. Add in bell peppers and broth and stir. Bring to a boil, lower the heat, and simmer for 20 minutes. Adjust the seasoning with salt and black pepper. Serve in soup bowls topped with parsley and thyme.

Cayenne Pumpkin Soup

Ingredients for 6 servings

1 (2-pound) pumpkin, sliced
3 tbsp olive oil
1 tsp salt
2 red bell peppers

1 onion, halved
1 head garlic
6 cups water
Zest and juice of 1 lime

¼ tsp cayenne pepper
½ tsp ground coriander
½ tsp ground cumin
Toasted pumpkin seeds

Directions and Total Time: 55 minutes

Preheat oven to 350 F.

Brush the pumpkin slices with oil and sprinkle with salt. Arrange the slices skin-side-down and on a greased baking dish and bake for 20 minutes. Brush the onion with oil. Cut the top of the garlic head and brush with oil.

When the pumpkin is ready, add in bell peppers, onion, and garlic, and bake for another 10 minutes. Allow cooling.

Take out the flesh from the pumpkin skin and transfer to a food processor. Cut the pepper roughly, peel and cut the onion, and remove the cloves from the garlic head. Transfer to the food processor and pour in the water, lime zest, and lime juice. Blend the soup until smooth. If it's very thick, add a bit of water to reach your desired consistency. Sprinkle with salt, cayenne, coriander, and cumin. Serve.

Cream Soup of Zucchini with Walnuts

Ingredients for 4 servings

3 zucchinis, chopped
2 tsp olive oil
Sea salt and black pepper to taste

1 onion, diced
4 cups vegetable stock
3 tsp ground sage

3 tbsp nutritional yeast
1 cup non-dairy milk
¼ cup toasted walnuts

Directions and Total Time: 45 minutes

Heat the oil in a skillet and place zucchini, onion, salt, and pepper; cook for 5 minutes. Pour in vegetable stock and bring to a boil. Lower the heat and simmer for 15 minutes. Stir in sage, nutritional yeast, and milk. Purée the soup with a blender until smooth. Serve garnished with toasted walnuts and pepper.

Homemade Ramen Soup

Ingredients for 4 servings

7 oz Japanese buckwheat noodles
4 tbsp sesame paste

1 cup canned pinto beans, drained
2 tbsp fresh cilantro, chopped

2 scallions, thinly sliced

Directions and Total Time: 25 minutes

In boiling salted water, add in the noodles and cook for 5 minutes over low heat. Remove a cup of the noodle water to a bowl and add in the sesame paste; stir until it has dissolved. Pour the sesame mix in the pot with the noodles, add in pinto beans, and stir until everything is hot. Serve topped with cilantro and scallions in individual bowls.

Black-Eyed Pea Soup

Ingredients for 6 servings

2 carrots, chopped
1 onion, chopped
2 cups canned dried black-eyed peas

1 tbsp soy sauce
3 tsp dried thyme
1 tsp onion powder

½ tsp garlic powder
Salt and black pepper to taste
¼ cup chopped pitted black olives

Directions and Total Time: 45 minutes

Place carrots, onion, black-eyed peas, 3 cups water, soy sauce, thyme, onion powder, garlic powder, and pepper in a pot. Bring to a boil, then reduce the heat to low. Cook for 20 minutes. Allow cooling for a few minutes. Transfer to a food processor and blend until smooth. Stir in black olives. Serve.

Cauliflower Soup with Leeks

Ingredients for 4 servings

2 tbsp olive oil	1 head cauliflower, cut into florets	Salt and black pepper to taste
3 leeks, thinly sliced	4 cups vegetable stock	3 tbsp chopped fresh chives

Directions and Total Time: 25 minutes

Heat the oil in a pot over medium heat. Place the leeks and sauté for 5 minutes. Add in broccoli, vegetable stock, salt, and pepper and cook for 10 minutes. Blend the soup until purée in a food processor. Top with chives and serve.

Lime Lentil Soup

Ingredients for 2 servings

1 tsp olive oil	½ tsp ground cinnamon	2 cups water
1 onion, chopped	Salt to taste	1 celery stalk, chopped
6 garlic cloves, minced	1 cup yellow lentils	2 cups chopped collard greens
1 tsp chili powder	1 cup canned crushed tomatoes	

Directions and Total Time: 35 minutes

Heat oil in a pot over medium heat. Place onion and garlic and cook for 5 minutes. Stir in chili powder, celery, cinnamon, and salt. Pour in lentils, tomatoes and juices, and water. Bring to a boil, then lower the heat and simmer for 15 minutes. Stir in collard greens. Cook for an additional 5 minutes. Serve.

Spinach, Rice & Bean Soup

Ingredients for 6 servings

6 cups baby spinach	2 garlic cloves, minced	Salt and black pepper to taste
2 tbsp olive oil	1 (15.5-oz) can black-eyed peas	½ cup brown rice
1 onion, chopped	6 cups vegetable broth	Tabasco sauce, for serving

Directions and Total Time: 45 minutes

Heat oil in a pot over medium heat. Place the onion and garlic and sauté for 3 minutes. Pour in broth and season with salt and pepper. Bring to a boil, then lower the heat and stir in rice. Simmer for 15 minutes. Stir in peas and spinach and cook for another 5 minutes. Serve topped with Tabasco sauce.

Ginger Broccoli Soup

Ingredients for 4 servings

1 onion, chopped	2 carrots, chopped	3 cups vegetable broth
1 tbsp minced peeled fresh ginger	1 head broccoli, chopped into florets	½ tsp turmeric
2 tsp olive oil	1 cup coconut milk	Salt and black pepper to taste

Directions and Total Time: 50 minutes

In a pot over medium heat, place the onion, ginger, and olive oil, cook for 4 minutes. Add in carrots, broccoli, broth, turmeric, pepper, and salt. Bring to a boil and cook for 15 minutes. Transfer the soup to a food processor and blend until smooth. Stir in coconut milk and serve warm.

Rice Noodle Soup with Beans

Ingredients for 6 servings

2 carrots, chopped	6 cups vegetable broth	1 (15-oz) can pinto beans
2 celery stalks, chopped	8 oz brown rice noodles	1 tsp dried herbs

Directions and Total Time: 10 minutes

Place a pot over medium heat and add in the carrots, celery, and vegetable broth. Bring to a boil. Add in noodles, beans, dried herbs, salt, and pepper. Reduce the heat and simmer for 5 minutes. Serve.

Vegetable & Rice Soup

Ingredients for 6 servings

3 tbsp olive oil
2 carrots, chopped
1 onion, chopped
1 celery stalk, chopped
2 garlic cloves, minced
2 cups chopped cabbage
½ red bell pepper, chopped
4 potatoes, unpeeled and quartered
6 cups vegetable broth
½ cup brown rice, rinsed
½ cup frozen green peas
2 tbsp chopped parsley

Directions and Total Time: 40 minutes

Heat the oil in a pot over medium heat. Place carrots, onion, celery, and garlic. Cook for 5 minutes. Add in cabbage, bell pepper, potatoes, and broth. Bring to a boil, then lower the heat and add the brown rice, salt, and pepper. Simmer uncovered for 25 minutes until vegetables are tender. Stir in peas and cook for 5 minutes. Top with parsley and serve warm.

Daikon & Sweet Potato Soup

Ingredients for 6 servings

6 cups water
2 tsp olive oil
1 chopped onion
3 garlic cloves, minced
1 tbsp thyme
2 tsp paprika
2 cups peeled and chopped daikon
2 cups chopped sweet potatoes
2 cups peeled and chopped parsnips
½ tsp sea salt
1 cup fresh mint, chopped
½ avocado
2 tbsp balsamic vinegar
2 tbsp pumpkin seeds

Directions and Total Time: 40 minutes

Heat the oil in a pot and place onion and garlic. Sauté for 3 minutes. Add in thyme, paprika, daikon, sweet potato, parsnips, water, and salt. Bring to a boil and cook for 30 minutes. Remove the soup to a food processor and add in balsamic vinegar; purée until smooth. Top with mint and pumpkin seeds to serve.

Chickpea & Vegetable Soup

Ingredients for 5 servings

2 tbsp olive oil
1 onion, chopped
1 carrot, chopped
1 celery stalk, chopped
1 eggplant, chopped
1 (28-oz) can diced tomatoes
2 tbsp tomato paste
1 (15.5-oz) can chickpeas, drained
2 tsp smoked paprika
1 tsp ground cumin
1 tsp za'atar spice
¼ tsp ground cayenne pepper
6 cups vegetable broth
4 oz whole-wheat vermicelli
2 tbsp minced cilantro

Directions and Total Time: 35 minutes

Heat the oil in a pot over medium heat. Place onion, carrot, and celery and cook for 5 minutes. Add in eggplant, tomatoes, tomato paste, chickpeas, paprika, cumin, za'atar spice, and cayenne pepper. Stir in broth and salt. Bring to a boil, then lower the heat and simmer for 15 minutes. Add in vermicelli and cook for another 5 minutes. Serve topped with cilantro.

Italian Bean Soup

Ingredients for 6 servings

3 tbsp olive oil
2 celery stalks, chopped
2 carrots, chopped
3 shallots, chopped
3 garlic cloves, minced
½ cup brown rice
6 cups vegetable broth
1 (14.5-oz) can diced tomatoes
2 bay leaves
Salt and black pepper to taste
2 (15.5-oz) cans white beans
¼ cup chopped basil

Directions and Total Time: 1 hour 25 minutes

Heat oil in a pot over medium heat. Place celery, carrots, shallots, and garlic and cook for 5 minutes. Add in brown rice, broth, tomatoes, bay leaves, salt, and pepper. Bring to a boil, then lower the heat and simmer uncovered for 20 minutes. Stir in beans and basil and cook for 5 minutes. Discard bay leaves and spoon into bowls. Sprinkle with basil and serve.

Brussels Sprouts & Tofu Soup

Ingredients for 4 servings

7 oz firm tofu, cubed
2 tsp olive oil
1 cup sliced mushrooms
1 cup shredded Brussels sprouts
1 garlic clove, minced
½-inch piece fresh ginger, minced
Salt to taste
2 tbsp apple cider vinegar
2 tbsp soy sauce
1 tsp pure date sugar
¼ tsp red pepper flakes
1 scallion, chopped

Directions and Total Time: 40 minutes

Heat the oil in a skillet over medium heat. Place mushrooms, Brussels sprouts, garlic, ginger, and salt. Sauté for 7-8 minutes until the veggies are soft. Pour in 4 cups of water, vinegar, soy sauce, sugar, pepper flakes, and tofu. Bring to a boil, then lower the heat and simmer for 5-10 minutes. Top with scallions and serve.

Rosemary White Bean Soup

Ingredients for 4 servings

2 tsp olive oil	2 garlic cloves, minced	1 cup dried white beans
1 carrot, chopped	1 tbsp rosemary, chopped	¼ tsp salt
1 onion, chopped	2 tbsp apple cider vinegar	2 tbsp nutritional yeast

Directions and Total Time: 30 minutes

Heat the oil in a pot over medium heat. Place carrots, onion, and garlic and cook for 5 minutes.

Pour in vinegar to deglaze the pot. Stir in 5 cups water and beans and bring to a boil. Lower the heat and simmer for 45 minutes until the beans are soft. Add in salt and nutritional yeast and stir. Serve topped with chopped rosemary.

Mushroom & Tofu Soup

Ingredients for 4 servings

4 cups water	4 white mushrooms, sliced	3 tbsp tahini
2 tbsp soy sauce	¼ cup chopped green onions	6 oz extra-firm tofu, diced

Directions and Total Time: 20 minutes

Pour the water and soy sauce in a pot and bring to a boil. Add in mushrooms and green onions. Lower the heat and simmer for 10 minutes. In a bowl, combine ½ cup of hot soup with tahini. Pour the mixture into the pot and simmer 2 minutes more, but not boil. Stir in tofu. Serve warm.

Butternut Squash Coconut Cream Soup

Ingredients for 5 servings

1 (2-lb) butternut squash, cubed	1 large onion, chopped	4 cups vegetable broth
1 red bell pepper, chopped	3 garlic cloves, minced	1 cup coconut cream

Directions and Total Time: 30 minutes

Place the squash, bell pepper, onion, garlic, and broth in a pot. Bring to a boil. Lower the heat and simmer for 20 minutes. Stir in coconut cream, salt and pepper. Transfer to a food processor purée the soup until smooth. Serve warm.

Coconut Mushroom Soup

Ingredients for 2 servings

2 tsp olive oil	2 cups chopped mushrooms	1 tsp dried rosemary
1 onion, chopped	Salt and black pepper to taste	4 cups vegetable broth
2 garlic cloves, minced	2 tbsp whole-wheat flour	1 cup coconut cream

Directions and Total Time: 20 minutes

In a pot over medium heat, warm the oil. Place the onion, garlic, mushrooms, and salt and cook for 5 minutes. Stir in the flour and cook for another 1-2 minutes. Add in rosemary, vegetable broth, coconut cream, and pepper. Lower the heat and simmer for 10 minutes. Serve.

Pomodoro Cream Soup

Ingredients for 5 servings

1 (28-oz) can tomatoes	2 cups vegetable broth	1 cup unsweetened non-dairy milk
2 tbsp olive oil	2 tsp dried herbs	Salt and black pepper to taste
1 tsp smoked paprika	1 red onion, chopped	

Directions and Total Time: 15 minutes

Place the tomatoes, olive oil, paprika, broth, dried herbs, onion, milk, salt, and pepper in a pot. Bring to a boil and cook for 10 minutes. Transfer to a food processor and blend the soup until smooth.

Pasta & Tomato Soup

Ingredients for 4 servings

4 cups cubed bread	8 oz whole-wheat pasta	2 tbsp minced parsley
¼ cup olive oil	1 (28-oz) can crushed tomatoes	Salt and black pepper to taste
2 garlic cloves, minced	4 cups vegetable broth	2 tbsp basil leaves, chopped

Directions and Total Time: 30 minutes

Preheat oven to 400 F. Arrange the bread cubes on a baking tray and toast for 10 minutes, shaking them once. Heat olive oil in a pot over medium heat. Place the garlic, cook for 1 minute. Add in pasta, tomatoes, broth, parsley, salt, and pepper. Bring to a boil, then lower the heat and simmer for 10 minutes. Share the toasted bread into soup bowls and spoon in the soup all over. Sprinkle with basil.

Mustard Green & Potato Soup

Ingredients for 6 servings

2 tbsp olive oil	2 garlic cloves, minced	1 lb sweet potatoes, diced
1 red onion, chopped	6 cups vegetable broth	¼ tsp crushed red pepper
1 leek, white part only, chopped	1 lb red potatoes, chopped	1 bunch mustard greens, chopped

Directions and Total Time: 30 minutes

Heat the oil in a pot over medium heat. Place onion, leek, and garlic and sauté for 5 minutes. Pour in broth, potatoes, and red pepper. Bring to a boil, then lower the heat and season with salt and pepper. Simmer for 15 minutes. Add in mustard greens, cook for 5 minutes until the greens are tender. Serve.

Sunday Soup

Ingredients for 5 servings

2 tbsp vegetable oil	3 small new potatoes, sliced	Salt and black pepper to taste
1 onion, chopped	1 zucchini, sliced	5 cups vegetable broth
1 carrot, chopped	1 yellow summer squash, sliced	2 cups chopped kale
2 garlic cloves, minced	2 ripe tomatoes, diced	¼ cup fresh basil leaves, chopped

Directions and Total Time: 45 minutes

Heat oil in a pot over medium heat. Place onion, carrot, and garlic and cook covered for 5 minutes. Add in potatoes, zucchini, yellow squash, tomatoes, salt, and pepper. Cook for 5 minutes. Stir in broth and bring to a boil. Lower the heat and simmer for 30 minutes. Stir in kale and basil. Serve in bowls.

Pumpkin Soup with Apples

Ingredients for 4 servings

1 tsp olive oil	1 tsp curry powder	3 cups canned pumpkin purée
1 onion, chopped	½ tsp pumpkin pie spice	Salt and black pepper to taste
1-inch piece fresh ginger, diced	½ tsp smoked paprika	½ cup almond milk
1 apple, cored and chopped	¼ tsp red pepper flakes	4 tbsp nutritional yeast

Directions and Total Time: 25 minutes

Warm the olive oil in a pot over medium heat. Place in the onion, ginger, and apple and cook for 5 minutes. Add in curry powder, pumpkin pie spice, paprika, and pepper flakes. Stir in 4 cups water, pumpkin, salt, and pepper. Cook for 10 minutes. Puree with an immersion blender until smooth. Pour in milk and nutritional yeast.

Potato Soup with Kale

Ingredients for 4 servings

2 tbsp olive oil	4 cups vegetable broth	⅛ tsp ground nutmeg
1 onion, chopped	⅓ cup plant butter	Salt and black pepper to taste
1 ½ lb potatoes, chopped	¼ tsp ground cayenne pepper	4 cups kale

Directions and Total Time: 45 minutes

Heat the oil in a pot over medium heat. Place in the onion and sauté for 5 minutes. Pour in potatoes and broth and cook for 20 minutes. Stir in butter, cayenne pepper, nutmeg, salt, and pepper. Add in kale and cook 5 minutes until wilted. Serve.

Mediterranean Soup

Ingredients for 4 servings

- 2 tsp olive oil
- 1 leek, chopped
- 4 garlic cloves, minced
- 2 carrots, peeled and chopped
- 1 tbsp dried herbs
- 4 cups vegetable broth
- 2 (15-oz) cans white beans
- 2 tbsp lemon juice
- 2 cups green beans

Directions and Total Time: 20 minutes

Heat the oil in a pot over medium heat. Place in leek, garlic, carrots, pepper, and salt. Cook for 5 minutes until fragrant. Season with dried herbs. Stir in broth, green beans, and white beans, reduce the heat and simmer for 10 minutes. Stir in lemon juice and serve.

Hot Bean & Corn Soup

Ingredients for 4 servings

- 3 tbsp olive oil
- 1 onion, chopped
- 3 garlic cloves, chopped
- 1 cup sweet corn
- 1 (14.5-oz) can crushed tomatoes
- 1 (15.5-oz) can black beans
- 1 (4-oz) can hot chilies
- 1 tsp ground cumin
- ½ tsp dried oregano
- 4 cups vegetable broth
- Salt and black pepper to taste
- ¼ cup chopped cilantro

Directions and Total Time: 30 minutes

Warm the olive oil in a pot over medium heat. Place in the onion and garlic and sauté for 3 minutes. Add in sweet corn, tomatoes, beans, chilies, cumin, oregano, broth, salt, and pepper. Reduce the heat and simmer for 15 minutes. Divide between bowls and garnish with cilantro to serve.

Vegetable Soup with Vermicelli

Ingredients for 6 servings

- 1 tbsp olive oil 1 onion, chopped
- 4 garlic cloves, minced
- 1 (14.5-oz) can diced tomatoes
- 6 cups vegetable broth
- 8 oz vermicelli
- 1 (5-oz) package baby spinach

Directions and Total Time: 20 minutes

Preparing the Ingredients

Warm the oil in a pot over medium heat. Place in onion and garlic and cook for 3 minutes. Stir in tomatoes, broth, salt, and pepper. Bring to a boil, then lower the heat and simmer for 5 minutes. Pour in vermicelli and spinach and cook for another 5 minutes. Serve warm.

Mushroom Curry Soup

Ingredients for 4 servings

- 1 tbsp coconut oil
- 1 red onion, sliced
- 1 carrot, chopped
- ½ cup sliced shiitake mushrooms
- 2 garlic cloves, minced
- 1 (13.5-oz) can coconut milk
- 4 cups vegetable stock
- 1 (8-oz) can tomato sauce
- 2 tbsp cilantro, chopped
- Juice from 1 lime
- Salt to taste
- 2 tbsp red curry paste

Directions and Total Time: 15 minutes

Melt coconut oil in a pot over medium heat. Place in onion, garlic, carrot, and mushrooms and sauté for 5 minutes. Pour in coconut milk, vegetable stock, tomato sauce, cilantro, lime juice, salt, and curry paste. Cook until heated through. Serve.

Garlicky Broccoli Soup

Ingredients for 6 servings

- 2 tbsp olive oil
- 3 spring onions, chopped
- 6 cups vegetable broth
- 3 potatoes, chopped
- 2 cups broccoli florets, chopped
- 2 garlic cloves, minced
- 1 cup plain unsweetened soy milk
- Salt and black pepper to taste
- 1 tbsp minced chives

Directions and Total Time: 35 minutes

Heat the oil in a pot over medium heat. Place in spring onions and garlic and sauté for 5 minutes until translucent. Add in broth, potatoes, and broccoli. Bring to a boil, then lower the heat and simmer for 20 minutes. Mix in soy milk, salt, and pepper. Cook for 5 more minutes. Serve topped with chives.

Vegetable & Black Bean Soup

Ingredients for 4 servings

2 tbsp olive oil
1 onion, chopped
1 celery stalk, chopped
2 medium carrots, chopped
1 small green bell pepper, chopped
2 garlic cloves, minced
2 tomatoes, chopped
4 cups vegetable broth
1 (15.5-oz) can black beans
1 tsp dried thyme
¼ tsp cayenne pepper
1 tbsp minced cilantro

Directions and Total Time: 50 minutes

Heat the oil in a pot over medium heat. Place in onion, celery, carrots, bell pepper, garlic, and tomatoes. Sauté for 5 minutes, stirring often. Stir in broth, beans, thyme, salt, and cayenne. Bring to a boil, then lower the heat and simmer for 15 minutes. Transfer the soup to a food processor and pulse until smooth. Serve in soup bowls garnished with cilantro.

Basil Coconut Soup

Ingredients for 4 servings

2 tbsp coconut oil
1 ½ cups vegetable broth
2 garlic cloves, minced
1 onion, chopped
1 tbsp minced fresh ginger
1 cup green bell peppers, sliced
1 (13.5-oz) can coconut milk
Juice of ½ lime
2 tbsp chopped basil
1 tbsp chopped cilantro
4 Lime wedges

Directions and Total Time: 15 minutes

Warm the coconut oil in a pot over medium heat. Place in onion, garlic, and ginger and sauté for 3 minutes. Add in bell peppers and broth. Bring to a boil, then lower the heat and simmer. Stir in coconut milk, lime juice, and chopped cilantro. Simmer for 5 minutes. Serve garnished with basil and lime.

Habanero Bean Soup with Brown Rice

Ingredients for 6 servings

2 tbsp olive oil
3 garlic cloves, minced
1 tbsp chili powder
1 tsp dried oregano
3 (15.5-oz) cans kidney beans
1 habanero pepper, chopped
¼ cup sun-dried tomatoes, chopped
6 cups vegetable broth
Salt and black pepper to taste
½ cup brown rice
1 tbsp chopped cilantro

Directions and Total Time: 40 minutes

Heat the oil in a pot over medium heat. Place in garlic and sauté for 1 minute. Add in chili powder, oregano, beans, habanero, tomatoes, broth, rice, salt, and pepper. Cook for 30 minutes.

Meanwhile, put the rice in a pot with boiling salted water and cook for 5 minutes. Spoon the soup in individual bowls and garnish with cilantro to serve.

Green Onion Corn & Bean Soup

Ingredients for 4 servings

2 tbsp olive oil
1 red onion, chopped
1 red bell pepper, chopped
1 carrot, chopped
2 garlic cloves, minced
1 tsp ground cumin
1 tsp dried oregano
1 (14.5-oz) can diced tomatoes
1 (15.5-oz) can pinto beans
4 cups vegetable broth
2 cups corn kernels
1 tsp fresh lemon juice
Salt and black pepper to taste
2 stalks green onions, chopped
Tabasco sauce for garnish

Directions and Total Time: 55 minutes

Heat the oil in a pot over medium heat. Place in onion, bell pepper, carrot, and garlic. Sauté for 5 minutes. Add in cumin, oregano, tomatoes, beans, salt, pepper, and broth. Bring to a boil, then lower the heat and simmer for 15 minutes.

In a food processor, transfer ⅓ of the soup and blend until smooth. Return to the pot and stir in the corn. Cook for 10 minutes. Drizzle with lemon juice before serving and garnish with green onions and hot sauce to serve.

Celery Butternut Squash Soup

Ingredients for 6 servings

2 tbsp olive oil
1 onion, chopped
1 celery stalk, chopped
½ tsp ground allspice
1 potato, peeled and chopped
1 lb butternut squash, chopped
6 cups vegetable broth
Salt to taste
2 tbsp fresh orange juice

Directions and Total Time: 30 minutes

Heat the oil in a pot over medium heat. Place in onion and celery and sauté for 5 minutes until tender. potato, squash, broth, and salt. Cook for 20 minutes. Stir in orange juice. Using an immersion blender, purée. Return to the pot and heat. Serve immediately.

Coconut & Tofu Soup

Ingredients for 4 servings

- 1 tbsp canola oil
- 1 onion, chopped
- 2 tbsp minced fresh ginger
- 2 tbsp soy sauce
- 1 cup shiitake mushrooms, sliced
- 1 tbsp pure date sugar
- 1 tsp chili paste
- 2 cups light vegetable broth
- 8 oz extra-firm tofu, chopped
- 2 (13.5-oz) cans coconut milk
- 1 tbsp fresh lime juice
- 3 tbsp chopped fresh cilantro

Directions and Total Time: 30 minutes

Heat the oil in a pot over medium heat. Place in onion and ginger and sauté for 3 minutes until softened. Add in soy sauce, mushrooms, sugar, and chili paste. Stir in broth. Bring to a boil, then lower the heat and simmer for 15 minutes. Strain the liquid and discard solids. Return the broth to the pot. Stir in tofu, coconut milk, and lime juice. Cook for 5 minutes. Garnish with cilantro and serve.

Garlic Veggie Bisque

Ingredients for 6 servings

- 1 red onion, chopped
- 2 carrots, chopped
- 1 potato, peeled and chopped
- 1 zucchini, sliced
- 1 ripe tomato, quartered
- 2 garlic cloves, crushed
- 3 tbsp olive oil
- ½ tsp dried rosemary
- Salt and black pepper to taste
- 6 cups vegetable broth
- 1 tbsp minced fresh parsley

Directions and Total Time: 25 minutes

Preheat oven to 400 F.

Arrange the onion, carrots, potato, zucchini, tomato, and garlic on a greased baking dish. Sprinkle with oil, rosemary, salt, and pepper. Cover with foil and roast for 30 minutes. Uncover and turn them. Roast for another 10 minutes.

Transfer the veggies into a pot and pour in the broth. Bring to a boil, lower the heat and simmer for 5 minutes. Transfer to a food processor and blend the soup until smooth. Return to the pot and cook until hot. Serve topped with parsley.

Ginger Squash Soup

Ingredients for 4 servings

- 1/3 cup toasted pumpkin seeds
- 1 tbsp chopped ginger paste
- 1 tbsp canola oil
- 1 onion, chopped
- 1 celery stalk, chopped
- 4 cups vegetable broth
- 1 acorn squash, peeled, chopped
- 1 tbsp soy sauce
- ¼ tsp ground allspice
- Salt and black pepper to taste
- 1 cup plain unsweetened soy milk

Directions and Total Time: 30 minutes

Heat the oil in a pot over medium heat. Place in onion and celery and sauté for 5 minutes until tender. Add in broth and squash, bring to a boil. Lower the heat and simmer for 20 minutes. Stir in soy sauce, ginger paste, allspice, salt, and pepper. Transfer to a food processor and blend the soup until smooth. Return to the pot. Mix in soy milk and cook until hot. Serve garnished with pumpkin seeds.

Easy Garbanzo Soup

Ingredients for 4 servings

- 2 tbsp olive oil
- 1 onion, chopped
- 1 green bell pepper, diced
- 1 carrot, peeled and diced
- 4 garlic cloves, minced
- 1 (15-oz) can garbanzo beans
- 1 cup spinach, chopped
- 4 cups vegetable stock
- ¼ tsp ground cumin
- Sea salt to taste
- ¼ cup chopped cilantro

Directions and Total Time: 25 minutes

Heat the oil in a pot over medium heat. Place in onion, garlic, bell pepper, and carrot and sauté for 5 minutes until tender. Stir in garbanzo beans, spinach, vegetable stock, cumin, and salt. Cook for 10 minutes. Mash the garbanzo using a potato masher, leaving some chunks. Top with cilantro and serve.

...dle Soup

Ingredients for 6 servings

2 tbsp olive oil
1 onion, chopped
1 carrot, sliced
2 garlic cloves, minced
1 (28-oz) can crushed tomatoes
1 cup Chana dal, rinsed and drained
1 tsp dried thyme
6 cups vegetable broth
4 oz soba noodles, broken into thirds

Directions and Total Time: 30 minutes

Warm the oil in a pot over medium heat. Place in onion, carrot, and garlic and sauté for 5 minutes. Add in tomatoes, chana dal, thyme, and broth. Bring to a boil, then lower the heat and season with salt and pepper. Simmer for 15 minutes. Stir in soba noodles, cook 5 minutes more. Serve immediately.

Hot Lentil Soup with Zucchini

Ingredients for 4 servings

2 tbsp olive oil
1 onion, chopped
1 zucchini, chopped
1 garlic clove, minced
1 tbsp hot paprika
1 (14.5-oz) can crushed tomatoes
1 cup red lentils, rinsed
4 cups vegetable broth
3 cups chopped Swiss chard

Directions and Total Time: 30 minutes

Heat the oil in a pot over medium heat. Place in onion, zucchini, and garlic and sauté for 5 minutes until tender. Add in paprika, tomatoes, lentils, broth, salt, and pepper. Bring to a boil, then lower the heat and simmer for 15 minutes, stirring often. Add in the Swiss chard and cook for another 3-5 minutes. Serve immediately.

Coconut Artichoke Soup with Almonds

Ingredients for 4 servings

1 tbsp olive oil
2 medium shallots, chopped
2 (10-oz) packages artichoke hearts
3 cups vegetable broth
1 tsp fresh lemon juice
Salt to taste
⅓ cup plant butter
⅛ tsp ground cayenne pepper
1 cup plain coconut cream
1 tbsp snipped fresh chives
2 tbsp sliced toasted almonds

Directions and Total Time: 30 minutes

Heat the oil in a pot over medium heat. Place in shallots and sauté until softened, about 3 minutes. Add in artichokes, broth, lemon juice, and salt. Bring to a boil, lower the heat, and simmer for 10 minutes. Stir in butter and cayenne pepper. Transfer to a food processor and blend until purée. Return to the pot. Mix in the coconut cream and simmer for 5 minutes. Serve topped with chives and almonds.

Classic Minestrone Soup

Ingredients for 4 servings

2 tbsp olive oil
1 onion, chopped
1 carrot, chopped
1 stalk celery, chopped
2 garlic cloves, minced
4 cups vegetable stock
1 cup green peas
½ cup orzo
1 (15-oz) can chopped tomatoes
2 tsp Italian seasoning
Sea salt and black pepper to taste

Directions and Total Time: 20 minutes

Heat the oil in a pot over medium heat. Place in onion, garlic, carrot, and celery and sauté for 5 minutes until tender. Stir in vegetable stock, green peas, orzo, tomatoes, salt, pepper, and Italian seasoning. Cook for 10 minutes. Serve right away.

Turnip & Rutabaga Soup

Ingredients for 5 servings

2 tbsp olive oil
1 onion, diced
3 garlic cloves, minced
1 carrot, chopped
1 rutabaga, chopped
1 turnip chopped
1 red potato, chopped
5 cups vegetable stock
2 tsp dried thyme

Directions and Total Time: 30 minutes

Heat the oil in a pot over medium heat. Place the onion and garlic and sauté for 3 minutes until translucent. Stir in carrot, rutabaga, turnip, potato, vegetable stock, salt, pepper, and thyme. Simmer for 10 minutes. In a food processor, put the soup and blend until purée. Serve warm.

Mushroom Rice Soup

Ingredients for 6 servings

3 tbsp olive oil
1 onion, chopped
1 carrot, chopped
1 celery stalk, chopped
1 cup wild mushrooms, sliced
½ cup brown rice
7 cups vegetable broth
1 tsp dried dill weed
Salt and black pepper to taste

Directions and Total Time: 30 minutes

Heat the oil in a pot over medium heat. Place in onion, carrot, and celery and sauté for 5 minutes. Add in mushrooms, rice, broth, dill weed, salt, and pepper. Bring to a boil, then lower the heat and simmer uncovered for 20 minutes. Serve.

Cold Vegetable Soup

Ingredients for 4 servings

2 lb tomatoes, chopped
1 cucumber, peeled, chopped
1 green bell pepper, chopped
1 cup cold water
1 slice whole-wheat bread
4 green onions, white part only
2 garlic cloves, minced
2 tbsp olive oil
2 tbsp white wine vinegar
Salt to taste
2 tbsp minced fresh parsley

Directions and Total Time: 15 minutes

In a food processor, place half of the tomatoes, cucumber, bell pepper, water, bread, green onions, and garlic. Blitz until smooth. Pour in oil, salt, and vinegar and pulse until combined. Transfer to a bowl and combine with remaining tomatoes. Close the lid and let chill in the fridge for 1-2 hours. Serve garnished with parsley.

Shallot Lentil Soup with Walnuts

Ingredients for 4 servings

2 tbsp olive oil
3 shallots, chopped
3 cups vegetable broth
1 cup apple juice
4 cups fresh spinach
½ cup lentils
1 tsp minced fresh sage
¼ tsp ground allspice
Salt and black pepper to taste
1 cup soy milk
¼ cup toasted walnuts, chopped

Directions and Total Time: 30 minutes

Heat the oil in a pot over medium heat. Place in the shallots and sauté for 3 minutes until translucent. Add in vegetable, apple juice, spinach, sage, allspice, salt, and pepper. Bring to a boil, lower the heat and simmer for 10 minutes. With an immersion blender, pulse the soup until purée. Mix in soy milk and heat until hot. Top with walnuts to serve.

Lime Pumpkin Soup

Ingredients for 4 servings

2 tsp olive oil
3 cups pumpkin, chopped
1 onion, chopped
1 garlic clove, minced
2 cups water
1 (15-oz) can black-eyed peas
2 tbsp lime juice
1 tbsp pure date sugar
1 tsp paprika
1 tbsp red pepper flakes
3 cups shredded cabbage
1 cup mushrooms, chopped

Directions and Total Time: 30 minutes

Warm the oil in a pot over medium heat. Place in pumpkin, onion, garlic, and salt. Cook for 5 minutes. Stir in water, peas, lime juice, sugar, paprika, and pepper flakes. Bring to a boil and cook for 15 minutes. Add in cabbage and mushrooms and cook for 5 minutes. Allow cooling before serving.

Brown Rice & Bean Chili

Ingredients for 6 servings

30 oz canned roasted tomatoes and peppers
3 tbsp olive oil
1 onion, chopped
4 garlic cloves, minced
1 (15-oz) can kidney beans, drained
½ cup brown rice
2 cups vegetable stock
3 tbsp chili powder
1 tsp sea salt

Directions and Total Time: 30 minutes

Heat the oil in a pot over medium heat. Place onion and garlic and cook for 3 minutes until fragrant. Stir in beans, rice, tomatoes and peppers, stock, chili powder, and salt. Cook for 20 minutes. Serve.

Spicy Potato Soup

Ingredients for 6 servings

3 tbsp olive oil
1 onion, chopped
1 garlic clove, minced
1 tbsp hot powder

1 lb carrots, chopped
2 potatoes, chopped
6 cups vegetable broth
Salt to taste

1 (13.5-oz) can coconut milk
1 tbsp minced fresh parsley
Chopped roasted cashews

Directions and Total Time: 25 minutes

Heat the oil in a pot over medium heat. Place in onion and garlic and cook for 3 minutes. Add in hot powder, cook for 30 seconds. Stir in carrots, potatoes, broth, and salt. Bring to a boil, lower the heat and simmer for 15 minutes.

With an immersion blender, blitz the soup until smooth. Sprinkle with salt and pepper. Mix in coconut milk and cook until hot. Garnish with parsley and chopped cashews to serve.

Sweet African Soup

Ingredients for 4 servings

1 tbsp canola oil
1 onion, chopped
1 carrot, chopped
1 garlic clove, minced

3 Granny Smith apples, chopped
2 tbsp curry powder
2 tsp tomato paste
3 cups vegetable broth

Salt to taste
1 cup soy milk
4 tsp sugar-free apricot preserves

Directions and Total Time: 45 minutes

Heat the oil in a pot over medium heat. Place onion, carrot, and garlic and sauté for 5 minutes. Stir in apples and cook for 5 minutes, until the apples soften. Add in tomato paste, broth, and salt. Cook for 10 minutes. Blend the soup in a food processor until smooth. Transfer to a bowl and mix with soy milk. Close the lid and let chill in the fridge for 3 hours. Serve topped with apricot preserves.

Spinach Soup with Gnocchi

Ingredients for 4 servings

1 tsp olive oil
1 cup green bell peppers
Salt and black pepper to taste
2 garlic cloves, minced

2 carrots, chopped
3 cups vegetable broth
1 cup gnocchi
¾ cup unsweetened non-dairy milk

¼ cup nutritional yeast
2 cups chopped fresh spinach
¼ cup pitted black olives, chopped
Croutons, for topping

Directions and Total Time: 25 minutes

Heat the oil in a pot over medium heat. Place in bell peppers, garlic, carrots, and salt and cook for 5 minutes. Stir in broth. Bring to a boil. Put in gnocchi, cook for 10 minutes. Add in spinach and cook for another 5 minutes. Stir in milk, nutritional yeast, and olives. Serve topped with croutons.

Celery & Potato Rice Soup

Ingredients for 6 servings

3 tbsp olive oil
1 onion, chopped
1 medium carrot, chopped
1 celery stalk, chopped

1 lb potatoes, chopped
½ cup long-grain brown rice
1 (14.5-oz) can crushed tomatoes
2 cups tomato juice

2 bay leaves
½ tsp ground cumin
Salt and black pepper to taste
1 tbsp minced fresh parsley

Directions and Total Time: 40 minutes

Heat oil in a pot and sauté onion, carrot, and celery for 10 minutes. Add in potatoes, rice, tomatoes, tomato juices, bay leaves, cumin, 6 cups water, salt, and pepper. Bring to a boil, then lower the heat and simmer uncovered for 20 minutes. Discard the bay leaves. Scatter with parsley. Serve immediately.

Rotini & Tomato Soup

Ingredients for 4 servings

1 tbsp olive oil
1 medium onion, chopped
1 celery rib, minced
3 garlic cloves, minced

1 (28-oz) can crushed tomatoes
3 cups chopped fresh ripe tomatoes
2 tbsp tomato paste
3 cups vegetable broth

2 bay leaves
1 cup plain unsweetened soy milk
½ cup whole-wheat rotini pasta
2 tbsp chopped fresh basil

Directions and Total Time: 25 minutes

Heat oil in a pot and sauté onion, celery, and garlic for 5 minutes. Add in tomatoes, tomato paste, broth, sugar, and bay leaves. Bring to a boil and add the rotini. Cook for 10 minutes. Discard bay leaves. Garnish with the basil and serve.

Rosemary Tomato Soup with Parmesan Croutons

Ingredients for 6 servings

3 tbsp flax seed powder	2 oz grated plant-based Parmesan	1 cup coconut cream
1 ¼ cups almond flour	2 lb fresh ripe tomatoes	½ tsp dried rosemary
2 tsp baking powder	4 cloves garlic, peeled only	½ tsp dried oregano
5 tbsp psyllium husk powder	1 small white onion, diced	2 tbsp chopped fresh basil
2 tsp plain vinegar	1 small red bell pepper, diced	Salt and black pepper to taste
3 oz plant butter	3 tbsp olive oil	Basil leaves to garnish

Directions and Total Time: 1 hour 25 minutes

In a medium bowl, mix the flax seed powder with 9 tbsp of water and set aside to soak for 5 minutes. Preheat oven to 350 F and line a baking sheet with parchment paper.

In another bowl, combine almond flour, baking powder, psyllium husk powder, and salt. When the vegan "flax egg" is ready, mix in 1 ¼ cups boiling water and plain vinegar. Add in the flour mixture and whisk for 30 seconds. Form 8 flat pieces out of the dough. Place the flattened dough on the baking sheet while leaving enough room between each to allow rising.

Bake for 40 minutes. Remove the croutons to cool and break them into halves. Mix the plant butter with plant-based Parmesan cheese and spread the mixture in the inner parts of the croutons. Increase the oven's temperature to 450 F and bake the croutons further for 5 minutes or until golden brown and crispier.

In a baking pan, add tomatoes, garlic, onion, red bell pepper, and drizzle with olive oil. Roast in the oven for 25 minutes and after broil for 3 to 4 minutes until some of the tomatoes are slightly charred. Transfer to a blender and add coconut cream, rosemary, oregano, basil, salt, and black pepper. Puree until smooth and creamy. Pour the soup into serving bowls, drop some croutons on top, garnish with basil leaves, and serve.

Butternut Squash Soup

Ingredients for 4 servings

2 tbsp olive oil	1 red bell pepper, chopped	½ cup plant butter
1 onion, chopped	4 cups vegetable broth	¼ cup toasted pumpkin seeds
½ lb butternut squash, chopped	Salt and black pepper to taste	

Directions and Total Time: 30 minutes

Heat oil in a pot over medium heat. Place in onion, squash, and bell pepper and sauté for 5 minutes until soft. Stir in broth, salt and pepper. Bring to a boil, then lower the heat and simmer for 20 minutes. Stir in butter and blend the soup using an immersion blender. Top with toasted seeds and serve.

Green Bean & Rice Soup

Ingredients for 4 servings

2 tbsp olive oil	2 garlic cloves minced	1 cup green beans, chopped
1 medium onion, minced	½ cup brown rice	2 tbsp chopped parsley

Directions and Total Time: 50 minutes

Heat oil in a pot over medium heat. Place in onion and garlic and sauté for 3 minutes. Add in rice, 4 cups water, salt, and pepper. Bring to a boil, lower the heat, and simmer for 15 minutes. Stir in beans and cook for 10 minutes. Top with parsley.

Pumpkin & Garbanzo Chili with Kale

Ingredients for 6 servings

¾ cup dried garbanzo beans, soaked	6 cups water	½ tsp garlic powder
1 (28-oz) can crushed tomatoes	2 tbsp chili powder	3 cups kale, chopped
2 cups chopped pumpkin	1 tsp onion powder	½ tsp salt

Directions and Total Time: 60 minutes

In a saucepan over medium heat, add garbanzo, tomatoes, pumpkin, 2 cups water, salt, chili, onion, and garlic powders. Bring to a boil. Reduce the heat and simmer for 50 minutes. Stir in kale and cook for 5 minutes until the kale wilts. Serve.

Spanish Gazpacho

Ingredients for 4 servings

3 tbsp olive oil
2 garlic cloves, crushed
Salt and black pepper to taste
2 cucumbers
2 tsp lemon juice
2 lb ripe plum tomatoes, chopped
1 (14.5-oz) can crushed tomatoes
1 cup tomato juice
2 tbsp chopped dill

Directions and Total Time: 15 minutes

In a food processor, put the garlic, olive oil, and salt and pulse until paste-like consistency forms. Add in 1 cucumber and lemon juice. Blitz until smooth. Put in tomatoes, tomato juice, salt, and pepper. Blend until smooth. Transfer to a bowl, close the lid, and let chill in the fridge before serving.

Green Bean & Zucchini Velouté

Ingredients for 6 servings

3 tbsp olive oil
1 onion, chopped
1 garlic clove, minced
2 cups green beans
4 cups vegetable broth
3 medium zucchini, sliced
½ tsp dried marjoram
½ cup plain almond milk
2 tbsp minced jarred pimiento

Directions and Total Time: 30 minutes

Heat oil in a pot and sauté onion and garlic for 5 minutes. Add in green beans and broth. Cook for 10 minutes. Stir in zucchini and cook for 10 minutes. Transfer to a food processor and pulse until smooth. Return to the pot and mix in almond milk; cook until hot. Serve topped with pimiento.

Cabbage & Red Bean Chili

Ingredients for 4 servings

2 tsp sesame oil
1 cup green onions, chopped
3 cloves garlic, minced
1 lb yellow squash, chopped
2 cups shredded napa cabbage
1 (14.5-oz) can red beans, drained
1 (14.5-oz) can diced tomatoes
2 cups vegetable broth
2 tbsp red miso paste
2 tbsp water
1 tbsp hot sauce
2 tsp tamari sauce

Directions and Total Time: 35 minutes

Heat the sesame oil in a pot over medium heat. Place in green onion, garlic and yellow squash, and cook for 5 minutes. Stir in cabbage, beans, tomatoes, and broth. Bring to a boil, then lower the heat and simmer covered for 15 minutes.

Meanwhile, mix the miso paste with hot water in a bowl. Remove the pot from heat and stir in the miso, tamari, and hot sauces. Adjust the seasoning and serve.

Vegetable Chili

Ingredients for 4 servings

1 onion, chopped
1 cup vegetable broth
2 garlic cloves, minced
1 potato, cubed
1 carrot, chopped
2 tsp olive oil
1 (28-oz) can tomatoes
1 tbsp tomato paste
1 (14-oz) can chickpeas
1 tsp chili powder
Salt and black pepper to taste
¼ cup parsley leaves, chopped

Directions and Total Time: 30 minutes

Heat oil in a pot over medium heat. Place in onion and garlic and sauté for 3 minutes. Add in potato, carrot, tomatoes, broth, tomato paste, chickpeas, and chili; season. Simmer for 20 minutes. Serve garnished with parsley.

Chili Gazpacho

Ingredients for 4 servings

2 tbsp olive oil
2 cups water
1 red onion, chopped
6 tomatoes, chopped
1 red bell pepper, diced
2 garlic cloves, minced
juice of 1 lemon
2 tbsp chopped fresh basil
½ tsp chili pepper

Directions and Total Time: 15 minutes

In a food processor, place the olive oil, half of the onion, half of the tomato, half of the bell pepper, garlic, lemon juice, basil, and chili pepper. Season with salt and pepper. Blitz until smooth. Transfer to a bowl and add in the reserved onion, tomatoes, and bell pepper. Let chill in the fridge before serving.

Carrot & Mushroom Broth

Ingredients for 6 servings

5 dried porcini mushrooms, soaked and liquid reserved
1 tbsp olive oil
1 onion, unpeeled and quartered
1 medium carrot, coarsely chopped
1 celery rib with leaves, chopped
8 oz Cremini mushrooms, chopped
1 onion, chopped
½ cup chopped fresh parsley
Salt and black pepper to taste
5 cups water

Directions and Total Time: 1 hour 15 minutes

Warm the oil in a pot over medium heat. Place in onion, carrot, celery, and cremini mushrooms. Cook for 5 minutes until softened. Add in the dried mushrooms and reserved liquid, onion, salt, and water. Bring to a boil and simmer for 1 hour. Let cool for a few minutes, then pour over a strainer into a pot. Divide between glass mason jars and allow cooling completely. Seal and store in the fridge up to 5 days or 1 month in the freezer.

Fennel & Corn Chowder

Ingredients for 4 servings

2 tbsp olive oil
1 onion, chopped
1 cup chopped fennel bulb
2 carrots, chopped
1 cup mushrooms, chopped
¼ cup whole-wheat flour
4 cups vegetable stock
2 cups canned corn
2 cups cubed red potatoes
1 cup almond milk
½ tsp chili paste
Sea salt and black pepper to taste

Directions and Total Time: 30 minutes

Heat the oil in a pot over medium heat. Place in onion, fennel, carrots, and mushrooms. Sauté for 5 minutes until tender. Stir in flour. Pour in vegetable stock. Lower the heat. Add in corn, potatoes, almond milk, and chili paste. Simmer for 20 minutes. Sprinkle with salt and pepper. Serve immediately.

Fennel & Parsnip Bisque

Ingredients for 6 servings

1 tbsp olive oil
2 green onions, chopped
½ fennel bulb, sliced
2 large carrots, shredded
2 parsnips, shredded
1 potato, chopped
2 garlic cloves, minced
½ tsp dried thyme
¼ tsp dried marjoram
6 cups vegetable broth
1 cup plain unsweetened soy milk
1 tbsp minced fresh parsley

Directions and Total Time: 30 minutes

Heat the oil in a pot over medium heat. Place in green onions, fennel, carrots, parsnips, potato, and garlic. Sauté for 5 minutes until softened. Add in thyme, marjoram, and broth. Bring to a boil, lower the heat, and simmer for 20 minutes. Transfer to a blender and pulse the soup until smooth. Return to the pot and mix in soy milk. Top with parsley to serve.

Pearl Barley & Vegetable Stew

Ingredients for 6 servings

3 tbsp olive oil
1 onion, chopped
2 garlic cloves, minced
2 turnips, chopped
4 potatoes, chopped
1 cup pearl barley
1 (28-oz) can diced tomatoes
3 tsp dried mixed herbs
Salt and black pepper to taste

Directions and Total Time: 30 minutes

Warm oil in a pot over medium heat. Add in onion and garlic and sauté for 3 minutes until fragrant. Stir in the turnips, potatoes, barley, tomatoes, 3 cups water, and herbs. Cook for 20 minutes. Serve.

Kale & Potato Stew

Ingredients for 4 servings

1 onion, diced
2 tbsp olive oil
2 potatoes, peeled and chopped
⅓ cup chunky almond butter
1 tsp paprika
¼ tsp red pepper flakes
Salt and black pepper to taste
2 cups kale, chopped

Directions and Total Time: 30 minutes

Warm oil in a saucepan over medium heat and cook onion for 3 minutes. Add in potatoes, almond butter, paprika, pepper flakes, 4 cups water, and salt; stir. Bring to a boil and simmer 20 for minutes. Add in the kale and cook for 5 minutes. Serve.

Mushroom, Chickpea & Eggplant Stew

Ingredients for 4 servings

2 tbsp olive oil
1 onion, chopped
1 eggplant, chopped
2 medium carrots, sliced
1 red potato, chopped

1 cup mushrooms, sliced
2 garlic cloves, minced
1 (15.5-oz) cans chickpeas, drained
1 (28-oz) can diced tomatoes
1 tbsp minced parsley

½ tsp dried oregano
½ tsp dried basil
1 tbsp soy sauce
½ cup vegetable broth
Salt and black pepper to taste

Directions and Total Time: 30 minutes

Heat the oil in a pot over medium heat. Place in onion, garlic, eggplant, and carrots and sauté for 5 minutes. Lower the heat and stir in potato, mushrooms, chickpeas, tomatoes, oregano, basil, soy sauce, salt, pepper, and broth. Simmer for 15 minutes. Serve sprinkled with parsley.

Caribbean Lentil Stew

Ingredients for 4 servings

2 tbsp olive oil
1 onion, chopped
1 carrot, sliced
2 garlic cloves, minced
1 sweet potato, chopped

¼ tsp crushed red pepper
1 cup red lentils, rinsed
1 (14.5-oz) can diced tomatoes
1 tsp hot curry powder
1 tsp chopped thyme

¼ tsp ground allspice
Salt and black pepper to taste
1 cup water
1 (13.5-oz) can coconut milk

Directions and Total Time: 50 minutes

Warm oil in a pot and sauté onion and carrot for 5 minutes, stirring occasionally until softened. Add in garlic, sweet potato, and crushed red pepper. Put in red lentils, tomatoes, curry powder, allspice, salt, and black pepper, stir to combine. Pour in water and simmer for 30 minutes until the vegetables are tender. Stir in coconut milk and simmer for 10 minutes. Serve hot topped with thyme.

Tomato Lentil Stew

Ingredients for 4 servings

2 tsp olive oil
4 carrots, chopped
1 onion, chopped

½ green bell pepper, chopped
1 tbsp paprika
2 garlic cloves, sliced

4 cups vegetable broth
1 (28-oz) can crushed tomatoes
2 (15-oz) cans lentils, drained

Directions and Total Time: 25 minutes

Heat the oil in a pot over medium heat. Place in carrots, onion, bell pepper, paprika, and garlic. Sauté for 5 minutes until tender. Stir in broth, tomatoes, and lentils. Bring to a boil, then lower the heat and simmer for 15 minutes. Sprinkle with salt and pepper. Serve warm.

Homemade Succotash Stew

Ingredients for 4 servings

1 cup canned chickpeas
2 tbsp olive oil
1 onion, chopped
2 russet potatoes, chopped
2 carrots, sliced

1 (14.5-oz) can diced tomatoes
1 (16-oz) package frozen succotash
2 cups vegetable broth
2 tbsp soy sauce
1 tsp dry mustard

½ tsp dried thyme
½ tsp ground allspice
¼ tsp ground cayenne pepper
Salt and black pepper to taste

Directions and Total Time: 30 minutes

Heat oil in a saucepan. Place in onion and sauté for 3 minutes. Stir in chickpeas, potatoes, carrots, tomatoes, succotash, broth, soy sauce, mustard, sugar, thyme, allspice, and cayenne pepper. Sprinkle with salt and pepper. Bring to a boil, then lower the heat and simmer for 20 minutes. Serve hot.

Sudanese Veggie Stew

Ingredients for 6 servings

3 potatoes, cubed
3 tbsp olive oil
2 carrots, sliced

4 shallots, chopped
2 garlic cloves, minced
1 tbsp ground turmeric

1 tsp ground ginger
1 ½ cups vegetable broth
4 cups shredded spinach

Directions and Total Time: 30 minutes

Cook the potatoes in salted water over medium heat, about 15 minutes. Drain and reserve. Heat the oil in a saucepan over medium heat. Place in carrots and shallots and cook for 5 minutes. Stir in garlic, turmeric, ginger, and salt. Cook for 1 minute more. Add in cooked potatoes and broth. Bring to a boil, then lower the heat. Stir in the spinach and cook for another 3 minutes until wilted.

Balsamic Veggie & Rice Stew

Ingredients for 6 servings

2 tsp olive oil	2 garlic cloves, minced	4 tbsp balsamic vinegar
1 cups bell peppers	1 tbsp dried herbs	1 cup frozen peas, thawed
Salt and black pepper to taste	1 cup brown rice	1 cup unsweetened non-dairy milk
1 onion, chopped	2 cups vegetable broth	2 cups chopped kale

Directions and Total Time: 30 minutes

Heat the oil in a pot over medium heat. Place in bell peppers, onion, garlic, and salt and cook for 5 minutes until tender. Put in dried herbs, brown rice, broth, vinegar, and pepper. Bring to a boil, then lower the heat and simmer for 20 minutes. Stir in peas, milk, and kale until the kale wilts. Serve.

Chicago-Style Vegetable Stew

Ingredients for 4 servings

2 tbsp olive oils	1 red bell pepper, chopped	2 Salt and black pepper to taste
3 shallots, chopped	1 ½ cups vegetable broth	3 cups fresh corn kernels
1 carrot, sliced	2 zucchini, sliced	1 cup green beans
½ cup dry white wine	1 yellow summer squash, sliced	¼ cup fresh basil
3 new potatoes, cubed	1 lb plum tomatoes, chopped	¼ cup chopped fresh parsley

Directions and Total Time: 35 minutes

Heat oil in a pot over medium heat. Place shallots and carrot and cook for 5 minutes. Pour in white wine, potatoes, bell pepper, and broth. Bring to a boil, lower the heat, and simmer for 5 minutes. Stir in zucchini, yellow squash and tomatoes. Sprinkle with salt and pepper. Simmer for 20 more minutes. Put in corn, green peas, basil, and parsley. Simmer an additional 5 minutes. Serve hot.

Moroccan Bean Stew

Ingredients for 4 servings

3 cups cooked red kidney beans	1 tsp grated fresh ginger	1 (4-oz) can diced green chiles, drained
2 tbsp olive oil	½ tsp ground cumin	1 ½ cups vegetable broth
1 yellow onion, chopped	1 tsp ras el hanout	Salt and black pepper to taste
2 carrots, sliced	2 russet potatoes, chopped	3 cups eggplants, chopped
3 garlic cloves, minced	1 (14.5-oz) can crushed tomatoes	⅓ cup chopped roasted peanuts

Directions and Total Time: 40 minutes

Heat the oil in a pot over medium heat. Place the onion, garlic, ginger, and carrots and sauté for 5 minutes until tender. Stir in cumin, ras el hanout, potatoes, beans, tomatoes, chiles, and broth. Season with salt and pepper. Bring to a boil, then lower the heat and simmer for 20 minutes. Add in eggplants and cook for 10 minutes. Serve garnished with peanuts.

Mushroom & Bean Stew

Ingredients for 4 servings

2 tbsp olive oil	½ cup capers	8 oz porcini mushrooms, sliced
1 onion, chopped	1 medium zucchini, chopped	3 cups fresh baby spinach
1 carrot, chopped	1 (14.5-oz) can diced tomatoes	1 (15.5-oz) can cannellini beans,
2 garlic cloves, minced	1 cup vegetable broth	½ tsp dried basil
1 red bell pepper, chopped	Salt and black pepper to taste	2 tbsp minced fresh parsley

Directions and Total Time: 35 minutes

Heat oil in a pot and sauté onion, carrot, garlic, mushrooms, and bell pepper for 5 minutes. Stir in capers, zucchini, tomatoes, broth, salt, and pepper. Bring to a boil, then lower the heat and simmer for 20 minutes. Add in beans and basil. Simmer an additional 2-3 minutes. Serve topped with parsley.

Asian Veggie Stew

Ingredients for 5 servings

- 2 tbsp canola oil
- 1 onion, chopped
- 2 garlic cloves, minced
- 2 fresh hot chilies, minced
- 1 tbsp grated fresh ginger
- 1 russet potato, chopped
- 1 medium eggplant, chopped
- 8 oz green peas
- 2 cups cauliflower florets
- 2 cups vegetable broth
- 1 (14.5-oz) can crushed tomatoes
- 2 tbsp soy sauce
- ½ tsp ground turmeric
- 1 (13.5-oz) can coconut milk
- 1 tbsp tamarind paste
- 2 tbsp fresh lime juice
- 3 tbsp minced fresh cilantro
- 2 tbsp minced scallions

Directions and Total Time: 40 minutes

Warm oil in a pot over medium heat. Place onion, garlic, chilies, and ginger and cook for 5 minutes. Stir in potato, eggplant, green peas, cauliflower, broth, tomatoes, soy sauce, and turmeric. Cook for 20 minutes. Lower the heat and pour in coconut milk, tamarind, salt, and pepper. Simmer for 5 minutes. Mix in lime juice. Top with cilantro and scallions to serve.

Mediterranean Vegetable Stew

Ingredients for 4 servings

- 2 tbsp olive oil
- 1 onions, chopped
- 2 carrots, chopped
- ½ tsp ground cumin
- ½ tsp ground ginger
- ½ tsp paprika
- ½ tsp saffron
- 1 (14.5-oz) can diced tomatoes
- ½ head broccoli, cut into florets
- 2 cups winter squash, chopped
- 1 russet potato, cubed
- 1 ½ cups vegetable broth
- 1 (15.5-oz) can chickpeas, drained
- 1 tsp lemon zest
- Salt and black pepper to taste
- ½ cup pitted green olives
- 1 tbsp minced cilantro for garnish
- ½ cup toasted slivered almonds

Directions and Total Time: 30 minutes

Heat the oil in a pot over medium heat. Place onions and carrots and sauté for 5 minutes. Add in cumin, ginger, paprika, salt, pepper, and saffron and cook for 30 seconds. Stir in tomatoes, broccoli, squash, potato, chickpeas, and broth. Bring to a boil, then lower the heat and simmer for 20 minutes. Add in olives and lemon zest and simmer for 2-3 minutes. Garnish with cilantro and almonds to serve.

Chili Cannellini Bean Stew

Ingredients for 4 servings

- 2 tbsp olive oil
- 1 onion, chopped
- 2 potatoes, chopped
- 2 (15.5-oz) cans cannellini beans
- 1 (28-oz) can crushed tomatoes
- 1 (4-oz) can mild chopped green chilies
- 2 tbsp tamarind paste
- ¼ cup pure agave syrup
- 1 cup vegetable broth
- 2 tbsp chili powder
- 1 tsp ground coriander
- ½ tsp ground cumin
- Salt and black pepper to taste
- 1 cup frozen peas, thawed

Directions and Total Time: 40 minutes

Heat the oil in a pot over medium heat. Place in the onion and sauté for 3 minutes until translucent. Stir in potatoes, beans, tomatoes, and chilies. Cook for 5 minutes more. In a bowl, whisk the tamarind paste with agave syrup and broth. Pour the mixture into the pot. Stir in chili powder, coriander, cumin, salt, and pepper. Bring to a boil, then lower the heat and simmer for 20 minutes until the potatoes are tender. Add in peas and cook for another 5 minutes. Serve warm.

Fall Medley Stew

Ingredients for 4 servings

- 2 tbsp olive oil
- 8 oz seitan, cubed
- 1 leek, chopped
- 2 garlic cloves, minced
- 1 russet potato, chopped
- 1 carrot, chopped
- 1 parsnip, chopped
- 1 cup butternut squash, cubed
- 1 head savoy cabbage, chopped
- 1 (14.5-oz) can diced tomatoes
- 1 (15.5-oz) can white beans
- 2 cups vegetable broth
- ½ cup dry white wine
- ½ tsp dried thyme
- ½ cup crumbled angel hair pasta

Directions and Total Time: 65 minutes

Heat oil in a pot over medium heat. Place in seitan and cook for 3 minutes. Sprinkle with salt and pepper. Add in leek and garlic and cook for another 3 minutes. Stir in potato, carrot, parsnip, and squash, cook for 10 minutes. Add in cabbage, tomatoes, white beans, broth, wine, thyme, salt, and pepper. Bring to a boil, lower the heat and simmer for 15 minutes. Put in pasta and cook for 5 minutes.

SALADS & ENTRÉES

Greek Salad

Ingredients for 2 servings

½ yellow bell pepper, cut into pieces
3 tomatoes cut into bite-size pieces
½ cucumber, cut into bite-size pieces
½ red onion, peeled and sliced
½ cup tofu cheese, cut into squares
10 Kalamata olives, pitted
½ tbsp red wine vinegar
4 tbsp olive oil
2 tsp dried oregano

Directions and Total Time: 10 minutes

Pour the bell pepper, tomatoes, cucumber, red onion, tofu cheese, and olives into a salad bowl. Drizzle the red wine vinegar and olive oil over the vegetables. Season with salt, black pepper, and oregano, and toss the salad with two spoons. Share the salad into two bowls and serve immediately.

Squash Salad

Ingredients for 4 servings

2 lb green squash, cubed
2 tbsp plant butter
Salt and black pepper to taste
3 oz fennel, sliced
2 oz chopped green onions
1 cup tofu mayonnaise
2 tbsp fresh chives, finely chopped
A pinch of mustard powder
Chopped dill to garnish

Directions and Total Time: 20 minutes

Put a pan over medium heat and melt plant butter. Fry in squash cubes until slightly softened but not browned, about 7 minutes. Allow the squash to cool. In a salad bowl, mix the cooled squash, fennel slices, green onions, tofu mayonnaise, chives, and mustard powder. Garnish with dill and serve.

Beet Tofu Salad

Ingredients for 4 servings

8 oz red beets
2 oz tofu, chopped into little bits
2 tbsp plant butter
½ red onion
1 cup tofu mayonnaise
1 small romaine lettuce, torn
Freshly chopped chives
Salt and black pepper to taste

Directions and Total Time: 50 minutes

Put beets in a pot, cover with water, and bring to a boil for 40 minutes. Melt plant butter in a non-stick pan over medium heat and fry tofu until browned. Set aside to cool. When the bits are ready, drain through a colander and allow cooling. Slip the skin off after and slice them. In a salad bowl, combine the beets, tofu, red onions, lettuce, salt, pepper, and tofu mayonnaise and mix until the vegetables are adequately coated with the mayonnaise. Garnish with chives and serve.

Mango Rice Salad with Lime Dressing

Ingredients for 4 servings

3 ½ cups cooked brown rice
½ cup chopped roasted peanuts
½ cup sliced mango
4 green onions, chopped
3 tbsp fresh lime juice
2 tsp agave nectar
1 tsp grated fresh ginger
1/3 cup grapeseed oil
Salt and black pepper to taste

Directions and Total Time: 15 minutes

In a bowl, mix the rice, peanuts, mango, and green onions. Set aside. In another bowl, whisk the lime juice, agave nectar, and ginger. Add in oil, salt and pepper, stir to combine. Pour over the rice bowl and toss to coat. Serve immediately.

Savory Pasta Salad with Cannellini Beans

Ingredients for 4 servings

2 ½ cups whole-wheat bow tie pasta
1 tbsp olive oil
1 medium zucchini, sliced
2 garlic cloves, minced
2 large tomatoes, chopped
1 (15 oz) can cannellini beans
1 (2 ¼ oz) can green olives, sliced
½ cup crumbled tofu cheese

Directions and Total Time: 35 minutes

Cook the pasta until al dente, 10 minutes. Drain and set aside. Heat olive oil in a skillet and sauté zucchini and garlic for 4 minutes. Stir in tomatoes, beans, and olives. Cook until the tomatoes soften, 10 minutes. Mix in pasta. Allow warming for 1 minute. Stir in tofu cheese and serve warm.

Bean & Farro Salad

Ingredients for 4 servings

1 (14-oz) can black beans
1 cup corn kernels
¼ cup fresh cilantro, chopped
Zest and juice of 1 lime
3 tsp chili powder
Sea salt and black pepper to taste

1 ½ cups cherry tomatoes, halved
1 red bell pepper, chopped
2 scallions, chopped
4 large whole-grain tortillas
2 tsp olive oil
1 tbsp oregano

1 tsp cayenne pepper
4 cups watercress and arugula mix
¾ cup cooked faro
¼ cup chopped avocado
¼ cup mango salsa

Directions and Total Time: 20 minutes

Combine black beans, corn, cilantro, lime juice, lime zest, chili powder, salt, pepper, cherry tomatoes, bell peppers, and scallions in a bowl. Set aside. Brush the tortillas with olive oil and season with salt, pepper, oregano, and cayenne pepper. Slice into 8 pieces. Line with parchment paper a baking sheet. Arrange tortilla pieces and bake for 3-5 minutes until browned. On a serving platter, put the watercress and arugula mix, top with faro, bean mixture, avocado, and sprinkle with mango salsa all over to serve.

Orange & Kale Salad

Ingredients for 4 servings

2 tbsp Dijon mustard
2 tbsp olive oil
¼ cup fresh orange juice

1 tsp agave nectar
2 tbsp minced fresh parsley
1 tbsp minced green onions

4 cups fresh kale, chopped
1 orange, peeled and segmented
½ red onion, sliced paper-thin

Directions and Total Time: 10 minutes

In a food processor, place the mustard, oil, orange juice, agave nectar, salt, pepper, parsley, and green onions. Blend until smooth. Set aside. In a bowl, combine the kale, orange, and onion. Pour over the dressing and toss to coat. Serve.

African Zucchini Salad

Ingredients for 2 servings

1 lemon, half zested and juiced, half cut into wedges
1 tsp olive oil 1 zucchini, chopped
½ tsp ground cumin
½ tsp ground ginger

¼ tsp turmeric
¼ tsp ground nutmeg
A pinch of salt
2 tbsp capers
1 tbsp chopped green olives

1 garlic clove, pressed
2 tbsp fresh mint, finely chopped
2 cups spinach, chopped

Directions and Total Time: 20 minutes

Warm olive oil in a skillet over medium heat. Place the zucchini and sauté for 10 minutes. Stir in cumin, ginger, turmeric, nutmeg, and salt. Pour in lemon zest, lemon juice, capers, garlic, and mint, cook for 2 minutes more. Divide the spinach between serving plates and top with the zucchini mixture. Garnish with lemon wedges and olives.

Tangy Nutty Brussel Sprout Salad

Ingredients for 4 servings

1 lb Brussels sprouts, grated
1 lemon, juiced and zested
½ cup olive oil

1 tbsp plant butter
1 tsp chili paste
2 oz pecans

1 oz pumpkin seeds
1 oz sunflower seeds
½ tsp cumin powder

Directions and Total Time: 20 minutes

Put Brussels sprouts in a salad bowl. In a small bowl, mix lemon juice, zest, olive oil, salt, and pepper, and drizzle the dressing over the Brussels sprouts. Toss and allow the vegetable to marinate for 10 minutes. Melt plant butter in a pan. Stir in chili paste and toss the pecans, pumpkin seeds, sunflower seeds, cumin powder, and salt in the chili butter. Sauté on low heat for 3-4 minutes just to heat the nuts. Allow cooling. Pour the nuts and seeds mix in the salad bowl, toss, and serve.

Warm Collard Salad

Ingredients for 2 servings

¾ cup coconut whipping cream
2 tbsp tofu mayonnaise
A pinch of mustard powder

2 tbsp coconut oil
1 garlic clove, minced
Salt and black pepper to taste

2 oz plant butter
1 cup collards, rinsed
4 oz tofu cheese

Directions and Total Time: 10 minutes

In a small bowl, whisk the coconut whipping cream, tofu mayonnaise, mustard powder, coconut oil, garlic, salt, and black pepper until well mixed; set aside. Melt the plant butter in a large skillet over medium heat and sauté the collards until wilted and brownish. Season with salt and black pepper to taste. Transfer the collards to a salad bowl and pour the creamy dressing over. Mix the salad well and crumble the tofu cheese over. Serve.

Roasted Mushrooms and Green Beans Salad

Ingredients for 4 servings

1 lb cremini mushrooms, sliced	3 tbsp melted plant butter	Juice of 1 lemon
½ cup green beans	Salt and black pepper to taste	4 tbsp toasted hazelnuts

Directions and Total Time: 25 minutes

Preheat oven to 450 F.

Arrange the mushrooms and green beans in a baking dish, drizzle the plant butter over, and sprinkle with salt and black pepper. Use your hands to rub the vegetables with the seasoning and roast in the oven for 20 minutes or until they are soft. Transfer the vegetables into a salad bowl, drizzle with the lemon juice, and toss the salad with the hazelnuts. Serve the salad immediately.

Bean & Couscous Salad

Ingredients for 4 servings

¼ cup olive oil	1 cup couscous	¼ cup golden raisins
1 medium shallot, minced	2 cups vegetable broth	¼ cup chopped roasted cashews
½ tsp ground coriander	1 yellow bell pepper, chopped	1 (15.5-oz) can white beans
½ tsp turmeric	1 carrot, shredded	2 tbsp minced fresh cilantro leaves
¼ tsp ground cayenne	½ cup chopped dried apricots	2 tbsp fresh lemon juice

Directions and Total Time: 15 minutes

Heat 1 tbsp of oil in a pot over medium heat. Place in shallot, coriander, turmeric, cayenne pepper, and couscous. Cook for 2 minutes, stirring often. Add in broth and salt. Bring to a boil. Turn the heat off and let sit covered for 5 minutes. Remove to a bowl and stir in bell pepper, carrot, apricots, raisins, cashews, beans, and cilantro. Set aside. In another bowl, whisk the remaining oil with lemon juice until blended. Pour over the salad and toss to combine. Serve immediately.

Seitan & Spinach Salad a la Puttanesca

Ingredients for 4 servings

4 tbsp olive oil	½ cup green olives, halved	2 tbsp balsamic vinegar
8 oz seitan, cut into strips	2 tbsp capers	2 tbsp torn fresh basil leaves
2 garlic cloves, minced	3 cups baby spinach, cut into strips	2 tbsp minced fresh parsley
½ cup Kalamata olives, halved	1 ½ cups cherry tomatoes, halved	1 cup pomegranate seeds

Directions and Total Time: 11 minutes

Heat half of the olive oil in a skillet over medium heat. Place the seitan and brown for 5 minutes on all sides. Add in garlic and cook for 30 seconds. Remove to a bowl and let cool. Stir in olives, capers, spinach, and tomatoes. Set aside.

In another bowl, whisk the remaining oil, vinegar, salt, and pepper until well mixed. Pour this dressing over the seitan salad and toss to coat. Top with basil, parsley, and pomegranate seeds. Serve.

Tomato & Avocado Lettuce Salad

Ingredients for 4 servings

1 garlic clove, chopped	¼ tsp pure date sugar	12 ripe grape tomatoes, halved
1 red onion, sliced	3 tbsp white wine vinegar	½ cup frozen peas, thawed
½ tsp dried basil	1/3 cup olive oil	8 black olives, pitted
Salt and black pepper to taste	1 head Iceberg lettuce, shredded	1 avocado, sliced

Directions and Total Time: 15 minutes

In a food processor, place the garlic, onion, oil, basil, salt, pepper, sugar, and vinegar. Blend until smooth. Set aside. Place the lettuce, tomatoes, peas, and olives on a nice serving plate. Top with avocado slices and drizzle the previously prepared dressing all over. Serve.

Fried Broccoli Salad with Tempeh & Cranberries

Ingredients for 4 servings

3 oz plant butter	1 lb broccoli florets	2 oz almonds
¾ lb tempeh slices, cubed	Salt and black pepper to taste	½ cup frozen cranberries

Directions and Total Time: 15 minutes

In a skillet, melt the plant butter over medium heat until no longer foaming, and fry the tempeh cubes until brown on all sides. Add the broccoli and stir-fry for 6 minutes. Season with salt and pepper. Turn the heat off. Stir in the almonds and cranberries to warm through. Share salad into bowls and serve.

Balsamic Lentil Salad

Ingredients for 4 servings

2 tsp olive oil	1 cup lentils	2 cups water
1 red onion, diced	1 tbsp dried basil	Sea salt to taste
1 garlic clove, minced	1 tbsp dried oregano	2 cups chopped Swiss chard
1 carrot, diced	1 tbsp balsamic vinegar	2 cups torn curly endive

Directions and Total Time: 40 minutes

In a bowl, mix the balsamic vinegar, olive oil, and salt. Set aside. Warm 1 tsp of oil in a pot over medium heat. Place the onion and carrot and cook for 5 minutes. Mix in lentils, basil, oregano, balsamic vinegar, and water and bring to a boil. Lower the heat and simmer for 20 minutes.

Mix in two-thirds of the dressing. Add in the Swiss chard and cook for 5 minutes on low. Let cool. Coat the endive with the remaining dressing. Transfer to a plate and top with lentil mixture to serve.

Warm Green Bean & Potato Salad

Ingredients for 4 servings

Salt and black pepper to taste	2 carrots, sliced	2 tsp dried dill
1 cup green beans, chopped	1 tbsp extra-virgin olive oil	1 cup cashew cream
4 potatoes, quartered	1 tbsp lime juice	

Directions and Total Time: 25 minutes

Pour salted water in a pot over medium heat. Add in potatoes, bring to a boil and cook for 8 minutes. Put in carrots and green beans and cook for 8 minutes. Drain and put in a bowl. Mix in olive oil, lime juice, dill, cashew cream, salt, and pepper. Toss to coat. Allow cooling before serving.

Millet Salad with Olives & Cherries

Ingredients for 4 servings

1 cup millet	3 green onions, minced	½ cup minced fresh parsley
1 (15.5-oz) can navy beans	½ cup chopped kalamata olives	1 garlic clove, pressed
1 celery stalk, finely chopped	½ cup dried cherries	3 tbsp sherry vinegar
1 carrot, shredded	½ cup toasted pecans, chopped	¼ cup grapeseed oil

Directions and Total Time: 40 minutes

Cook the millet in salted water for 30 minutes. Remove to a bowl. Mix in beans, celery, carrot, green onions, olives, cherries, pecans, and parsley. Set aside. In another bowl, whisk the garlic, vinegar, salt, and pepper until well mixed. Pour over the millet mixture and toss to coat. Serve immediately.

Daikon Salad with Caramelized Onion

Ingredients for 4 servings

1 lb daikon, peeled	2 tsp olive oil	1 tbsp rice vinegar
2 cups sliced sweet onions	Salt to taste	

Directions and Total Time: 50 minutes

Place the daikon in a pot with salted water and cook 25 minutes, until tender. Drain and let cool. In a skillet over low heat, warm olive oil and add the onion. Sauté for 10-15 minutes until caramelized. Sprinkle with salt. Remove to a bowl. Chop the daikon into wedges and add to the onion bowl. Stir in the vinegar. Serve.

Quick Fresh Salad

Ingredients for 4 servings

- 1 lb carrots, shredded
- 2 oranges, chopped
- ½ cup roasted walnuts
- ¼ cup chopped fresh parsley
- 2 tbsp fresh orange juice
- 2 tbsp fresh lime juice
- 2 tsp pure date sugar
- Salt and black pepper to taste
- ¼ cup olive oil

Directions and Total Time: 15 minutes

In a bowl, mix the carrots, oranges, walnuts, and parsley. Set aside. In another bowl, whisk the orange juice, lime juice, sugar, salt, pepper, and oil. Mix until blended. Pour over the carrots mixture and toss to coat. Adjust the seasoning. Serve.

Radish & Tomato Salad

Ingredients for 4 servings

- 2 tomatoes, sliced
- 6 small red radishes, sliced
- 2 ½ tbsp white wine vinegar
- ½ tsp chopped chervil
- Salt and black pepper to taste
- ¼ cup olive oil

Directions and Total Time: 15 minutes

Mix the tomatoes and radishes in a bowl. Set aside.

In another bowl, whisk the vinegar, chervil, salt, and pepper until mixed. Pour over the salad and toss to coat. Serve.

Carrot & Cabbage Salad with Avocado & Capers

Ingredients for 4 servings

- 1 carrot, shredded
- 1 cup finely shredded red cabbage
- 1 cup cherry tomatoes, halved
- 1 yellow bell pepper, cut into sticks
- 1 (15.5-oz) can chickpeas
- ¼ cup capers
- 1 avocado, sliced
- ¼ cup olive oil
- 1 ½ tbsp fresh lemon juice

Directions and Total Time: 15 minutes

Combine the carrot, cabbage, tomatoes, bell pepper, chickpeas, capers, and avocado in a bowl. In another bowl, mix the oil, lemon juice, salt, and pepper until thoroughly combined. Pour over the cabbage mixture and toss to coat. Serve.

Chickpea & Celery Salad

Ingredients for 4 servings

- 1 (15.5-oz) can chickpeas
- 1 head fennel bulb, sliced
- ½ cup sliced red onion
- ½ cup celery leaves, chopped
- ¼ cup vegan mayonnaise
- Salt and black pepper to taste

Directions and Total Time: 5 minutes

In a bowl, mash the chickpeas until chunky. Stir in fennel bulb, onion, celery, vegan mayonnaise, salt, and pepper. Serve.

Mexican Bean Salad

Ingredients for 4 servings

- ¼ cup vegan salad dressing
- 1 tsp chili powder
- 2 (14.5-oz) cans kidney beans
- 2 cups frozen corn, thawed
- 1 cup cooked pearl barley
- 1 head chopped Iceberg lettuce

Directions and Total Time: 15 minutes

Mix the salad dressing and chili powder in a bowl. Add in kidney beans, corn, barley and lettuce. Serve.

Traditional Lebanese Salad

Ingredients for 4 servings

- 1 cup cooked bulgur
- 1 cup boiling water
- Zest and juice of 1 lemon
- 1 garlic clove, pressed
- Sea salt to taste
- 1 tbsp olive oil
- ½ cucumber, sliced
- 1 tomato, sliced
- 1 cup fresh parsley, chopped
- ¼ cup fresh mint, chopped
- 2 scallions, chopped
- 4 tbsp sunflower seeds

Directions and Total Time: 25 minutes

In a bowl, mix the lemon juice, lemon zest, garlic, salt, and olive oil. Stir in cucumber, tomato, parsley, mint, and scallions. Toss to coat. Fluff the bulgur and put into the cucumber mix. Stir to combine. Top with sunflower seeds and serve.

Cucumber, Lettuce & Tomato Salad

Ingredients for 4 servings

- ¾ cup olive oil
- ¼ cup white wine vinegar
- 2 tsp Dijon mustard
- 1 garlic clove
- 1 tbsp minced green onions
- ½ head romaine lettuce, chopped
- ½ head iceberg lettuce, chopped
- 1 (15.5-oz) can lentils, drained
- 2 ripe tomatoes, chopped
- 1 cucumber, peeled and chopped
- 1 carrot, chopped
- ½ cup halved pitted kalamata olives
- 3 small red radishes, chopped
- 2 tbsp chopped fresh parsley
- 1 ripe avocado, chopped

Directions and Total Time: 15 minutes

Put the oil, vinegar, mustard, garlic, green onions, salt, and pepper in a food processor. Pulse until blended. Set aside. In a bowl, place the lettuces, lentils, tomatoes, cucumber, carrot, olives, radishes, parsley, and avocado. Pour enough dressing over the salad and toss to coat. Serve immediately.

Tropical Salad

Ingredients for 4 servings

- ½ tsp minced garlic
- ½ tsp grated fresh ginger
- ¼ cup olive oil
- ¼ tsp crushed red pepper
- 3 tbsp rice vinegar
- 3 tbsp water
- 1 tbsp soy sauce
- 2 cups snow peas, sliced and blanched
- 3 papaya, chopped
- 1 large carrot, shredded
- 1 cucumber, peeled and sliced
- 3 cups shredded romaine lettuce
- ½ cup chopped roasted almonds
- Salt to taste

Directions and Total Time: 15 minutes

Combine the garlic, ginger, olive oil, red pepper, vinegar, water, salt, and soy sauce in a bowl. Set aside.

In another bowl, add in papaya, snow peas, cucumber slices, and carrot. Drizzle with the dressing and toss to coat. Place a bed of lettuce on a plate and top with the salad. Serve topped with almonds.

Mediterranean Pasta Salad

Ingredients for 4 servings

- 8 oz whole-wheat pasta
- 1 (15.5-oz) can chickpeas
- ½ cup pitted black olives
- ½ cup minced sun-dried tomatoes
- 1 (6-oz) jar dill pickles, sliced
- 2 roasted red peppers, chopped
- ½ cup frozen peas, thawed
- 1 tbsp capers
- 3 tsp dried chives
- ½ cup olive oil
- ¼ cup white wine vinegar
- ½ tsp dried basil
- 1 garlic clove, minced
- Salt and black pepper to taste

Directions and Total Time: 15 minutes

Cook the pasta in salted water for 8-10 minutes until al dente. Drain and remove to a bowl. Stir in chickpeas, olives, tomatoes, dill pickles, roasted peppers, peas, capers, and chives. In another bowl, whisk oil, vinegar, basil, garlic, sugar, salt, and pepper. Pour over the pasta and toss to coat. Serve.

Zucchini & Bell Pepper Salad with Beans

Ingredients for 2 servings

- 1 tbsp olive oil
- 2 tbsp balsamic vinegar
- 1 tsp minced fresh chives
- 1 garlic clove, minced
- 1 tbsp fresh rosemary, chopped
- 1 tbsp fresh oregano, chopped
- A pinch of salt
- 1 (14-oz) can cannellini beans
- 1 green bell pepper, sliced
- 1 zucchini, diced
- 2 carrots, diced
- 2 tbsp fresh basil, chopped

Directions and Total Time: 40 minutes

In a bowl, mix the olive oil, balsamic vinegar, chives, garlic, rosemary, oregano, and salt. Stir in the beans, bell pepper, zucchini, carrots, and basil. Serve.

Bulgur & Kale Salad

Ingredients for 4 servings

- 1 avocado, peeled and pitted
- 1 tbsp fresh lemon juice
- 1 tbsp fresh dill
- 1 small garlic clove, pressed
- 1 scallion, chopped
- Sea salt to taste
- 8 large kale leaves, chopped
- ½ cup chopped green beans, steamed
- 1 cup cherry tomatoes, halved
- 1 bell pepper, chopped
- 2 scallions, chopped
- 2 cups cooked bulgur

Directions and Total Time: 30 minutes

In a food processor, place the avocado, lemon juice, dill, garlic, scallion, salt, and ¼ cup water. Blend until smooth. Set aside the dressing. Put kale, green beans, cherry tomatoes, bell pepper, scallions, and bulgur in a serving bowl. Add in the dressing and toss to coat. Serve.

Cashew & Raisin Salad with & Haricots Verts

Ingredients for 4 servings

3 cups haricots verts, chopped
2 carrots, sliced
3 cups shredded cabbage
1/3 cup golden raisins
¼ cup roasted cashew

1 garlic clove, minced
1 medium shallot, chopped
1 ½ tsp grated fresh ginger
⅓ cup creamy peanut butter
2 tbsp soy sauce

2 tbsp fresh lemon juice
Salt to taste
⅛ tsp ground cayenne
¾ cup coconut milk

Directions and Total Time: 15 minutes

Place the haricots verts, carrots, and cabbage in a pot with water and steam for 5 minutes. Drain and transfer to a bowl. Add in raisins and cashew. Let cool. In a food processor, put the garlic, shallot, and ginger. Pulse until puréed. Add in peanut butter, soy sauce, lemon juice, salt, cayenne pepper. Blitz until smooth. Stir in coconut milk. Sprinkle the salad with the dressing and toss to coat.

Lettuce & Tomato Salad with Quinoa

Ingredients for 4 servings

1 ½ cups dry quinoa, drained
2 ¼ cups water
⅓ cup white wine vinegar

2 tbsp extra-virgin olive oil
1 tbsp chopped fresh dill
Salt and black pepper to taste

2 cups sliced sweet onions
2 tomatoes, sliced
4 cups shredded lettuce

Directions and Total Time: 25 minutes

Place the quinoa in a pot with salted water. Bring to a boil. Lower the heat and simmer covered for 15 minutes. Turn the heat off and let sit for 5 minutes. Using a fork, fluff the quinoa and set aside. In a small bowl, whisk the vinegar, olive oil, dill, salt, and pepper; set aside. In a serving plate, combine onions, tomatoes, quinoa, and lettuce. Pour in the dressing and toss to coat. Serve.

Minty Eggplant Salad

Ingredients for 2 servings

1 lemon, half zested and juiced, half cut into wedges
1 tsp olive oil
1 eggplant, chopped
½ tsp ground cumin
½ tsp ground ginger

¼ tsp turmeric
¼ tsp ground nutmeg
Sea salt to taste
2 tbsp capers

1 tbsp chopped green olives
1 garlic clove, pressed
2 tbsp fresh mint, finely chopped
2 cups watercress, chopped

Directions and Total Time: 45 minutes

In a skillet over medium heat, warm the oil. Place the eggplant and cook for 5 minutes. Add in cumin, ginger, turmeric, nutmeg, and salt. Cook for another 10 minutes. Stir in lemon zest, lemon juice, capers, olives, garlic, and mint. Cook for 1-2 minutes more. Place some watercress on each plate and top with the eggplant mixture. Serve immediately.

Potato & Green Bean Salad

Ingredients for 4 servings

1 ½ lb small potatoes, unpeeled
1 cup frozen green beans, thawed
½ cup shredded carrots
4 green onions, chopped

1 tbsp grapeseed oil
1 garlic clove, minced
1/3 cup peanut butter
½ tsp Asian chili paste

2 tbsp soy sauce
1 tbsp rice vinegar
¾ cup coconut milk
3 tbsp chopped roasted peanuts

Directions and Total Time: 30 minutes

Place the potatoes in a pot with boiling salted water and cook for 20 minutes. Drain and let cool. Chop into chunks and place in a bowl. Stir in green beans, carrots, and green onions. Set aside.

Heat oil in a pot over medium heat. Place in garlic and cook for 30 seconds. Add in peanut butter, chili, soy sauce, vinegar, coconut milk. Cook for 5 minutes, stirring often. Pour over the potatoes and toss to coat. Serve garnished with peanuts.

Artichoke & Potato Salad

Ingredients for 4 servings

1 (10-oz) package frozen artichoke hearts, cooked
1 ½ lb potatoes, chopped
2 cups halved cherry tomatoes
½ cup sweet corn
3 green onions, minced
1 tbsp minced fresh parsley
⅓ cup olive oil
2 tbsp fresh lemon juice
1 garlic clove, minced
Salt and black pepper to taste

Directions and Total Time: 30 minutes

Place the potatoes in a pot with salted water and boil for 15 minutes. Drain and remove to a bowl.
Cut the artichokes by quarts and mix into the potato bowl. Stir in tomatoes, corn, green onions, and parsley. Set aside. Whisk the oil, lemon juice, garlic, salt, and pepper in a bowl. Pour over the potatoes and toss to coat. Let sit for 20 minutes.

Italian Vegetable Relish

Ingredients for 6 servings

¼ cup sliced pimiento-stuffed green olives
1 carrot, sliced
1 medium red bell pepper, sliced
1 cup cauliflower florets
2 celery stalks, chopped
½ cup chopped red onion
1 garlic clove, minced
1 jalapeño pepper, chopped
3 tbsp white wine vinegar
⅓ cup olive oil

Directions and Total Time: 15 minutes

Combine the carrot, bell pepper, cauliflower, celery, and onion in a bowl. Add in salt and cold water. Cover and transfer to the fridge for 4-6 hours. Strain and wash the veggies. Remove to a bowl and mix in olives. Set aside. In another bowl, mix the garlic, jalapeño pepper, vinegar, and oil. Pour over the veggies and toss to coat. Let chill in the fridge and serve.

Colorful Quinoa Salad

Ingredients for 6 servings

1 cup canned mandarin oranges in juice, drained
3 tbsp olive oil
Juice of 1 ½ lemons
1 tsp garlic powder
½ tsp dried oregano
1 bunch baby spinach
2 cups cooked tricolor quinoa
1 cup diced yellow summer squash
1 red bell pepper, diced
½ red onion, sliced
½ cup dried cranberries
½ cup slivered almonds

Directions and Total Time: 15 minutes

Mix the oil, lemon juice, garlic powder, and oregano in a bowl. In another bowl, place the spinach and pour over the dressing, toss to coat. Stir in quinoa, oranges, squash, bell pepper, and red onion. Share into bowls and garnish with cranberries and almonds to serve.

Radish & Cabbage Ginger Salad

Ingredients for 4 servings

8 oz napa cabbage, cut crosswise into strips
1 cup grated carrots
1 cup sliced radishes
2 green onions, minced
2 tbsp chopped fresh parsley
2 tbsp rice vinegar
2 tsp toasted sesame oil
1 tbsp soy sauce
1 tsp grated fresh ginger
½ tsp dry mustard
Salt and black pepper to taste
2 tbsp chopped roasted hazelnuts

Directions and Total Time: 15 minutes

Place the napa cabbage, carrot, radishes, green onions, and parsley in a bowl, stir to combine. In another bowl, mix vinegar, sesame oil, soy sauce, ginger, mustard, salt, and pepper. Pour over the slaw and toss to coat. Marinate covered in the fridge for 2 hours. Serve topped with hazelnuts.

Coleslaw & Spinach Salad with Grapefruit

Ingredients for 4 servings

1 large grapefruit
2 cups coleslaw mix
2 cups green leaf lettuce, torn
2 cups baby spinach
1 bunch watercress
6 radishes, sliced
Juice of 1 lemon
2 tsp date syrup
1 tsp white wine vinegar
Sea salt and black pepper
¼ cup extra-virgin olive oil

Directions and Total Time: 10 minutes

Slice the grapefruit by cutting the ends, peeling all the white pith, and making an incise in the membrane to take out on each segment. Transfer to a bowl. Stir in coleslaw, lettuce, spinach, watercress, and radishes. In a bowl, mix the lemon juice, date syrup, vinegar, salt, and pepper. Gently beat the olive oil until emulsified. Pour over the salad and toss to coat.

Lemon Potato Salad with Kalamata Olives

Ingredients for 4 servings

4 potatoes, chopped
Salt and black pepper to taste
¼ cup olive oil
2 tbsp apple cider vinegar
2 tbsp lemon juice
1 tsp dried dill
½ cucumber, chopped
¼ red onion, diced
¼ cup chopped kalamata olives

Directions and Total Time: 30 minutes

In a pot with salted water, place the potatoes. Bring to a boil and cook for 20 minutes. Drain and let cool. Mix the olive oil, vinegar, lemon juice, and dill in a bowl. Add in cucumber, red onion, and olives. Toss to coat. Stir in the potatoes. Season with salt and pepper. Serve.

Beet & Cucumber Salad with Balsamic Dressing

Ingredients for 2 servings

3 beets, peeled and sliced
1 tsp olive oil
1 cucumber, sliced
2 cups mixed greens
4 tbsp balsamic dressing
2 tbsp chopped almonds

Directions and Total Time: 40 minutes

Preheat oven to 390 F.

In a bowl, stir the beets, oil, and salt. Toss to coat. Transfer to a baking dish and roast for 20 minutes, until golden brown. Once the beets are ready, divide between 2 plates and place a cucumber slice on each beet. Top with mixed greens. Pour over the dressing and garnish with almonds to serve.

Chinese-Style Cabbage Salad

Ingredients for 6 servings

4 cups shredded red cabbage
2 cups thinly sliced napa cabbage
1 cup red radishes, sliced
¼ cup fresh orange juice
2 tbsp Chinese black vinegar
1 tbsp soy sauce
2 tbsp toasted sesame oil
1 tsp grated fresh ginger
1 tbsp black sesame seeds

Directions and Total Time: 15 minutes

Mix the red cabbage, napa cabbage, and radishes in a bowl. In another bowl, whisk the orange juice, vinegar, soy sauce, sesame oil, and ginger. Pour over the slaw and toss to coat. Marinate covered in the fridge for 2 hours. Serve topped with sesame seeds.

Radicchio & Cabbage Coleslaw

Ingredients for 2 servings

½ head white cabbage, shredded
¼ head radicchio, shredded
1 large carrot, shredded
¾ cup vegan mayonnaise
¼ cup soy milk
1 tbsp cider vinegar
½ tsp dry mustard
¼ tsp celery seeds
Salt and black pepper to taste

Directions and Total Time: 10 minutes

Combine cabbage, radicchio, and carrot in a bowl. In another bowl, whisk mayonnaise, soy milk, mustard, vinegar, celery seeds, salt, and pepper. Pour over the slaw and toss to coat. Serve immediately.

Avocado Salad with Sesame Seeds

Ingredients for 4 servings

2 medium avocados, sliced
3 tbsp sesame oil
2 tbsp soy sauce
1 tbsp mirin
2 tsp rice vinegar
2 tbsp toasted sesame seeds

Directions and Total Time: 15 minutes

Place the avocado in a bowl. Set aside. In another bowl, mix the oil, soy sauce, mirin, and vinegar. Pour over the avocado and toss to coat. Let sit for 10 minutes. Serve in bowls topped with sesame seeds.

Cilantro Chickpea & Corn Salad

Ingredients for 4 servings

- 1 cup corn kernels
- 1 (15.5-oz) can chickpeas
- 1 celery stalk, sliced
- 2 green onions, minced
- 2 tbsp chopped fresh cilantro
- ¼ cup olive oil
- 2 tbsp white wine vinegar
- ½ tsp ground cumin
- Salt and black pepper to taste

Directions and Total Time: 10 minutes

Combine the corn, chickpeas, celery, green onions, and cilantro in a bowl. Set aside. In another bowl, mix the oil, vinegar, cumin, salt, and pepper. Pour over the salad and toss to coat. Serve immediately.

Easy Pineapple & Jicama Salad

Ingredients for 6 servings

- 1 jicama, peeled and grated
- 1 pineapple, peeled and sliced
- ¼ cup non-dairy milk
- 2 tbsp fresh basil, chopped
- 1 large scallion, chopped
- Sea salt to taste
- 1 ½ tbsp tahini
- Arugula for serving
- Chopped cashews

Directions and Total Time: 15 minutes

Place jicama in a bowl. In a food processor, put the pineapple and enough milk. Blitz until puréed. Add in basil, scallions, tahini, and salt. Pour over the jicama and cover. Transfer to the fridge and marinate for 1 hour. Place a bed of arugula on a plate and top with the salad. Serve garnished with cashews.

Broccoli & Mango Rice Salad

Ingredients for 4 servings

- ½ cup brown rice, rinsed
- 3 cups broccoli florets, blanched
- 1 mango, chopped
- 1 small red bell pepper, chopped
- 1 jalapeño, seeded and minced
- 1 tsp grated fresh ginger
- 2 tbsp fresh lemon juice
- 3 tbsp grapeseed oil
- 1/3 cup roasted almonds, chopped

Directions and Total Time: 25 minutes

Place the rice in a bowl with salted water and cook for 18-20 minutes. Remove to a bowl. Stir in broccoli, mango, bell pepper, and chili. In another bowl, mix the ginger, lemon juice, and oil. Pour over the rice and toss to combine. Top with almonds to serve.

Mom´s Caesar Salad

Ingredients for 4 servings

- ½ cup cashews
- ½ cup water
- 3 tbsp olive oil
- Juice of ½ lime
- 1 tbsp white miso paste
- 1 tsp soy sauce
- 1 tsp Dijon mustard
- 1 tsp garlic powder
- Sea salt and black pepper to taste
- 2 heads romaine lettuce, chopped
- 2 tsp capers
- 1 cup cherry tomatoes, halved
- Plant-based Parmesan cheese
- Whole-what bread croutons

Directions and Total Time: 10 minutes

In a blender, put cashews, water, olive oil, lime juice, miso paste, soy sauce, mustard, garlic powder, salt, and pepper. Blend until smooth. Mix the lettuce with half of dressing in a bowl. Divide in individual bowls and add in capers, tomatoes, and plant-based Parmesan cheese. Serve topped with croutons.

Baked Potato & Black-Eyed Pea Salad

Ingredients for 4 servings

- 1 ½ lb potatoes, chopped
- 1 red onion, sliced
- ¼ cup olive oil
- Salt and black pepper to taste
- 3 tbsp white wine vinegar
- 1 (15.5-oz) can black-eyed peas
- 1/3 cup chopped sun-dried tomatoes
- ¼ cup green olives, halved
- ¼ cup chopped fresh parsley

Directions and Total Time: 25 minutes

Preheat oven to 420 F.

In a bowl, mix the potatoes, onion, and 1 tbsp of oil. Sprinkle with salt and pepper. Spread on a baking sheet and roast for 20 minutes. Remove to a bowl and let cool. In another bowl, combine the remaining oil, vinegar and pepper. Stir the peas, tomatoes, olives, and parsley into the potato bowl. Pour over the dressing and toss to coat. Adjust seasonings and serve.

Fantastic Green Salad

Ingredients for 4 servings

1 head Iceberg lettuce
8 asparagus spears, chopped
2 mini seedless cucumbers, sliced
1 small zucchini, cut into ribbons
1 carrot, cut into ribbons
1 avocado, sliced
½ cup vegan green dres[sing]
2 scallions, thinly slice[d]

Directions and Total Time: 10 minutes

Share the lettuce into 4 bowls and add in some asparagus, cucumber, zucchini, carrot, and avocado. Sprinkle each bowl with 2 tbsp of dressing. Serve garnished with scallions.

Chickpea & Quinoa Salad with Capers

Ingredients for 4 servings

1 cup quinoa, rinsed
1 (15.5-oz) can chickpeas
1 cup cherry tomatoes, halved
2 green onions, minced
½ cucumber, peeled and chopped
¼ cup capers
2 tbsp toasted pine nuts
1 medium shallot, sliced
1 garlic clove, chopped
1 tsp Dijon mustard
2 tbsp white wine vinegar
¼ cup olive oil

Directions and Total Time: 25 minutes

Boil salted water in a pot over medium heat. Add in quinoa, lower the heat and simmer for 15 minutes. Remove to a bowl. Stir in chickpeas, tomatoes, green onions, cucumber, capers, and pine nuts. Set aside. In a food processor, put the shallot, garlic, mustard, vinegar, oil, salt, and pepper. Pulse until blend. Pour over the salad and toss to coat. Serve immediately.

Apple & Spinach Salad with Walnut Crunch

Ingredients for 4 servings

¼ cup tahini
2 tbsp Dijon mustard
3 tbsp maple syrup
1 tbsp lemon juice
½ cup finely chopped walnuts
2 tsp soy sauce
1 lb baby spinach
1 green apple, cored and sliced

Directions and Total Time: 20 minutes

Preheat oven to 360 F. Line with parchment paper a baking sheet. In a bowl, mix the tahini, mustard, 2 tbsp maple syrup, lemon juice, and salt. Set aside the dressing.

In another bowl, combine the walnuts, soy sauce, and the remaining maple syrup. Spread evenly on the baking sheet and bake for 5 minutes, shaking once until crunchy. Allow cooling for 3 minutes. Combine the spinach and apples in a bowl. Pour over the dressing and toss to coat. Serve garnished with the walnut crunch.

Dijon Potato Salad

Ingredients for 4 servings

1 ½ lb small potatoes, unpeeled
2 celery stalks, sliced
¼ cup sweet pickle relish
3 tbsp minced green onions
¾ cup vegan mayonnaise
1 tbsp soy milk
1 tbsp white wine vinegar
1 tsp Dijon mustard
10 black olives, pitted and sliced

Directions and Total Time: 25 minutes

Place the potatoes in a pot with boiling salted water and cook for 20 minutes. Drain and let cool. Once the potatoes are cooled, peel them and cut into small cubes. Remove to a bowl. Stir in celery, pickle relish, and green onions. In another bowl, mix the mayonnaise, soy milk, vinegar, mustard, salt, and pepper. Pour over the salad and toss to coat. Serve.

Apple & Arugula Salad with Walnuts

Ingredients for 4 servings

¼ cup chopped walnuts
10 oz arugula
1 apple, thinly sliced
1 tbsp finely minced shallot
2 tbsp champagne vinegar
2 tbsp olive oil
Sea salt and black pepper to taste
¼ tsp English mustard

Directions and Total Time: 20 minutes

Preheat oven to 360 F.

In a baking sheet, spread the walnuts and toast for 6 minutes. Let cool. In a bowl, combine the walnuts, arugula, and apple. In another bowl, mix the shallot, vinegar, olive oil, salt, pepper, and mustard. Pour over the salad and toss to coat. Serve.

Bean & Roasted Parsnip Salad

Ingredients for 3 servings

4 parsnips, sliced	Salt to taste	⅓ cup pomegranate seeds
2 tsp olive oil	1 (15-oz) can cannellini beans	⅓ cup sunflower seeds
½ tsp ground cinnamon	3 cups chopped spinach	¼ cup raspberry vinaigrette

Directions and Total Time: 40 minutes

Preheat oven to 390 F.

In a bowl, combine the parsnips, olive oil, cinnamon, and salt. Spread on a baking tray and roast for 15 minutes. Flip the parsnips and add the beans. Roast for another 15 minutes. Allow cooling. Divide the spinach among plates and place the pomegranate seeds, sunflower seeds, and roasted parsnips and beans. Sprinkle with raspberry vinaigrette and serve.

Christmas Potato Salad

Ingredients for 4 servings

1 ½ lb potatoes, chopped	1 bunch green onions, chopped	⅓ cup white wine vinegar
½ cup olive oil	1 tbsp whole-wheat flour	¼ cup water
4 portobello mushrooms, chopped	2 tbsp pure date sugar	Salt and black pepper to taste

Directions and Total Time: 15 minutes

Place the potatoes in a pot with boiling salted water and cook for 20 minutes. Drain and remove to a bowl. Heat oil in a skillet over medium heat. Place the mushrooms and sauté for 5 minutes. Add the mushrooms to the potatoes. To the skillet, add in green onions and cook for 1 minute. Mix in flour, sugar, vinegar, water, salt, and pepper. Bring to a boil and cook until creamy. Pour the resulting sauce over the potatoes and mushrooms and toss to coat. Serve immediately.

Apple & Kale Salad with Raspberry Vinaigrette

Ingredients for 2 servings

1 cup kale	¼ red onion, thinly sliced	2 tbsp raisins
½ apple, cored and chopped	2 tbsp sunflower seeds	2 tbsp raspberry vinaigrette

Directions and Total Time: 5 minutes

Place the kale on a plate. Add in apple, red onion, sunflower seeds, and raisins. Sprinkle with the vinaigrette and serve.

Carrot Salad with Cherries & Pecans

Ingredients for 4 servings

1 lb carrots, shredded	2 ½ cups toasted pecans	3 tbsp avocado oil
1 cup sweetened dried cherries	3 tbsp fresh lemon juice	Black pepper to taste

Directions and Total Time: 15 minutes

Combine the carrots, cherries, and pecans in a bowl. In another bowl, mix the lemon juice, avocado oil, and pepper. Pour over the salad and toss to coat. Serve immediately.

Beet Slaw with Apples

Ingredients for 4 servings

2 tbsp olive oil	½ beet, shredded	2 apples, peeled and julienned
Juice of 1 lemon	Sea salt to taste	4 cups shredded red cabbage

Directions and Total Time: 10 minutes

Mix the olive oil, lemon juice, beet, and salt in a bowl. In another bowl, combine the apples and cabbage. Pour over the vinaigrette and toss to coat. Serve right away.

Spinach Salad with Blackberries & Pecans

Ingredients for 4 servings

10 oz baby spinach	¼ red onion, thinly sliced	¾ cup olive oil
1 cup raisins	½ cup chopped pecans	Sea salt and black pepper to taste
1 cup fresh blackberries	¼ cup balsamic vinegar	

Directions and Total Time: 10 minutes

Combine the spinach, raisins, blackberries, red onion, and pecans in a bowl. In another bowl, mix the vinegar, olive oil, salt, and pepper. Pour over the salad and toss to coat. Serve immediately.

Festive Nicoise Salad Potato Salad

Ingredients for 4 servings

1 ½ lb small potatoes, unpeeled
1 cup firm tofu, drained and cubed
2 tbsp minced fresh parsley
1 tbsp minced fresh chives
1 tsp minced fresh tarragon
⅓ cup olive oil
2 tbsp white wine vinegar
Black pepper to taste

Directions and Total Time: 25 minutes

Place the potatoes in a pot with boiling salted water and cook for 20 minutes. Drain, cool, and slice. Remove to a bowl. Stir in tofu, parsley, chives, and tarragon. In another bowl, mix the oil, vinegar, and pepper. Pour over the salad and toss to coat. Let chill and serve.

Cowboy Salad

Ingredients for 4 servings

2 heads romaine lettuce, chopped
2 cups cherry tomatoes, halved
1 avocado, peeled, pitted, and diced
1 cup corn kernels
1 large cucumber, peeled and diced
4 oz soy chorizo
4 scallions, thinly sliced
Vegan ranch dressing

Directions and Total Time: 15 minutes

Place a bed of romaine lettuce in a serving bowl. Layer tomatoes, avocado, corn, cucumber, and soy chorizo. Serve topped with scallions and vegan ranch dressing.

Bell Pepper & Quinoa Salad

Ingredients for 4 servings

2 cups cooked quinoa
½ red onion, diced
1 red bell pepper, diced
1 orange bell pepper, diced
1 carrot, diced
¼ cup olive oil
2 tbsp rice vinegar
1 tbsp soy sauce
1 garlic clove, minced
1 tbsp grated fresh ginger
Sea salt and black pepper to taste

Directions and Total Time: 15 minutes

Combine the quinoa, onion, bell peppers, and carrots in a bowl. In another bowl, mix the olive oil, rice vinegar, soy sauce, garlic, ginger, salt, and pepper. Pour over the quinoa and toss to coat. Serve.

Dijon Potato & Carrot Salad

Ingredients for 4 servings

6 potatoes, chopped
2 carrots, chopped
Salt to taste
½ cup tahini dressing
1 tsp dried dill
1 tsp Dijon mustard
4 celery stalks, chopped
2 scallions, chopped

Directions and Total Time: 25 minutes

Place the potatoes and carrots in a pot with salted water. Bring to a boil and cook for 20 minutes. Drain and let cool. In a bowl, mix the dressing, dill, and mustard. Add in celery and scallions, toss to coat. Stir in carrots and potatoes. Serve.

Tomato Bean & Bulgur Salad

Ingredients for 4 servings

3 cups water
1 ½ cups bulgur, rinsed
Salt and black pepper to taste
1 (15.5-oz) can black beans
4 ripe plum tomatoes, sliced
1 red onion, sliced
¼ cup chopped fresh parsley
¼ cup olive oil
2 tbsp sherry vinegar

Directions and Total Time: 25 minutes

Place the bulgur in a pot with boiling salted water. Lower the heat and simmer for 20 minutes. Remove to a bowl. Stir in black beans, tomatoes, onion, and parsley. In another bowl, mix the olive oil, vinegar, salt, and pepper. Pour over the bulgur mixture and toss to coat. Let sit covered for 20 minutes. Serve.

Cucumber & Pear Rice Salad

Ingredients for 4 servings

1 cup brown rice	¼ cup orange juice	½ cucumber, diced
¼ cup olive oil	1 pear, cored and diced	¼ cup raisins

Directions and Total Time: 15 minutes

Place the rice in a pot with 2 cups of salted water. Bring to a boil, then lower the heat and simmer for 15 minutes. In a bowl, whisk together the olive oil, orange juice, salt, and pepper. Stir in the pear, cucumber, raisins, and cooked rice. Serve.

Lemony Ditalini Salad with Chickpeas

Ingredients for 4 servings

¼ cup olive oil	1 ½ cups canned chickpeas	1 cup chopped cucumber
2 tbsp freshly squeezed lemon juice	2 cups cooked ditalini pasta	¼ red onion, finely diced
A pinch of salt	2 cups raw spinach, finely chopped	

Directions and Total Time: 25 minutes

Mix the olive oil, lemon juice, and salt in a bowl. Stir in chickpeas and ditalini pasta. Add in spinach, cucumber and red onion, stir to combine. Serve.

Apple & Spinach Salad with Nuts & Cranberries

Ingredients for 4 servings

Juice of 1 lemon	1 (5-oz) package baby spinach	2 apples, cored and sliced
2 tbsp olive oil	1 cup corn kernels	½ cup pine nuts
1 tbsp maple syrup	½ red onion, thinly sliced	¼ cup dried cranberries

Directions and Total Time: 10 minutes

Mix the lemon juice, oil, maple syrup, and salt in a bowl. Combine the spinach, corn, red onion, and apples in another bowl. Pour over the lemon dressing and toss to coat. Separate into 4 plates and serve topped with pine nuts and cranberries.

Chickpea & Faro Entrée

Ingredients for 4 servings

2 tbsp olive oil	½ cup dried apricots, quartered	1 tsp turmeric
½ cup chopped green onions	¼ cup golden raisins	1/3 cup pomegranate molasses
2 tsp minced fresh ginger	¼ tsp ground cumin	1 (15.5-oz) can chickpeas, drained
1 cup faro	¼ tsp ground cayenne	¼ cup minced fresh cilantro

Directions and Total Time: 30 minutes

Heat oil in a pot and sauté green onions, ginger, apricots, raisins, cumin, cayenne, turmeric, salt, and pepper for 2 minutes. Add in pomegranate molasses, faro, and 2 cups water. Bring to a boil, lower the heat, and simmer for 10 minutes. Stir in chickpeas and cilantro and cook for 10 minutes. Serve warm.

Corn & Bean Quesadillas

Ingredients for 4 servings

1 tsp olive oil	1 (7 oz) can chopped tomatoes	4 whole-wheat tortillas
1 small onion, chopped	1 (7 oz) can black beans, drained	1 cup grated plant-based cheddar
½ red bell pepper, chopped	1 (7 oz) can sweet corn kernels	

Directions and Total Time: 35 minutes

Heat olive oil in a skillet and sauté onion and bell pepper for 3 minutes. Mix in tomatoes, black beans, sweet corn, and cook until the tomatoes soften, 10 minutes. Season with salt and black pepper.

Heat another medium skillet over medium heat and lay in one tortilla. Spread a quarter of the tomato mixture on top, scatter a quarter of the plant cheese on the sauce, and cover with another tortilla. Cook until the cheese melts. Flip and cook further for 2 minutes. Transfer to a plate and make one more piece using the remaining ingredients. Cut each tortilla set into quarters and serve immediately.

LUNCH

Tofu Cabbage Stir-Fry

Ingredients for 4 servings

2 ½ cups baby bok choy, quartered
5 oz plant butter
2 cups tofu, cubed
1 tsp garlic powder

1 tsp onion powder
1 tbsp plain vinegar
2 garlic cloves, minced
1 tsp chili flakes

1 tbsp fresh ginger, grated
3 green onions, sliced
1 tbsp sesame oil
1 cup tofu mayonnaise

Directions and Total Time: 45 minutes

Melt half of the butter in a wok over medium heat, add the bok choy, and stir-fry until softened. Season with salt, black pepper, garlic powder, onion powder, and plain vinegar. Sauté for 2 minutes; set aside. Melt the remaining butter in the wok, add and sauté garlic, chili flakes, and ginger until fragrant. Put the tofu in the wok and cook until browned on all sides. Add the green onions and bok choy, heat for 2 minutes, and add the sesame oil. Stir in tofu mayonnaise, cook for 1 minute, and serve.

Smoked Tempeh with Broccoli Fritters

Ingredients for 4 servings

4 tbsp flax seed powder
1 tbsp soy sauce
3 tbsp olive oil
1 tbsp grated ginger
3 tbsp fresh lime juice

Cayenne pepper to taste
10 oz tempeh slices
1 head broccoli, grated
8 oz tofu, grated
3 tbsp almond flour

½ tsp onion powder
4 ¼ oz plant butter
½ cup mixed salad greens
1 cup tofu mayonnaise
Juice of ½ a lemon

Directions and Total Time: 40 minutes

In a bowl, mix the flax seed powder with 12 tbsp water and set aside to soak for 5 minutes. In another bowl, combine soy sauce, olive oil, grated ginger, lime juice, salt, and cayenne pepper. Brush the tempeh slices with the mixture. Heat a grill pan over medium and grill the tempeh on both sides until golden brown and nicely smoked. Remove the slices into a plate.

In another bowl, mix the tofu with broccoli. Add in vegan "flax egg," almond flour, onion powder, salt, and black pepper. Mix and form 12 patties out of the mixture. Melt the plant butter in a skillet and fry the patties on both sides until golden brown. Remove to a plate. Add the grilled tempeh with the broccoli fritters and salad greens. Mix the tofu mayonnaise with the lemon juice and drizzle over the salad.

Cheesy Cauliflower Casserole

Ingredients for 4 servings

2 oz plant butter
1 white onion, finely chopped
½ cup celery stalks, finely chopped

1 green bell pepper, chopped
Salt and black pepper to taste
1 small head cauliflower, chopped

1 cup tofu mayonnaise
4 oz grated plant-based Parmesan
1 tsp red chili flakes

Directions and Total Time: 35 minutes

Preheat oven to 400 F. Season onion, celery, and bell pepper with salt and black pepper. In a bowl, mix cauliflower, tofu mayonnaise, Parmesan cheese, and red chili flakes. Pour the mixture into a greased baking dish and add the vegetables; mix to distribute. Bake for 20 minutes. Remove and serve warm.

Spicy Veggie Steaks with Green Salad

Ingredients for 2 servings

1 eggplant, sliced
1 zucchini, sliced
¼ cup coconut oil
Juice of ½ a lemon

5 oz plant-based cheddar, cubed
10 Kalamata olives
2 tbsp pecans
1 oz mixed salad greens

½ cup tofu mayonnaise
Salt to taste
½ tsp Cayenne pepper to taste

Directions and Total Time: 35 minutes

Set oven to broil and line a baking sheet with parchment paper. Arrange eggplant and zucchini on the baking sheet. Brush with coconut oil and sprinkle with cayenne pepper. Broil for 15-20 minutes.

Remove to a serving platter and drizzle with the lemon juice. Arrange the plant-based cheddar cheese, Kalamata olives, pecans, and mixed greens by the grilled veggies. Top with tofu mayonnaise and serve.

Mushroom Curry Pie

Ingredients for 6 servings

Piecrust:

1 tbsp flax seed powder + 3 tbsp water
¾ cup coconut flour
4 tbsp chia seeds

4 tbsp almond flour
1 tbsp psyllium husk powder
1 tsp baking powder

1 pinch of salt
3 tbsp olive oil
4 tbsp water

Filling:

1 cup chopped shiitake mushrooms
1 cup tofu mayonnaise
3 tbsp flax seed powder + 9 tbsp water

½ red bell pepper, finely chopped
1 tsp turmeric
½ tsp paprika

½ tsp garlic powder
½ cup cashew cream cheese
1 ¼ cups grated plant-based Parmesan

Directions and Total Time: 70 minutes

In two separate bowls, mix the different portions of flax seed powder with the respective quantity of water and set aside to absorb for 5 minutes.

Preheat oven to 350 F. When the vegan "flax egg" is ready, pour the smaller quantity into a food processor, add in the pie crust ingredients and blend until a ball forms out of the dough. Line a springform pan with parchment paper and grease with cooking spray. Spread the dough on the bottom of the pan and bake for 15 minutes. In a bowl, add the remaining flax egg and all the filling ingredients, combine the mixture, and fill the piecrust. Bake for 40 minutes. Serve sliced.

Tofu & Spinach Lasagna with Red Sauce

Ingredients for 4 servings

2 tbsp plant butter
1 white onion, chopped
1 garlic clove, minced
2 ½ cups crumbled tofu
3 tbsp tomato paste

½ tbsp dried oregano
Salt and black pepper to taste
1 cup baby spinach
8 tbsp flax seed powder
1 ½ cup cashew cream cheese

5 tbsp psyllium husk powder
2 cups coconut cream
5 oz grated plant-based mozzarella
2 oz grated plant-based Parmesan
½ cup fresh parsley, finely chopped

Directions and Total Time: 65 minutes

Melt plant butter in a medium pot and sauté onion and garlic until fragrant and soft, about 3 minutes. Stir in tofu and cook until brown. Mix in tomato paste, oregano, salt, and black pepper. Pour ½ cup of water into the pot, stir, and simmer the ingredients until most of the liquid has evaporated.

Preheat oven to 300 F. Mix flax seed powder with 1 ½ cups water in a bowl to make vegan "flax egg." Allow sitting to thicken for 5 minutes. Combine vegan "flax egg" with cashew cream cheese and salt. Add psyllium husk powder a bit at a time while whisking and allow the mixture to sit for a few minutes. Line a baking sheet with parchment paper and spread the mixture in. Cover with another parchment paper and flatten the dough into the sheet. Bake for 10-12 minutes. Slice the pasta into sheets.

In a bowl, combine coconut cream and two-thirds of the plant-based mozzarella cheese. Fetch out 2 tablespoons of the mixture and reserve. Mix in plant-based Parmesan cheese, salt, pepper, and parsley. Set aside. Grease a baking dish with cooking spray, layer a single line of pasta, spread with some tomato sauce, 1/3 of the spinach, and ¼ of the coconut cream mixture. Repeat layering the ingredients twice in the same manner , making sure to top the final layer with the coconut cream mixture and the reserved cream cheese. Bake for 30 minutes at 400 F. Slice and serve with salad.

Curried Tofu with Buttery Cabbage

Ingredients for 4 servings

2 cups tofu, cubed
1 tbsp + 3 ½ tbsp coconut oil
½ cup grated coconut

1 tsp yellow curry powder
½ tsp onion powder
2 cups Napa cabbage, grated

4 oz plant butter
Salt and black pepper to taste
Lemon wedges for serving

Directions and Total Time: 55 minutes

Drizzle 1 tablespoon of coconut oil on the tofu. In a bowl, mix the shredded coconut, yellow curry powder, salt, and onion powder. Toss the tofu cubes in the spice mixture. Heat the remaining coconut oil in a non-stick skillet and fry the coated tofu until golden brown on all sides. Transfer to a plate.

In another skillet, melt half of the plant butter, add, and sauté the cabbage until slightly caramelized. Then, season with salt and black pepper. Dish the cabbage into serving plates with the tofu and lemon wedges. Melt the remaining plant butter in the skillet and drizzle over the cabbage and tofu. Serve.

Avocado Coconut Pie

Ingredients for 4 servings

Piecrust:

1 tbsp flax seed powder + 3 tbsp water	1 tbsp psyllium husk powder	3 tbsp coconut oil
1 cup coconut flour	1 tsp baking soda	4 tbsp water
4 tbsp chia seeds	1 pinch salt	

Filling:

2 ripe avocados, chopped	2 tbsp fresh parsley, chopped	¼ tsp salt
1 cup tofu mayonnaise	1 jalapeno, finely chopped	½ cup cream cheese
3 tbsp flax seed powder + 9 tbsp water	½ tsp onion powder	1 ¼ cups grated plant-based Parmesan

Directions and Total Time: 80 minutes

In 2 separate bowls, mix the different portions of flax seed powder with the respective quantity of water. Allow absorbing for 5 minutes.

Preheat oven to 350 F. In a food processor, add the piecrust ingredients and the smaller portion of the vegan "flax egg." Blend until the resulting dough forms into a ball. Line a springform pan with parchment paper and spread the dough in the pan. Bake for 10-15 minutes.

Put the avocado in a bowl and add the tofu mayonnaise, remaining vegan "flax egg," parsley, jalapeno, onion powder, salt, cream cheese, and plant-based Parmesan. Combine well. Remove the piecrust when ready and fill with the creamy mixture. Bake for 35 minutes. Cool before slicing and serving.

Green Avocado Carbonara

Ingredients for 4 servings

8 tbsp flax seed powder	1 ¾ cups coconut cream	¼ cup olive oil
1 ½ cups cashew cream cheese	Juice of ½ lemon	Salt and black pepper to taste
5 ½ tbsp psyllium husk powder	1 teaspoon onion powder	½ cup grated plant-based Parmesan
1 avocado, chopped	½ teaspoon garlic powder	4 tbsp toasted pecans

Directions and Total Time: 30 minutes

Preheat oven to 300 F.

In a medium bowl, mix the flax seed powder with 1 ½ cups water and allow sitting to thicken for 5 minutes. Add the cashew cream cheese, salt, and psyllium husk powder. Whisk until smooth batter forms. Line a baking sheet with parchment paper, pour in the batter, and cover with another parchment paper. Use a rolling pin to flatten the dough into the sheet. Bake for 10-12 minutes. Remove, take off the parchment papers and use a sharp knife to slice the pasta into thin strips lengthwise. Cut each piece into halves, pour into a bowl, and set aside.

In a blender, combine avocado, coconut cream, lemon juice, onion powder, and garlic powder; puree until smooth. Pour the olive oil over the pasta and stir to coat properly. Pour the avocado sauce on top and mix. Season with salt and black pepper. Divide the pasta into serving plates, garnish with Parmesan cheese and pecans, and serve immediately.

Mushroom & Green Bean Biryani

Ingredients for 4 servings

1 cup brown rice	¼ tsp cinnamon powder	3 large tomatoes, diced
3 tbsp plant butter	2 tsp garam masala	2 green chilies, minced
3 medium white onions, chopped	½ tsp cardamom powder	1 tbsp tomato puree
6 garlic cloves, minced	½ tsp cayenne powder	1 cup chopped cremini mushrooms
1 tsp ginger puree	½ tsp cumin powder	1 cup chopped mustard greens
1 tbsp turmeric powder + for dusting	1 tsp smoked paprika	1 cup plant-based yogurt

Directions and Total Time: 50 minutes

Melt the butter in a large pot and sauté the onions until softened, 3 minutes. Mix in the garlic, ginger, turmeric, cardamom powder, garam masala, cardamom powder, cayenne pepper, cumin powder, paprika, and salt. Stir-fry for 1-2 minutes.

Stir in the tomatoes, green chili, tomato puree, and mushrooms. Once boiling, mix in the rice and cover with water. Cover the pot and cook over medium heat until the liquid absorbs and the rice is tender, 15-20 minutes. Open the lid and fluff in the mustard greens and half of the parsley. Dish the food, top with the coconut yogurt, garnish with the remaining parsley, and serve warm.

Baked Cheesy Spaghetti Squash

Ingredients for 4 servings

2 lb spaghetti squash
1 tbsp coconut oil
Salt and black pepper to taste
2 tbsp melted plant butter
½ tbsp garlic powder
1/5 tsp chili powder
1 cup coconut cream
2 oz cashew cream cheese
1 cup plant-based mozzarella
2 oz grated plant-based Parmesan
2 tbsp fresh cilantro, chopped
Olive oil for drizzling

Directions and Total Time: 40 minutes

Preheat oven to 350 F.

Cut the squash in halves lengthwise and spoon out the seeds and fiber. Place on a baking dish, brush with coconut oil, and season with salt and pepper. Bake for 30 minutes. Remove and use two forks to shred the flesh into strands.

Empty the spaghetti strands into a bowl and mix with plant butter, garlic and chili powders, coconut cream, cream cheese, half of the plant-based mozzarella and plant-based Parmesan cheeses. Spoon the mixture into the squash cups and sprinkle with the remaining mozzarella cheese. Bake further for 5 minutes. Sprinkle with cilantro and drizzle with some oil. Serve.

Kale & Mushroom Pierogis

Ingredients for 4 servings

Stuffing:

2 tbsp plant butter
2 garlic cloves, finely chopped
1 small red onion, finely chopped
3 oz baby Bella mushrooms, sliced
2 oz fresh kale
½ tsp salt
¼ tsp freshly ground black pepper
½ cup dairy-free cream cheese
2 oz plant-based Parmesan, grated

Pierogi:

1 tbsp flax seed powder
½ cup almond flour
4 tbsp coconut flour
½ tsp salt
1 tsp baking powder
1 ½ cups grated plant-based Parmesan
5 tbsp plant butter
Olive oil for brushing

Directions and Total Time: 45 minutes

Put the plant butter in a skillet and melt over medium heat, then add and sauté the garlic, red onion, mushrooms, and kale until the mushrooms brown. Season the mixture with salt and black pepper and reduce the heat to low. Stir in the cream cheese and plant-based Parmesan cheese and simmer for 1 minute. Turn the heat off and set the filling aside to cool.

Make the pierogis: In a small bowl, mix the flax seed powder with 3 tbsp water and allow sitting for 5 minutes. In a bowl, combine almond flour, coconut flour, salt, and baking powder. Put a small pan over low heat, add, and melt the plant-based Parmesan cheese and plant butter while stirring continuously until smooth batter forms. Turn the heat off.

Pour the vegan "flax egg" into the cream mixture, continue stirring while adding the flour mixture until a firm dough forms. Mold the dough into four balls, place on a chopping board, and use a rolling pin to flatten each into ½ inch thin round pieces. Spread a generous amount of stuffing on one-half of each dough, then fold over the filling, and seal the dough with your fingers. Brush with olive oil, place on a baking sheet, and bake for 20 minutes at 380 F. Serve with salad.

Vegan Mushroom Pizza

Ingredients for 4 servings

2 tsp plant butter
1 cup chopped button mushrooms
½ cup sliced mixed bell peppers
Salt and black pepper to taste
1 pizza crust
1 cup tomato sauce
1 cup plant-based Parmesan cheese
5-6 basil leaves

Directions and Total Time: 35 minutes

Melt plant butter in a skillet and sauté mushrooms and bell peppers for 10 minutes until softened. Season with salt and black pepper. Put the pizza crust on a pizza pan, spread the tomato sauce all over, and scatter vegetables evenly on top. Sprinkle with plant-based Parmesan cheese. Bake for 20 minutes until the cheese has melted. Garnish with basil and serve.

Grilled Zucchini with Spinach Avocado Pesto

Ingredients for 4 servings

3 oz spinach, chopped
1 ripe avocado, chopped
Juice of 1 lemon
1 garlic clove, minced
2 oz pecans
Salt and black pepper to taste
¾ cup olive oil
2 zucchini, sliced
1 tbsp fresh lemon juice
2 tbsp melted plant butter
1 ½ lb tempeh slices

Directions and Total Time: 20 minutes

Place the spinach in a food processor along with the avocado, lemon juice, garlic, and pecans. Blend until smooth and then season with salt and black pepper. Add the olive oil and process a little more. Pour the pesto into a bowl and set aside.

Place zucchini in a bowl. Season with the remaining lemon juice, salt, black pepper, and the plant butter. Also, season the tempeh with salt and black pepper, and brush with olive oil. Preheat a grill pan and cook both the tempeh and zucchini slices until browned on both sides. Plate the tempeh and zucchini, spoon some pesto to the side, and serve immediately.

Eggplant Fries with Chili Aioli & Beet Salad

Ingredients for 4 servings

Eggplant Fries:

2 tbsp flax seed powder
2 eggplants, sliced
2 cups almond flour
Salt and black pepper to taste
2 tbsp olive oil

Beet salad:

3½ oz beets, peeled and thinly cut
3½ oz red cabbage, grated
2 tbsp fresh cilantro
2 tbsp olive oil
1 tbsp freshly squeezed lime juice
Salt and black pepper to taste

Spicy Aioli:

1 tbsp flax seed powder
2 garlic cloves, minced
¾ cup light olive oil
½ tsp red chili flakes
1 tbsp freshly squeezed lemon juice
3 tbsp dairy-free yogurt

Directions and Total Time: 35 minutes

Preheat oven to 400 F. In a bowl, combine the flax seed powder with 6 tbsp water and allow sitting to thicken for 5 minutes. In a deep plate, mix almond flour, salt, and black pepper. Dip the eggplant slices into the vegan "flax egg," then in the almond flour, and then in the vegan "flax egg," and finally in the flour mixture. Place the eggplants on a greased baking sheet and drizzle with olive oil. Bake until the fries are crispy and brown, about 15 minutes.

For the aioli, mix the flax seed powder with 3 tbsp water in a bowl and set aside to thicken for 5 minutes. Whisk in garlic while pouring in the olive oil gradually. Stir in red chili flakes, salt, black pepper, lemon juice, and dairy-free yogurt. Adjust the taste with salt, garlic, or yogurt as desired.

For the beet salad, in a salad bowl, combine the beets, red cabbage, cilantro, olive oil, lime juice, salt, and black pepper. Use two spoons to toss the ingredients until properly combined. Serve the eggplant fries with the chili aioli and beet salad.

Tofu Skewers with Salsa Verde & Squash Mash

Ingredients for 4 servings

7 tbsp fresh cilantro, finely chopped
4 tbsp fresh basil, finely chopped
2 garlic cloves
Juice of ½ lemon
4 tbsp capers
2/3 cup olive oil
1 lb extra firm tofu, cubed
½ tbsp sugar-free BBQ sauce
1 tbsp melted plant butter
3 cups butternut squash, cubed
½ cup cold plant butter
2 oz grated plant-based Parmesan

Directions and Total Time: 20 minutes

In a blender, add cilantro, basil, garlic, lemon juice, capers, olive oil, salt, and pepper. Process until smooth; set aside. Thread the tofu cubes on wooden skewers. Season with salt and brush with BBQ sauce. Melt plant butter in a grill pan and fry the tofu until browned. Remove to a plate. Pour the squash into a pot, add some lightly salted water, and bring the vegetable to a boil until soft, about 6 minutes. Drain and pour into a bowl. Add the cold plant butter, plant-based Parmesan cheese, salt, and black pepper. Mash the vegetable with an immersion blender until the consistency of mashed potatoes is achieved. Serve the tofu skewers with the mashed cauliflower and salsa verde.

Mushroom Lettuce Wraps

Ingredients for 4 servings

2 tbsp plant butter
4 oz baby Bella mushrooms, sliced
1 ½ lb tofu, crumbled
1 iceberg lettuce, leaves extracted
1 cup grated plant-based cheddar
1 large tomato, sliced

Directions and Total Time: 25 minutes

Melt the plant butter in a skillet, add in mushrooms and sauté until browned and tender, about 6 minutes. Transfer to a plate. Add the tofu to the skillet and cook until brown, about 10 minutes. Spoon the tofu and mushrooms into the lettuce leaves, sprinkle with the plant-based cheddar cheese, and share the tomato slices on top. Serve the burger immediately.

Chili Bean & Brown Rice Tortillas

Ingredients for 4 servings

1 cups brown rice
Salt and black pepper to taste
1 tbsp olive oil
1 medium red onion, chopped
1 green bell pepper, diced

2 garlic cloves, minced
1 tbsp chili powder
1 tsp cumin powder
1/8 tsp red chili flakes
1 (15 oz) can black beans, rinsed

4 whole-wheat flour tortillas, warmed
1 cup salsa
1 cup coconut cream for topping
1 cup grated plant-based cheddar

Directions and Total Time: 50 minutes

Add 2 cups of water and brown rice to a medium pot, season with some salt, and cook over medium heat until the water absorbs and the rice is tender, 15 to 20 minutes.

Heat the olive oil in a medium skillet over medium heat and sauté the onion, bell pepper, and garlic until the softened and fragrant, 3 minutes.

Mix in the chili powder, cumin powder, red chili flakes, and season with salt and black pepper. Cook for 1 minute or until the food releases fragrance. Stir in the brown rice, black beans, and allow warming through, 3 minutes. Lay the tortillas on a clean, flat surface and divide the rice mixture in the center of each. Top with the salsa, coconut cream, and plant cheddar cheese. Fold the sides and ends of the tortillas over the filling to secure. Serve immediately.

Cashew Buttered Quesadillas with Leafy Greens

Ingredients for 4 servings

3 tbsp flax seed powder
½ cup cashew cream cheese
1 ½ tsp psyllium husk powder

1 tbsp coconut flour
½ tsp salt
1 tbsp cashew butter

5 oz grated plant-based cheddar
1 oz leafy greens

Directions and Total Time: 30 minutes

Preheat oven to 400 F.

In a bowl, mix flax seed powder with ½ cup water and allow sitting to thicken for 5 minutes. Whisk cashew cream cheese into the vegan "flax egg" until the batter is smooth. In another bowl, combine psyllium husk powder, coconut flour, and salt. Add the flour mixture to the flax egg batter and fold in until incorporated. Allow sitting for a few minutes. Line a baking sheet with wax paper and pour in the mixture. Spread and bake for 5-7 minutes. Slice into 8 pieces. Set aside.

For the filling, spoon a little cashew butter into a skillet and place a tortilla in the pan. Sprinkle with some plant-based cheddar cheese, leafy greens, and cover with another tortilla. Brown each side of the quesadilla for 1 minute or until the cheese melts. Transfer to a plate. Repeat assembling the quesadillas using the remaining cashew butter. Serve.

Asparagus with Creamy Puree

Ingredients for 4 servings

4 tbsp flax seed powder
2 oz plant butter, melted
3 oz cashew cream cheese

½ cup coconut cream
Powdered chili pepper to taste
1 tbsp olive oil

½ lb asparagus, hard stalks removed
3 oz plant butter
Juice of ½ a lemon

Directions and Total Time: 15 minutes

In a safe microwave bowl, mix the flax seed powder with ½ cup water and set aside to thicken for 5 minutes. Warm the vegan "flax egg" in the microwave for 1-2 minutes, then pour it into a blender. Add in plant butter, cashew cream cheese, coconut cream, salt, and chili pepper. Puree until smooth.

Heat olive oil in a saucepan and roast the asparagus until lightly charred. Season with salt and black pepper and set aside. Melt plant butter in a frying pan until nutty and golden brown. Stir in lemon juice and pour the mixture into a sauce cup. Spoon the creamy blend into the center of four serving plates and use the back of the spoon to spread out lightly. Top with the asparagus and drizzle the lemon butter on top. Serve immediately.

Kale Mushroom Galette

Ingredients for 4 servings

1 tbsp flax seed powder
½ cup grated plant-based mozzarella
1 tbsp plant butter
½ cup almond flour
¼ cup coconut flour

½ tsp onion powder
1 tsp baking powder
3 oz cashew cream cheese, softened
1 garlic clove, finely minced
Salt and black pepper to taste

1 cup kale, chopped
2 oz cremini mushrooms, sliced
2 oz grated plant-based mozzarella
1 oz grated plant-based Parmesan
Olive oil for brushing

Directions and Total Time: 35 minutes

Preheat oven to 375 F. Line a baking sheet with parchment paper and grease with cooking spray.

In a bowl, mix flax seed powder with 3 tbsp water and allow sitting to thicken for 5 minutes. Place a pot over low heat, add in plant-based mozzarella and plant butter, and melt both whiles stirring continuously; remove. Stir in almond and coconut flours, onion powder, baking powder, and ¼ tsp salt. Pour in the vegan "flax egg" and combine until a quite sticky dough forms. Transfer dough to the baking sheet, cover with another parchment paper, and use a rolling pin to flatten into a 12-inch circle.

After, remove the parchment paper and spread the cashew cream cheese on the dough, leaving about a 2-inch border around the edges. Sprinkle with garlic, salt, and black pepper. Spread kale on top of the cheese, followed by the mushrooms. Sprinkle the plant-based mozzarella and plant-based Parmesan cheese on top. Fold the ends of the crust over the filling and brush with olive oil. Bake until the cheese has melted and the crust golden brown, about 25-30 minutes. Slice and serve with arugula salad.

White Pizza with Mixed Mushrooms

Ingredients for 4 servings

2 tbsp flax seed powder	1 tsp baking powder	Salt and black pepper to taste
½ cup tofu mayonnaise	2 oz mixed mushrooms, sliced	½ cup coconut cream
¾ cup almond flour	1 tbsp plant-based basil pesto	¾ cup grated plant-based Parmesan
1 tbsp psyllium husk powder	2 tbsp olive oil	

Directions and Total Time: 35 minutes

Preheat oven to 350 F.

Combine flax seed powder with 6 tbsp water and allow sitting to thicken for 5 minutes. Whisk in tofu mayonnaise, almond flour, psyllium husk powder, baking powder, and salt. Allow sitting for 5 minutes. Pour the batter into a baking sheet and spread out with a spatula. Bake for 10 minutes.

In a bowl, mix mushrooms with the pesto, olive oil, salt, and black pepper. Remove the crust from the oven and spread the coconut cream on top. Add the mushroom mixture and plant-based Parmesan cheese. Bake the pizza further until the cheese has melted, 5-10 minutes. Slice and serve with salad.

Seitan Cakes with Broccoli Mash

Ingredients for 4 servings

1 tbsp flax seed powder	2 oz olive oil	2 oz grated plant-based Parmesan
1 ½ lb crumbled seitan	1 lb broccoli	4 oz plant butter, room temperature
½ white onion	5 oz cold plant butter	2 tbsp lemon juice

Directions and Total Time: 30 minutes

Preheat oven to 220 F. In a bowl, mix the flax seed powder with 3 tbsp water and allow sitting to thicken for 5 minutes. When the vegan "flax egg" is ready, add in crumbled seitan, white onion, salt, and pepper. Mix and mold out 6-8 cakes out of the mixture. Melt plant butter in a skillet and fry the patties on both sides until golden brown. Remove onto a wire rack to cool slightly.

Pour salted water into a pot, bring to a boil, and add in broccoli. Cook until the broccoli is tender but not too soft. Drain and transfer to a bowl. Add in cold plant butter, plant-based Parmesan, salt, and pepper. Puree the ingredients until smooth and creamy. Set aside. Mix the soft plant butter with lemon juice, salt, and pepper in a bowl. Serve the seitan cakes with the broccoli mash and lemon butter.

Spicy Cheese with Tofu Balls

Ingredients for 4 servings

1/3 cup tofu mayonnaise	1 tbsp mustard powder	1 tbsp flax seed powder
¼ cup pickled jalapenos	1 pinch cayenne pepper	2 ½ cup crumbled tofu
1 tsp paprika powder	4 oz grated plant-based cheddar	2 tbsp plant butter

Directions and Total Time: 40 minutes

In a bowl, mix tofu mayonnaise, jalapeños, paprika, mustard powder, cayenne powder, and plant-based cheddar cheese; set aside. In another bowl, combine flax seed powder with 3 tbsp water and allow absorbing for 5 minutes. Add the vegan "flax egg" to the cheese mixture, crumbled tofu, salt, and pepper and combine well. Form meatballs out of the mix. Melt plant butter in a skillet and fry the tofu balls until browned. Serve the tofu balls with roasted cauliflower mash.

Quinoa & Veggie Burgers

Ingredients for 4 servings

1 cup quick-cooking quinoa
1 tbsp olive oil
1 shallot, chopped
2 tbsp chopped fresh celery
1 garlic clove, minced
1 (15 oz) can pinto beans, drained
2 tbsp whole-wheat flour
¼ cup chopped fresh basil
2 tbsp pure maple syrup
4 whole-grain hamburger buns, split
4 small lettuce leaves for topping
½ cup tofu mayonnaise for topping

Directions and Total Time: 35 minutes

Cook the quinoa with 2 cups of water in a medium pot until the liquid absorbs, 10 to 15 minutes. Heat the olive oil in a medium skillet over medium heat and sauté the shallot, celery, and garlic until softened and fragrant, 3 minutes.

Transfer the quinoa and shallot mixture to a medium bowl and add the pinto beans, flour, basil, maple syrup, salt, and black pepper. Mash and mold 4 patties out of the mixture and set aside.

Heat a grill pan to medium heat and lightly grease with cooking spray. Cook the patties on both sides until light brown, compacted, and cooked through, 10 minutes. Place the patties between the burger buns and top with the lettuce and tofu mayonnaise. Serve.

Baked Tofu with Roasted Peppers

Ingredients for 4 servings

3 oz cashew cream cheese
¾ cup tofu mayonnaise
2 oz cucumber, diced
1 large tomato, chopped
2 tsp dried parsley
4 medium orange bell peppers
2 ½ cups cubed tofu
1 tbsp melted plant butter
1 tsp dried basil

Directions and Total Time: 20 minutes

Preheat oven's broiler to 450 F and line a baking sheet with parchment paper. In a salad bowl, combine cashew cream cheese, tofu mayonnaise, cucumber, tomato, salt, pepper, and parsley. Refrigerate.

Arrange the bell peppers and tofu on the baking sheet, drizzle with melted plant butter, and season with basil, salt, and pepper. Bake for 10-15 minutes or until the peppers have charred lightly and the tofu browned. Remove from the oven and serve with the salad.

Zoodle Bolognese

Ingredients for 4 servings

3 oz olive oil
1 white onion, chopped
1 garlic clove, minced
3 oz carrots, chopped
3 cups crumbled tofu
2 tbsp tomato paste
1 ½ cups crushed tomatoes
Salt and black pepper to taste
1 tbsp dried basil
1 tbsp vegan Worcestershire sauce
2 lb zucchini, spiralized
2 tbsp plant butter

Directions and Total Time: 45 minutes

Pour olive oil into a saucepan and heat over medium heat. Add in onion, garlic, and carrots and sauté for 3 minutes or until the onions are soft and the carrots caramelized. Pour in tofu, tomato paste, tomatoes, salt, pepper, basil, and Worcestershire sauce. Stir and cook for 15 minutes. Mix in some water if the mixture is too thick and simmer further for 20 minutes. Melt plant butter in a skillet and toss in the zoodles quickly, about 1 minute. Season with salt and black pepper. Divide into serving plates and spoon the Bolognese on top. Serve immediately.

Zucchini Boats with Vegan Cheese

Ingredients for 2 servings

1 medium-sized zucchini
4 tbsp plant butter
2 garlic cloves, minced
1 ½ oz baby kale
Salt and black pepper to taste
2 tbsp unsweetened tomato sauce
1 cup grated plant-based mozzarella
Olive oil for drizzling

Directions and Total Time: 40 minutes

Preheat oven to 375 F.

Use a knife to slice the zucchini in halves and scoop out the pulp with a spoon into a plate. Keep the flesh. Grease a baking sheet with cooking spray and place the zucchini boats on top. Put the plant butter in a skillet and melt over medium heat.

Sauté the garlic for 1 minute. Add in kale and zucchini pulp. Cook until the kale wilts; season with salt and black pepper. Spoon tomato sauce into the boats and spread to coat the bottom evenly. Then, spoon the kale mixture into the zucchinis and sprinkle with the plant-based mozzarella cheese. Bake for 20-25 minutes. Serve immediately.

Roasted Butternut Squash with Chimichurri

Ingredients for 4 servings

Zest and juice of 1 lemon
½ medium red bell pepper, chopped
1 jalapeno pepper, chopped

1 cup olive oil
½ cup chopped fresh parsley
2 garlic cloves, minced

Directions and Total Time: 15 minutes

In a bowl, add the lemon zest and juice, red bell pepper, jalapeno, olive oil, parsley, g
immersion blender to grind the ingredients until your desired consistency is achieved;

Slice the butternut squash into rounds and remove the seeds. Drizzle with the plant bu
pepper. Preheat a grill pan over medium heat and cook the squash for 2 minutes on e
the squash to serving plates, scatter the pine nuts on top, and serve with the chimichu

Sweet and Spicy Brussel Sprout Stir-Fry

Ingredients for 4 servings

4 oz plant butter + more to taste
4 shallots, chopped

1 tbsp apple cider vinegar
Salt and black pepper to taste

1 lb Brussels sprouts
Hot chili sauce

Directions and Total Time: 15 minutes

Put the plant butter in a saucepan and melt over medium heat. Pour in the shallots and sauté for 2 minutes, to caramelize and slightly soften. Add the apple cider vinegar, salt, and black pepper. Stir and reduce the heat to cook the shallots further with continuous stirring, about 5 minutes. Transfer to a plate after.

Trim the Brussel sprouts and cut in halves. Leave the small ones as wholes. Pour the Brussel sprouts into the saucepan and stir-fry with more plant butter until softened but al dente. Season with salt and black pepper, stir in the onions and hot chili sauce, and heat for a few seconds. Serve immediately.

Black Bean Burgers with BBQ Sauce

Ingredients for 4 servings

3 (15 oz) cans black beans, drained
2 tbsp whole-wheat flour
2 tbsp quick-cooking oats

¼ cup chopped fresh basil
2 tbsp pure barbecue sauce
1 garlic clove, minced

Salt and black pepper to taste
4 whole-grain hamburger buns, split

For topping:

Red onion slices
Tomato slices

Fresh basil leaves
Additional barbecue sauce

Directions and Total Time: 20 minutes

In a medium bowl, mash the black beans and mix in the flour, oats, basil, barbecue sauce, garlic salt, and black pepper until well combined. Mold 4 patties out of the mixture and set aside.

Heat a grill pan to medium heat and lightly grease with cooking spray. Cook the bean patties on both sides until light brown and cooked through, 10 minutes. Place the patties between the burger buns and top with the onions, tomatoes, basil, and some barbecue sauce. Serve warm.

Creamy Brussels Sprouts Bake

Ingredients for 4 servings

3 tbsp plant butter
1 cup tempeh, cut into 1-inch cubes
1 ½ lb halved Brussels sprouts

5 garlic cloves, minced
1 ¼ cups coconut cream
10 oz grated plant-based mozzarella

¼ cup grated plant-based Parmesan
Salt and black pepper to taste

Directions and Total Time: 26 minutes

Preheat oven to 400 F.

Melt the plant butter in a large skillet over medium heat and fry the tempeh cubes until browned on both sides, about 6 minutes. Remove onto a plate and set aside. Pour the Brussels sprouts and garlic into the skillet and sauté until fragrant.

Mix in coconut cream and simmer for 4 minutes. Add tempeh cubes and combine well. Pour the sauté into a baking dish, sprinkle with plant-based mozzarella cheese, and plant-based Parmesan cheese. Bake for 10 minutes or until golden brown on top. Serve with tomato salad.

...an Panini

...servings

...l pesto
..., juiced
...he panini:
. tbsp basil pesto
8 thick slices whole-wheat ciabatta

1 garlic clove, minced
1/8 tsp salt

Olive oil for brushing
8 slices plant-based mozzarella

1 cup chopped seitan

1 yellow bell pepper, chopped
¼ cup grated plant Parmesan cheese

Directions and Total Time: 15 minutes+ cooling time

In a medium bowl, mix the pesto, lemon juice, garlic, and salt. Add the seitan and coat well with the marinade. Cover with a plastic wrap and marinate in the refrigerator for 30 minutes.

Preheat a large skillet over medium heat and remove the seitan from the fridge. Cook the seitan in the skillet until brown and cooked through, 2-3 minutes. Turn the heat off.

Preheat a panini press to medium heat. In a small bowl, mix the pesto in the inner parts of two slices of bread. On the outer parts, apply some olive oil and place a slice with (the olive oil side down) in the press. Lay 2 slices of plant-based mozzarella cheese on the bread, spoon some seitan on top. Sprinkle with some bell pepper and some plant-based Parmesan cheese. Cover with another bread slice.

Close the press and grill the bread for 1 to 2 minutes. Flip the bread, and grill further for 1 minute or until the cheese melts and golden brown on both sides. Serve warm.

Jalapeño Quinoa Bowl with Lima Beans

Ingredients for 4 servings

1 tbsp olive oil
1 lb extra firm tofu, cubed
Salt and black pepper to taste
1 medium yellow onion, finely diced
½ cup cauliflower florets
1 jalapeño pepper, minced

2 garlic cloves, minced
1 tbsp red chili powder
1 tsp cumin powder
1 (8 oz) can sweet corn kernels
1 (8 oz) can lima beans, rinsed
1 cup quick-cooking quinoa

1 (14 oz) can diced tomatoes
2 ½ cups vegetable broth
1 cup grated plant-based cheddar
2 tbsp chopped fresh cilantro
2 limes, cut into wedges
1 avocado, pitted, sliced and peeled

Directions and Total Time: 30 minutes

Heat olive oil in a pot and cook the tofu until golden brown, 5 minutes. Season with salt, pepper, and mix in onion, cauliflower, and jalapeño pepper. Cook until the vegetables soften, 3 minutes.

Stir in garlic, chili powder, and cumin powder; cook for 1 minute. Mix in sweet corn kernels, lima beans, quinoa, tomatoes, and vegetable broth. Simmer until the quinoa absorbs all the liquid, 10 minutes. Fluff quinoa. Top with the plant-based cheddar cheese, cilantro, lime wedges, and avocado. Serve.

Caprese Casserole

Ingredients for 4 servings

1 cup plant-based mozzarella, cut into pieces
1 cup cherry tomatoes, halved
2 tbsp basil pesto

1 cup tofu mayonnaise
2 oz plant-based Parmesan

1 cup arugula
4 tbsp olive oil

Directions and Total Time: 25 minutes

Preheat oven to 350 F.

In a baking dish, mix the cherry tomatoes, vegan mozzarella, basil pesto, tofu mayonnaise, half of the plant-based Parmesan cheese, salt, and black pepper. Level the ingredients with a spatula and sprinkle the remaining plant-based Parmesan cheese on top. Bake for 20 minutes or until the top of the casserole is golden brown. Remove and allow cooling for a few minutes. Slice and dish into plates, top with some arugula, and drizzle with olive oil.

Tempeh Garam Masala Bake

Ingredients for 4 servings

3 tbsp plant butter
3 cups tempeh slices

2 tbsp garam masala
1 green bell pepper, finely diced

1 ¼ cups coconut cream
1 tbsp fresh cilantro, finely chopped

Directions and Total Time: 30 minutes

Preheat oven to 400 F.

Place a skillet over medium heat, add, and melt the plant butter. Meanwhile, season the tempeh with some salt. Fry the tempeh in the plant butter until browned on both sides, about 4 minutes. Stir half of the garam masala into the tempeh until evenly mixed; turn the heat off. Transfer the tempeh with the spice into a baking dish.

Then, in a small bowl, mix the green bell pepper, coconut cream, cilantro, and remaining garam masala. Pour the mixture over the tempeh and bake in the oven for 20 minutes or until golden brown on top. Garnish with cilantro and serve.

American-Style Tempeh Bake with Garden Peas

Ingredients for 4 servings

16 oz whole-wheat bow-tie pasta
2 tbsp olive oil, divided
2/3 lb tempeh, cut into 1-inch cubes
Salt and black pepper to taste
1 medium yellow onion, chopped

½ cup sliced white mushrooms
2 tbsp whole-wheat flour
¼ cup white wine
¾ cup vegetable stock
¼ cup oats milk

2 tsp chopped fresh thyme
¼ cup chopped cauliflower
½ cup grated plant-based Parmesan
3 tbsp whole-wheat breadcrumbs

Directions and Total Time: 50 minutes

Cook the pasta in 8 cups of slightly salted water for 10 minutes or until al dente. Drain and set aside.

Preheat the oven to 375 F. Heat the 1 tbsp of olive oil in a skillet, season the tempeh with salt and pepper, and cook until golden brown all around. Mix in onion, mushrooms, and cook for 5 minutes. Stir in flour and cook for 1 more minute.

Mix in wine and add two-thirds of the vegetable stock. Cook for 2 minutes while occasionally stirring and then add milk; continue cooking until the sauce thickens, 4 minutes. Season with thyme, salt, black pepper, and half of the Parmesan cheese. Once the cheese melts, turn the heat off and allow cooling.

Add the rest of the vegetable stock and cauliflower to a food processor and blend until smooth. Pour the mixture into a bowl, add in the sauce, and mix in pasta until combined. Grease a baking dish with cooking spray and spread in the mixture. Drizzle the remaining olive oil on top, breadcrumbs, some more thyme, and remaining cheese. Bake until the cheese melts and is golden brown on top, 30 minutes. Remove the dish from the oven, allow cooling for 3 minutes, and serve.

Seitan Cauliflower Gratin

Ingredients for 4 servings

2 oz plant butter
1 leek, coarsely chopped
1 white onion, coarsely chopped
2 cups broccoli florets

1 cup cauliflower florets
2 cups crumbled seitan
1 cup coconut cream
2 tbsp mustard powder

5 oz grated plant-based Parmesan
4 tbsp fresh rosemary
Salt and black pepper to taste

Directions and Total Time: 40 minutes

Preheat oven to 450 F.

Melt half of the plant butter in a pot over medium heat. Add in leek, white onion, broccoli, and cauliflower and cook for about 6 minutes. Transfer the vegetables to a baking dish.

Melt the remaining butter in a skillet over medium heat and cook the seitan until browned. Mix the coconut cream and mustard powder in a bowl. Pour the mixture over the vegetables. Scatter the seitan and plant-based Parmesan cheese on top and sprinkle with rosemary, salt, and pepper. Bake for 15 minutes. Remove to cool for a few minutes and serve.

Tomato Artichoke Pizza

Ingredients for 4 servings

2 tbsp flax seed powder
4 ¼ oz grated broccoli
6 ¼ oz grated plant-based Parmesan

2 tbsp tomato sauce
2 oz plant-based mozzarella
2 oz canned artichoke wedges

1 garlic clove, thinly sliced
1 tbsp dried oregano
Green olives for garnish

Directions and Total Time: 40 minutes

Preheat oven to 350 F and line a baking sheet with parchment paper. In a bowl, mix flax seed powder and 6 tbsp water and allow thicken for 5 minutes. When the vegan "flax egg" is ready, add broccoli, 4 ½ oz of plant-based Parmesan cheese, salt, and stir to combine. Pour the mixture into the baking sheet and spread out with a spatula. Bake until the crust is lightly browned, about 20 minutes. Remove from the oven and spread the tomato sauce on top, sprinkle with the remaining plant-based Parmesan cheese, plant-based mozzarella, add the artichokes, and the slices of garlic. Spread the oregano on top. Bake the pizza further for 5-10 minutes at 420 F. Slice the pizza, garnish with the olives, and serve.

Zesty Rice Bowls with Tempeh

Ingredients for 4 servings

2 tbsp olive oil
1 ½ cups crumbled tempeh
1 tsp Creole seasoning
2 red bell peppers, sliced

1 cup brown rice
2 cups vegetable broth
Salt to taste
1 lemon, zested and juiced

1 (8 oz) can black beans, drained
2 chives, chopped
2 tbsp freshly chopped parsley

Directions and Total Time: 50 minutes

Heat the olive oil in a medium pot and cook in the tempeh until golden brown, 5 minutes. Season with the Creole seasoning and stir in the bell peppers. Cook until the peppers slightly soften, 3 minutes. Stir in the brown rice, vegetable broth, salt, and lemon zest. Cover and cook until the rice is tender and all the liquid is absorbed, 15 to 25 minutes. Mix in the lemon juice, beans, and chives. Allow warming for 3 to 5 minutes and dish the food. Garnish with the parsley and serve warm.

Vegan Cordon Bleu Casserole

Ingredients for 4 servings

2 cups grilled tofu
1 cup smoked seitan
1 cup cashew cream cheese

1 tbsp mustard powder
1 tbsp plain vinegar
1 ¼ cup grated plant-based cheddar

Salt and black pepper to taste
½ cup baby spinach
4 tbsp olive oil

Directions and Total Time: 30 minutes

Preheat oven to 400 F. Place the tofu and seitan on a chopping board and chop both into small cubes. Mix the cashew cream cheese, mustard powder, plain vinegar, and plant-based cheddar cheese in a baking dish.

After, top with the tofu, seitan, and season with salt and black pepper. Bake in the oven until the casserole is golden brown on top, about 15 to 20 minutes. Serve with some baby spinach and a generous drizzle of olive oil.

Tempeh Coconut Curry Bake

Ingredients for 4 servings

1 oz plant butter, for greasing
2 ½ cups chopped tempeh
Salt and black pepper to taste

4 tbsp plant butter
2 tbsp red curry paste
1 ½ cups coconut cream

½ cup fresh parsley, chopped
15 oz cauliflower, cut into florets

Directions and Total Time: 30 minutes

Preheat oven to 400 F and grease a baking dish with 1 ounce of plant butter.

Arrange the tempeh in the baking dish, sprinkle with salt and black pepper, and top each tempeh with a slice of the remaining plant butter. In a bowl, mix the red curry paste with the coconut cream and parsley. Pour the mixture over the tempeh. Bake in the oven for 20 minutes or until the tempeh is cooked.

While baking, season the cauliflower with salt, place in a microwave-safe bowl, and sprinkle with some water. Steam in the microwave for 3 minutes or until the cauliflower is soft and tender within. Remove and serve with tempeh.

Savoy Cabbage Rolls with Tofu & Buckwheat

Ingredients for 4 servings

2 tbsp plant butter
2 cups extra-firm tofu, crumbled
½ medium sweet onion, chopped
2 garlic cloves, minced

Salt and black pepper to taste
1 cup buckwheat groats
1 ¾ cups vegetable stock
1 bay leaf

2 tbsp chopped cilantro
1 head Savoy cabbage, leaves separated (scraps kept)
1 (23 oz) canned chopped tomatoes

Directions and Total Time: 30 minutes

Melt the plant butter in a large bowl and cook the tofu until golden brown, 8 minutes. Stir in the onion and garlic until softened and fragrant, 3 minutes. Season with salt and black pepper and mix in the buckwheat, bay leaf, and vegetable stock. Close the lid, allow boiling, and then simmer until all the liquid is absorbed. Open the lid, remove the bay leaf, and adjust the taste with salt and pepper.

Lay the cabbage leaves on a flat surface and add 3 to 4 tablespoons of the cooked buckwheat onto each leaf. Roll the leaves to firmly secure the filling.

Pour the tomatoes with juices into a medium pot, season with a little salt, black pepper, and lay the cabbage rolls in the sauce. Cook over medium heat until the cabbage softens, 5 to 8 minutes. Turn the heat off and dish the food onto serving plates. Garnish with more cilantro and serve warm.

Tofu Loaf with Nuts

Ingredients for 4 servings

- 2 tbsp olive oil + extra for brushing
- 2 white onions, finely chopped
- 4 garlic cloves, minced
- 1 lb firm tofu, pressed and crumbled
- 2 tbsp soy sauce
- ¾ cup chopped mixed nuts
- ¼ cup flaxseed meal
- 1 tbsp sesame seeds
- 1 cup chopped mixed bell peppers
- Salt and black pepper to taste
- 1 tbsp Italian seasoning
- ½ tsp pure date syrup
- ½ cup tomato sauce

Directions and Total Time: 65 minutes

Preheat the oven to 350 F and grease a loaf pan with olive oil.

Heat 1 tbsp of olive oil in a small skillet and sauté the onion and garlic until softened and fragrant, 2 minutes. Pour the onion mixture into a large bowl and mix with the tofu, soy sauce, nuts, flaxseed meal, sesame seeds, bell peppers, salt, black pepper, Italian seasoning, and date syrup until well combined. Spoon the mixture into the loaf pan, press to fit and spread the tomato sauce on top. Bake the tofu loaf in the oven for 45 minutes to 1 hour or until well compacted. Remove the loaf pan from the oven, invert the tofu loaf onto a chopping board, and cool for 5 minutes. Slice and serve warm.

Mexican-Style Soy Chorizo & Rice Bowls

Ingredients for 4 servings

- 2 tbsp olive oil
- 2 cups chopped soy chorizo
- 1 tsp taco seasoning
- 2 green bell peppers, sliced
- 1 cup brown rice
- 2 cups vegetable broth
- ¼ cup salsa
- 1 lemon, zested and juiced
- 1 (8 oz) can pinto beans, drained
- 1 (7 oz) can sweet corn kernels
- 2 green onions, chopped
- 2 tbsp freshly chopped parsley

Directions and Total Time: 50 minutes

Heat the olive oil in a medium pot and cook the soy chorizo until golden brown, 5 minutes. Season with the taco seasoning and stir in the bell peppers; cook until the peppers slightly soften, 3 minutes. Stir in the brown rice, vegetable broth, salt, salsa, and lemon zest.

Close the lid and cook the food until the rice is tender and all the liquid is absorbed, 15 to 25 minutes. Mix in the lemon juice, pinto beans, corn kernels, and green onions. Allow warming for 3-5 minutes and dish the food. Garnish with the parsley and serve.

Pesto Mushroom Pizza

Ingredients for 4 servings

- 2 tbsp flax seed powder
- ½ cup tofu mayonnaise
- ¾ cup whole-wheat flour
- 1 tsp baking powder
- 1 cup sliced mixed mushrooms
- 2 tbsp olive oil
- 1 tbsp basil pesto
- ½ cup red pizza sauce
- ¾ cup grated plant-based Parmesan

Directions and Total Time: 40 minutes

Preheat the oven to 350 F.

In a bowl, mix the flax seed powder with 6 tbsp water and allow thicken for 5 minutes to make the vegan "flax egg." Mix in tofu mayonnaise, whole-wheat flour, baking powder, and salt until dough forms. Spread the dough on a pizza pan and bake in the oven for 10 minutes or until the dough sets.

In a medium bowl, mix the mushrooms, olive oil, basil pesto, salt, and black pepper. Remove the pizza crust spread the pizza sauce on top. Scatter mushroom mixture on the crust and top with plant-based Parmesan cheese. Bake further until the cheese melts, and the mushrooms soften, about 10-15 minutes. Remove the pizza, slice, and serve.

Tomato & Alfredo Fettuccine

Ingredients for 4 servings

- 2 cups almond milk
- 1 ½ cups vegetable broth
- 3 tbsp plant butter
- 1 large garlic clove, minced
- 16 oz whole-wheat fettuccine
- ½ cup coconut cream
- ¼ cup halved cherry tomatoes
- ¾ cup grated plant-based Parmesan
- Chopped fresh parsley to garnish

Directions and Total Time: 20 minutes

Bring almond milk, vegetable broth, butter, and garlic to a boil in a large pot, 5 minutes. Mix in the fettuccine and cook until tender, while frequently tossing for about 10 minutes. Mix in coconut cream, tomatoes, plant Parmesan cheese, salt, and pepper. Cook for 3 minutes or until the cheese melts. Garnish with some parsley and serve warm.

Green Beans & Grilled Tempeh

Ingredients for 4 servings

1 tbsp plant butter, melted
1 lb tempeh, sliced into 4 pieces
1 lb green beans, trimmed
Salt and black pepper to taste
2 sprigs thyme
2 tbsp olive oil
1 tbsp pure corn syrup
1 lemon, juiced

Directions and Total Time: 15 minutes

Preheat a grill pan over medium heat and brush with the plant butter.

Season the tempeh and green beans with the salt, black pepper, and place the thyme in the pan. Grill the tempeh and green beans on both sides until golden brown and tender, 10 minutes. Transfer to serving plates. In a small bowl, whisk the olive oil, corn syrup, lemon juice, and drizzle all over the food. Serve warm.

Pea & Basil Fettuccine

Ingredients for 4 servings

16 oz whole-wheat fettuccine
Salt and black pepper to taste
¾ cup flax milk
½ cup cashew butter, softened
1 tbsp olive oil
2 garlic cloves, minced
1 ½ cups frozen peas
½ cup chopped fresh basil

Directions and Total Time: 25 minutes

Add the fettuccine and 10 cups of water to a large pot, and cook over medium heat until al dente, 10 minutes. Drain the pasta through a colander and set aside. In a bowl, whisk the flax milk, cashew butter, and salt until smooth. Set aside.

Heat the olive oil in a large skillet and sauté the garlic until fragrant, 30 seconds. Mix in the peas, fettuccine, and basil. Toss well until the pasta is well-coated in the sauce and season with some black pepper. Dish the food and serve warm.

Scallion Sweet Potatoes with Chili Corn Salad

Ingredients for 4 servings

3 tbsp olive oil
4 sweet potatoes, cubed
2 limes, juiced
¼ tsp cayenne pepper
2 scallions, thinly sliced
1 (15 oz) can sweet corn kernels
½ tbsp plant butter, melted
1 large green chili, minced
1 tsp cumin powder

Directions and Total Time: 35 minutes

Preheat the oven to 400 F and lightly grease a baking sheet with cooking spray.

In a medium bowl, add the sweet potatoes, lime juice, salt, black pepper, and cayenne pepper. Toss well and spread the mixture on the baking sheet. Bake until the potatoes soften, 20-25 minutes. Transfer to a serving plate and garnish with scallions. In a bowl, mix corn kernels, butter, green chili, and cumin powder. Serve the sweet potatoes with the corn salad.

Plant-Based Cheddar Broccoli Gratin

Ingredients for 4 servings

1 tbsp olive oil
2 cups broccoli florets
1 (10 oz) can cream mushroom soup
1 cup tofu mayonnaise
3 tbsp coconut cream
1 medium red onion, chopped
2 cups grated plant-based cheddar
¾ cup whole-wheat bread crumbs
3 tbsp plant butter, melted

Directions and Total Time: 50 minutes

Preheat the oven to 350 F.

Heat the olive oil in a medium skillet and sauté the broccoli florets until softened, 8 minutes. Turn the heat off and mix in the mushroom soup, mayonnaise, salt, black pepper, coconut cream, and onion. Spread the mixture into the baking sheet. In a small bowl, mix the breadcrumbs with the plant butter and distribute the mixture on top. Add the cheddar cheese and bake the casserole in the oven until golden on top and the cheese melts. Remove the casserole from the oven, allow cooling for 5 minutes, dish, and serve warm.

Stuffed Zucchini Rolls with Tempeh & Tofu

Ingredients for 4 servings

3 zucchinis, sliced lengthwise
1 tbsp olive oil
¾ lb crumbled tempeh
1 cup crumbled tofu cheese
1/3 cup grated plant-based Parmesan
¼ cup chopped fresh basil leaves
2 garlic cloves, minced
1 ½ cups marinara sauce, divided
2 cups grated plant-based mozzarella

Directions and Total Time: 60 minutes

Line a baking sheet with paper towels and lay the zucchini slices in a single layer. Sprinkle each side with some salt and allow releasing of liquid for 15 minutes.

Heat the olive oil in a skillet and cook tempeh for 10 minutes; set aside. In a bowl, mix tempeh, tofu cheese, plant-based Parmesan cheese, basil, and garlic.

Preheat the oven to 400 F. Spread 1 cup of marinara sauce onto the bottom of a baking pan and set aside. Spread 1 tbsp of the cheese mixture evenly along with each zucchini slices; sprinkle with 1 tbsp of plant mozzarella cheese. Roll up the zucchini slices over the filling and arrange in the baking pan. Top with the remaining marinara sauce and sprinkle with the remaining plant-based mozzarella cheese. Bake for 25-30 minutes or until the cheese begins to brown. Serve immediately.

Hot Seitan with Rice

Ingredients for 4 servings

2 tbsp olive oil	1 tsp garlic powder	1 tsp oregano
1 lb seitan, cut into cubes	1 yellow onion, chopped	1 cup chopped tomatoes
Salt and black pepper to taste	2 celery stalks, chopped	3 green chilies, chopped
1 tsp chili powder	2 carrots diced	1 lime, juiced
1 tsp onion powder	4-5 cloves garlic	1 cup brown rice
1 tsp cumin powder	1 cup vegetable broth	

Directions and Total Time: 50 minutes

Add brown rice, 2 cups of water, and salt to a pot. Cook for 15-20 minutes.

Heat the olive oil in a large pot, season the seitan with salt, black pepper, and cook in the oil until brown, 10 minutes. Stir in the chili powder, onion powder, cumin powder, garlic powder, and cook until fragrant, 1 minute. Mix in the onion, celery, carrots, garlic, and cook until softened. Pour in the vegetable broth, 1 cup of water, oregano, tomatoes, and green chilies.

Cover the pot and cook until the tomatoes soften and the liquid reduces by half, 10 to 15 minutes. Open the lid, adjust the taste with salt, black pepper, and mix in the lime juice. Dish and serve warm with the brown rice.

Oat & Chickpea Burgers with Avocado Dip

Ingredients for 4 servings

1 large avocado, pitted and peeled	2 tbsp almond flour	1 garlic clove, minced
1 tomato, chopped	2 tbsp quick-cooking oats	¼ tsp garlic salt
1 small red onion, chopped	¼ cup chopped fresh parsley	1/8 tsp black pepper
3 (15 oz) cans chickpeas, drained	1 tbsp hot sauce	4 whole-grain hamburger buns, split

Directions and Total Time: 20 minutes

In a medium bowl, mash avocados and mix in the tomato and onion. Set aside the dip.

In another bowl, mash the chickpeas and mix in the almond flour, oats, parsley, hot sauce, garlic, garlic salt, and black pepper. Mold 4 patties out of the mixture and set aside.

Heat a grill pan to medium heat and lightly grease with cooking spray. Cook the bean patties on both sides until light brown and cooked through, 10 minutes. Place each patty between each burger bun and top with the avocado dip.

Bell Pepper & Tempeh Balls with Asparagus

Ingredients for 4 servings

1 tbsp flax seed powder	1 tbsp almond flour	2 tbsp plant butter
1 lb tempeh, crumbled	1 tsp garlic powder	1 lb asparagus, hard part trimmed
¼ cup chopped red bell pepper	1 tsp onion powder	2 tbsp pure maple syrup
Salt and black pepper to taste	1 tsp tofu mayonnaise	1 tbsp freshly squeezed lemon juice

Directions and Total Time: 40 minutes

Preheat the oven to 400 F and line a baking sheet with parchment paper. In a bowl, mix flax seed powder with 3 tbsp water and allow thicken for 5 minutes. Add in tempeh, bell pepper, salt, pepper, almond flour, garlic powder, onion powder, and tofu mayonnaise. Mix and form 1-inch balls from the mixture. Arrange on the baking sheet, brush with cooking spray, and bake for 15-20 minutes; set aside.

Melt butter in a skillet and sauté asparagus until softened with some crunch, 7 minutes. Mix in maple syrup and lemon juice. Cook for 2 minutes and plate the asparagus. Serve warm with the tempeh balls.

Bean & Spinach Casserole

Ingredients for 6 servings

3 tbsp olive oil
1 onion, chopped
2 carrots, chopped
1 celery stalk, chopped
2 garlic cloves, minced

1 (15.5-oz) can Navy beans
1 (15.5-oz) can Great Northern beans
1 cup baby spinach
3 tomatoes, chopped
1 cup vegetable broth

1 tbsp fresh parsley, chopped
1 tsp dried thyme
Salt and black pepper to taste
½ cup breadcrumbs

Directions and Total Time: 35 minutes

Preheat oven to 380 F.

Heat the oil in a skillet over medium heat. Place in onion, carrots, celery, and garlic. Sauté for 5 minutes. Remove into a greased casserole. Add in beans, spinach, tomatoes, broth, parsley, thyme, salt, and pepper and stir to combine. Cover with foil and bake in the oven for 15 minutes.

Next, take out the casserole from the oven, remove the foil, and spread the breadcrumbs all over. Bake for another 10 minutes until the top is crispy and golden. Serve warm.

Chickpea & Bean Patties

Ingredients for 4 servings

1 (15 oz) can chickpea, drained
1 (15 oz) can pinto beans, drained
1 (15 oz) can red kidney beans
2 tbsp whole-wheat flour

¼ cup dried mixed herbs
¼ tsp hot sauce
½ tsp garlic powder
Salt and black pepper to taste

4 slices cashew cheese
4 whole-grain hamburger buns, split
4 small lettuce leaves for topping

Directions and Total Time: 30 minutes

In a medium bowl, mash the chickpea, pinto beans, kidney beans and mix in the flour, mixed herbs, hot sauce, garlic powder, salt, and black pepper. Mold 4 patties out of the mixture and set aside.

Heat a grill pan to medium heat and grease with cooking spray. Cook the bean patties on both sides until light brown and cooked through, 10 minutes. Lay a cashew cheese slice on each and allow slight melting, 2 minutes. Remove the patties between the burger buns and top with the lettuce and serve.

Vegetable & Hummus Pizza

Ingredients for 4 servings

3 ½ cups whole-wheat flour
1 tsp yeast
1 tsp salt
1 pinch sugar

3 tbsp olive oil
1 cup hummus
10 cremini mushrooms, sliced
½ cup fresh baby spinach

½ cup cherry tomatoes, halved
½ cup sliced Kalamata olives
½ medium onion, sliced
2 tsp dried oregano

Directions and Total Time: 30 minutes

Preheat the oven the 350 F and lightly grease a pizza pan with cooking spray.

In a medium bowl, mix the flour, nutritional yeast, salt, sugar, olive oil, and 1 cup warm water until smooth dough forms. Allow rising for an hour or until the dough doubles in size. Spread the dough on the pizza pan and apply the hummus on the dough. Add the mushrooms, spinach, tomatoes, olives, onion, and top with the oregano. Bake for 20 minutes. Cool for 5 minutes, slice, and serve.

Black Olive & Chickpea Lunch

Ingredients for 4 servings

2 tbsp olive oil
2 cups chopped onion
2 garlic cloves, minced
2 carrots, cut into thick slices

1/3 cup white wine
3 cups cherry tomatoes
2/3 cup vegetable stock
1 1/3 cups canned chickpeas

½ cup pitted black olives
1 tbsp chopped fresh oregano
Salt and black pepper to taste

Directions and Total Time: 15 minutes

Heat the olive oil in a medium pot and sauté the onion, garlic, and carrots until softened, 5 minutes. Mix in the white wine, reduce one-third, and mix in the tomatoes and vegetable stock.

Cover the lid and cook until the tomatoes break, soften, and the liquid reduces by half. Stir in the chickpeas, olives, oregano, and season with salt and pepper. Cook for 3 minutes to warm the chickpeas.

Basil & Tofu Stuffed Portobello Mushrooms

Ingredients for 4 servings

4 large portobello mushrooms, stems removed
Garlic salt and black pepper to taste
½ tsp olive oil
1 small onion, chopped
1 cup chopped fresh kale
¼ cup crumbled tofu cheese
1 tbsp chopped fresh basil

Directions and Total Time: 25 minutes

Preheat the oven to 350 F and grease a baking sheet with cooking spray.

Lightly oil the mushrooms with some cooking spray and season with the black pepper and garlic salt. Arrange the mushrooms on the baking sheet and bake in the oven until tender, 10 to 15 minutes.

Heat olive oil in a skillet and sauté onion until tender, 3 minutes. Stir in kale until wilted, 3 minutes. Spoon the mixture into the mushrooms and top with the tofu cheese and basil. Serve.

Kale Pizza with Grilled Zucchini

Ingredients for 4 servings

¼ cup capers
½ cup grated plant Parmesan cheese
3 ½ cups whole-wheat flour
1 tsp yeast
1 tsp salt
1 pinch sugar
3 tbsp olive oil
1 cup marinara sauce
2 large zucchinis, sliced
½ cup chopped kale
1 tsp oregano

Directions and Total Time: 30 minutes

Preheat the oven the 350 F and lightly grease a pizza pan with cooking spray. In a bowl, mix flour, nutritional yeast, salt, sugar, olive oil, and 1 cup of warm water until smooth dough forms. Allow rising for an hour or until the dough doubles in size. Spread the dough on the pizza pan and apply marinara sauce and oregano on top.

Heat a grill pan, season the zucchinis with salt, black pepper, and cook in the pan until slightly charred on both sides. Sit the zucchini on the pizza crust and top with kale, capers, and plant-based Parmesan cheese. Bake for 20 minutes. Cool for 5 minutes, slice, and serve.

Amazing Tofu Burgers

Ingredients for 4 servings

1 tbsp flax seed powder
2/3 lb crumble tofu
1 tbsp quick-cooking oats
1 tbsp toasted almond flour
½ tsp garlic powder
½ tsp onion powder
¼ tsp curry powder
3 tbsp whole-grain breadcrumbs
4 whole-wheat burger buns, halved

Directions and Total Time: 20 minutes

In a small bowl, mix the flax seed powder with 3 tbsp water and allow thicken for 5 minutes to make the vegan "flax egg." Set aside. In a bowl, mix tofu, oats, almond flour, garlic powder, onion powder, salt, pepper, and curry powder. Mold 4 patties out of the mixture and brush both sides with the vegan "flax egg." Pour the breadcrumbs onto a plate and coat the cakes in the crumbs until well covered.

Heat a pan over medium heat and grease with cooking spray. Cook the patties on both sides for 10 minutes. Place each patty between each burger bun and top with the guacamole. Serve immediately.

Bean Gyros

Ingredients for 6 servings

1 (14-oz) can white beans
2 scallions, minced
¼ cup fresh parsley, chopped
2 tbsp Kalamata olives, chopped
1 tbsp tahini
1 tbsp lemon juice
½ tsp ground cumin
¼ tsp paprika
4 tsp olive oil
6 whole-grain wraps, warm
1 cup hummus
1 cup arugula, chopped
2 tomatoes, chopped
1 cucumber, chopped
¼ cup chopped avocado

Directions and Total Time: 60 minutes

In a blender, place the white beans, scallions, parsley, and olives. Pulse until finely chopped. In a bowl, beat the tahini with lemon juice. Add in cumin, paprika, and salt. Transfer into beans mixture and mix well to combine. Shape the mixture into balls; flatten to make 6 patties.

In a skillet over medium heat, warm the oil and cook the patties for 8-10 minutes on both sides; reserve. Spread each wrap with hummus and top with patties, tomatoes, cucumber, and avocado. Roll the wraps up to serve.

Saucy Seitan with Sesame Seeds

Ingredients for 4 servings

4 tsp olive oil	1/3 tsp allspice	1 ½ tbsp olive oil
½ tsp freshly grated ginger	1/2 cup soy sauce	1 lb seitan, cut into 1-inch pieces
3 garlic cloves, minced	½ cup + 2 tbsp pure date sugar	1 tbsp toasted sesame seeds
1/3 tsp red chili flakes	2 tsp cornstarch	1 tbsp sliced scallions

Directions and Total Time: 20 minutes

Heat half of the olive oil in a wok and sauté ginger and garlic until fragrant, 30 seconds. Mix in red chili flakes, allspice, soy sauce, and date sugar. Allow the sugar to melt and set aside. In a small bowl, mix cornstarch and 2 tbsp of water. Stir the cornstarch mixture into the sauce and allow thicken for 1 minute. Heat the remaining olive oil in a medium skillet over medium heat and fry the seitan on both sides until crispy, 10 minutes. Mix the seitan into the sauce and warm over low heat. Dish the food, garnish with the sesame seeds and scallions. Serve warm.

Gingery Pea & Potato Skillet

Ingredients for 4 servings

4 medium potatoes, diced	1 tsp red chili powder	¼ tsp turmeric powder
2 tbsp olive oil	1 tsp fresh ginger-garlic paste	Salt and black pepper to taste
1 medium onion, chopped	1 tsp cumin powder	1 cup fresh green peas

Directions and Total Time: 21 minutes

Steam potatoes in a safe microwave bowl in the microwave for 8-10 minutes or until softened. Heat the olive oil in a wok and sauté the onion until softened, 3 minutes. Mix in the chili powder, ginger-garlic paste, cumin powder, turmeric powder, salt, and black pepper. Cook until the fragrant releases, 1 minute. Stir in the green peas, potatoes, and cook until softened, 2 to 3 minutes. Serve warm.

Broccoli Stuffed Cremini Mushrooms

Ingredients for 4 servings

½ head broccoli, cut into florets	1 onion, finely chopped	1 tsp Cajun seasoning mix
1 lb cremini mushroom caps	1 tsp garlic, minced	Salt and black pepper, to taste
2 tbsp olive oil	1 bell pepper, chopped	¼ cup plant-based mozzarella

Directions and Total Time: 35 minutes

Preheat oven to 360 F. Bake mushroom caps in a greased baking dish for 10-12 minutes. In a food processor, place broccoli and pulse until it become like small rice-like granules. In a heavy-bottomed skillet, warm olive oil; stir in bell pepper, garlic, and onion and sauté until fragrant. Place in pepper, salt, and Cajun seasoning mix. Fold in broccoli rice. Divide the filling mixture among mushroom caps. Top with plant-based mozzarella cheese and bake for 17 more minutes. Serve warm.

Tempeh & Vegetable Stir-Fry

Ingredients for 4 servings

1 can (28 oz) whole plum tomatoes	1 can (8 oz) tomato sauce	1 tsp dried mixed herbs
1 lb crumbled tempeh	2 tbsp plain vinegar	1 small head cabbage, thinly sliced
1 large yellow onion, chopped	1 tbsp pure date sugar	1 green bell pepper, cut into strips

Directions and Total Time: 30 minutes

Drain the tomatoes and reserve their liquid. Chop the tomatoes and set aside.

Add the tempeh to a large skillet and cook until brown, 10 minutes. Mix in the onion, tomato sauce, vinegar, date sugar, mixed herbs, and chopped tomatoes. Close the lid and cook until the liquid reduces, 10 minutes. Stir in the cabbage and bell pepper; cook until softened, 5 minutes. Serve.

Watercress & Mushroom Spaghetti

Ingredients for 4 servings

1 lb whole-wheat spaghetti	2 garlic cloves, minced	1 tsp hot sauce
3 tbsp plant butter	½ lb chopped button mushrooms	A handful fresh watercress
2 tbsp olive oil	1 tbsp sake	¼ cup chopped fresh parsley
2 shallots, finely chopped	3 tbsp soy sauce	Black pepper to taste

Directions and Total Time: 30 minutes

Cook spaghetti in lightly salted water in a large pot over medium heat until al dente, 10 minutes. Drain and set aside. Heat butter and olive oil in a skillet and sauté shallots, garlic, and mushrooms for 5 minutes. Stir in sake, soy sauce, and hot sauce. Cook for 1 minute. Toss spaghetti in the sauce along with watercress and parsley. Season with the black pepper. Dish the food and serve warm.

Rice with Green Lentil & Celery

Ingredients for 4 servings

2 tbsp olive oil	1 tsp cumin powder	1 tsp oregano
1 lb tempeh, cut into cubes	2 celery stalks, chopped	1 cup green lentils, rinsed
1 yellow onion, chopped	2 carrots diced	¼ cup chopped tomatoes
Salt and black pepper to taste	4 garlic cloves, minced	1 lime, juiced
1 tsp chili powder	3 cups vegetable broth	1 cup brown rice

Directions and Total Time: 50 minutes

Heat the olive oil in a large pot, season the tempeh with salt, pepper, and cook for 10 minutes. Stir in chili powder, cumin powder, onion, celery, carrots, garlic, and cook for 5 minutes. Pour in vegetable broth, oregano, green lentils, tomatoes, brown rice, and green chilies. Cover the pot and cook for 18-20 minutes. Open the lid, adjust the taste with salt, black pepper, and mix in the lime juice. Serve.

Spinach & Chickpea Pizza with Avocado

Ingredients for 4 servings

3 tbsp olive oil	1 tsp salt	1 (15 oz) can chickpeas, drained
1 tsp oregano	1 pinch sugar	1 avocado, chopped
3 ½ cups whole-wheat flour	1 cup red pizza sauce	¼ cup grated plant-based Parmesan
1 tsp yeast	1 cup baby spinach	

Directions and Total Time: 40 minutes

Preheat the oven the 350 F and lightly grease a pizza pan with cooking spray. In a bowl, mix flour, nutritional yeast, salt, sugar, olive oil, and 1 cup of warm water until smooth dough forms. Allow rising for an hour or until the dough doubles in size. Spread the dough on the pizza pan and apply the pizza sauce on top. Top with oregano, baby spinach, chickpeas, avocado, and plant Parmesan cheese. Bake for 20 minutes or until the cheese melts. Remove from the oven, cool for 5 minutes, slice, and serve.

Herby Quinoa with Walnuts

Ingredients for 4 servings

1 cup quinoa, well-rinsed	2 tbsp finely chopped parsley	1 tbsp olive oil
2 cups vegetable broth	2 tbsp finely chopped basil	½ tsp lemon zest
2 garlic cloves, minced, divided	2 tbsp finely chopped mint	1 tbsp fresh lemon juice
¼ cup chopped chives	2 tbsp chopped sundried tomatoes	2 tbsp minced walnuts

Directions and Total Time: 20 minutes

In a pot, combine quinoa, vegetable broth, and garlic. Boil until the quinoa is tender and the liquid absorbs, 10-15 minutes. Fuff with a fork and stir in chives, parsley, basil, mint, tomatoes, olive oil, zest, lemon juice, and walnuts. Warm for 5 minutes. Serve.

Pasta Primavera with Cherry Tomatoes

Ingredients for 4 servings

2 tbsp olive oil	2 garlic cloves, minced	3 tbsp plant butter, cubed
8 oz whole-wheat fidelini pasta	1 cup dry white wine	1 lemon, zested and juiced
½ tsp paprika	Salt and black pepper to taste	1 cup packed fresh basil leaves
1 small red onion, sliced	2 cups cherry tomatoes, halved	

Directions and Total Time: 25 minutes

Heat olive oil in a pot and mix in fidelini, paprika, onion, garlic, and stir-fry for 2-3 minutes. Mix in white wine, salt, and pepper. Cover with water. Cook until the water absorbs and the fidelini al dente, 5 minutes. Mix in the cherry tomatoes, butter, lemon zest, lemon juice, and basil leaves. Serve warm.

Cherry & Quinoa Tacos

Ingredients for 4 servings

½ cup brown quinoa
2 tsp olive oil
1 ½ cups shredded carrots
1 ¼ cups fresh cherries, halved
4 scallions, chopped
2 tbsp plain vinegar
2 tbsp soy sauce
1 tbsp pure maple syrup
4 (8-inch) tortilla wraps

Directions and Total Time: 25 minutes

Cook the quinoa in 1 cup of slightly salted water in a pot for 15 minutes. Fluff and set aside. Heat olive oil in a skillet and sauté carrots, cherries, and scallions. In a small bowl, mix vinegar, soy sauce, and maple syrup. Stir the mixture into the vegetable mixture. Simmer for 5 minutes. Spread the tortillas on a flat surface, spoon the mixture at the center, fold the sides and ends to wrap in the filling. Serve.

Quinoa a la Puttanesca

Ingredients for 4 servings

1 cup brown quinoa
2 cups water
1/8 tsp salt
4 cups plum tomatoes, chopped
4 pitted green olives, sliced
4 pitted Kalamata olives, sliced
1 ½ tbsp capers, rinsed and drained
2 garlic cloves, minced
1 tbsp olive oil
1 tbsp chopped fresh parsley
¼ cup chopped fresh basil
1/8 tsp red chili flakes

Directions and Total Time: 30 minutes

Add quinoa, water, and salt to a medium pot and cook for 15 minutes. In a bowl, mix tomatoes, green olives, olives, capers, garlic, olive oil, parsley, basil, and red chili flakes. Allow sitting for 5 minutes. Serve the puttanesca with the quinoa.

Acorn Squash Stuffed with Beans & Spinach

Ingredients for 4 servings

2 lb large acorn squash
2 tbsp olive oil
3 garlic cloves, minced
1 (15 oz) can white beans, drained
1 cup chopped spinach leaves
½ cup vegetable stock
Salt and black pepper to taste
½ tsp cumin powder
½ tsp chili powder

Directions and Total Time: 60 minutes

Preheat the oven to 350 F. Cut the squash into half and scoop out the seeds. Season with salt and pepper and place face down on a sheet pan. Bake for 45 minutes.

Heat olive oil in a pot over medium heat. Sauté garlic until fragrant, 30 seconds and mix in beans and spinach, allow wilting for 2 minutes and season with salt, black pepper, cumin powder, and chili powder. Cook for 2 minutes and turn the heat off. When the squash is fork-tender, remove from the oven and fill the holes with the bean and spinach mixture. Serve.

Cabbage & Bean Stir-Fry

Ingredients for 2 servings

1 cup canned white beans
1 tsp olive oil
2 carrots, julienned
1 cup sliced red cabbage
1 red bell pepper, sliced
2 scallions, chopped
3 tbsp fresh mint, chopped
1 cup bean sprouts
¼ cup peanut sauce
¼ cup fresh cilantro, chopped
2 tbsp roasted peanuts, chopped
Fresh lime wedges

Directions and Total Time: 20 minutes

Heat oil in a skillet and cook carrots, cabbage, and bell pepper for 10-15 minutes. Stir in scallions, mint and bean sprouts, cook for 1-2 minutes. Remove to a bowl. Mix in white beans and peanut sauce; toss to combine. Garnish with cilantro and peanuts. Serve with lime wedges on the side.

Hot Paprika Lentils

Ingredients for 6 servings

1 onion, chopped
3 tbsp olive oil
1 tbsp hot paprika
2 ¼ cups lentils, drained
3 garlic cloves, minced
½ tsp dried thyme

Directions and Total Time: 20 minutes

Heat the oil in a pot over medium heat. Place the onion and garlic and sauté for 3 minutes. Add in paprika, salt, pepper, 5 cups water, lentils, and thyme. Bring to a boil, lower the heat and simmer for 15 minutes until tender, stirring often.

Lemony Green Bean Risotto

Ingredients for 4 servings

2 tsp plant butter
2 cloves minced garlic
1 cup brown rice
2 cups vegetable broth
2 cups green be[ans]
2 tbsp parsley,

Directions and Total Time: 25 minutes

Melt the butter in a skillet over medium heat. Place in garlic and cook for 1 minute. Stir in ric[e]
Bring to a boil, then lower the heat and simmer for 10 minutes. Put in the green beans and cook for an[other]
Fluff the rice with a fork, sprinkle with parsley and serve.

Chipotle Kidney Bean Chili

Ingredients for 4 servings

2 tbsp olive oil
1 onion, chopped
2 garlic cloves, minced
1 (16-oz) can tomato sauce
1 (4-oz) can green chilies, chopped
1 tbsp chili powder
1 canned chipotle chili, minced
1 tsp ground cumin
½ tsp dried marjoram
1 (15.5-oz) can kidney beans
Salt and black pepper to taste
½ tsp cayenne pepper

Directions and Total Time: 30 minutes

Heat the oil in a pot over medium heat. Place in onion and garlic and sauté for 3 minutes. Put in tomato sauce, green chilies, chili powder, cumin, cayenne pepper, marjoram, salt, and pepper and cook for 5 minutes. Stir in kidney beans and 2 cups of water. Bring to a boil, then lower the heat and simmer for 15 minutes, stirring often. Serve immediately.

Carrot & Black Bean Chili

Ingredients for 4 servings

2 tbsp olive oil
1 onion, finely chopped
2 carrots, chopped
1 tsp grated fresh ginger
1 green bell pepper, chopped
2 tbsp chili powder
1 (28-oz) can diced tomatoes
1 (15.5-oz) can black beans
3 minced green onions

Directions and Total Time: 25 minutes

Heat the oil in a pot over medium heat. Place in onion, carrot, ginger, bell pepper, and chili powder and sauté for 5 minutes until tender. Stir in tomatoes, 2 cups of water, black beans, salt, and pepper. Bring to a boil, then lower the heat and simmer for 15 minutes. Serve topped with green onions.

Special Butternut Squash Chili

Ingredients for 4 servings

1 butternut squash, cubed
2 tbsp olive oil
1 onion, chopped
3 cups tomato salsa
1 (15.5-oz) can garbanzo beans
1 cup frozen green peas
1 cup corn kernels
½ tsp cayenne pepper
½ tsp ground allspice

Directions and Total Time: 60 minutes

Heat the oil in a saucepan over medium heat. Place in onion and squash and cook for 10 minutes until tender. Add in tomato salsa, garbanzo beans, green peas, corn, cayenne pepper, allspice, salt, and pepper. Pour in 2 cups of water. Bring to a boil, then lower the heat and simmer for 15 minutes. Serve.

Mediterranean Chickpeas with Vegetables

Ingredients for 6 servings

3 tbsp olive oil
1 red onion, chopped
2 carrots, chopped
1 celery stalk, chopped
2 garlic cloves, minced
1 tsp grated fresh ginger
1 tsp ground cumin
½ tsp turmeric
2 parsnips, peeled and chopped
8 oz green beans, chopped
1 (15.5-oz) can chickpeas, drained
1 (14.5-oz) can diced tomatoes
1 ½ cups vegetable broth
2 tbsp minced cilantro
1 tsp fresh lemon juice

Directions and Total Time: 40 minutes

Heat the oil in a pot over medium heat. Place in onion, carrots, celery, garlic, and ginger. Sauté for 5 minutes. Add in cumin, turmeric, parsnips, green beans, chickpeas, tomatoes and juices, and broth. Bring to a boil, then lower the heat and sprinkle with salt and pepper. Simmer for 30 minutes. Sprinkle with lemon juice and cilantro and serve.

...ern Bean Salad

Ingredients for 4 servings

- ...omato, chopped
- ... red bell pepper, chopped
- 1 green bell pepper, chopped
- 1 small red onion, sliced
- 1 (14.5-oz) can black-eyed peas
- 1 (14.5-oz) can black beans
- ¼ cup capers
- 2 avocados, pitted
- 1 tbsp lemon juice
- ¼ cup sake
- 1 tsp dried oregano
- Salt to taste
- 2 tbsp olive oil
- 1 cup leafy greens, chopped

Directions and Total Time: 15 minutes

In a bowl, mix the tomato, peppers, onion, black-eyed peas, beans, and capers. Put the avocados, lemon juice, sake, olive oil, oregano, and salt in a food processor and blitz until smooth. Add the dressing to the bean bowl and toss to combine. Transfer to a plate and top with leafy greens to serve.

Hot Coconut Beans with Vegetables

Ingredients for 4 servings

- 2 tbsp olive oil
- 1 onion, chopped
- 1 red bell pepper, chopped
- 2 garlic cloves, minced
- 1 tbsp hot powder
- 2 tbsp plant butter
- 1 (13.5-oz) can coconut milk
- 2 (15.5-oz) cans white beans
- 1 (14.5-oz) can diced tomatoes
- 3 cups fresh baby spinach
- Salt and black pepper to taste
- Chopped toasted walnuts

Directions and Total Time: 18 minutes

Heat the oil in a pot over medium heat. Place in onion, garlic, hot powder, and bell pepper and sauté for 5 minutes, stirring occasionally. Put in butter and coconut milk and whisk until well mixed. Add in white beans, tomatoes, spinach, salt, and pepper and cook for 5 minutes until the spinach wilts. Transfer to a platter, garnish with walnuts and serve.

Seitan & Lentil Chili

Ingredients for 4 servings

- 2 tbsp olive oil
- 1 onion, chopped
- 8 oz seitan, chopped
- 1 cup lentils
- 1 (14.5-oz) can diced tomatoes
- 1 tbsp soy sauce
- 1 tbsp chili powder
- 1 tsp ground cumin
- 1 tsp ground allspice
- ½ tsp ground oregano
- ¼ tsp ground cayenne
- Salt and black pepper to taste

Directions and Total Time: 35 minutes

Heat the oil in a pot over medium heat. Place in onion and seitan and cook for 10 minutes. Add in lentils, diced tomatoes, 2 cups of water, soy sauce, chili powder, cumin, allspice, sugar, oregano, cayenne pepper, salt, and pepper. Bring to a boil, then lower the heat and simmer for 20 minutes.

White Salad with Walnut Pesto

Ingredients for 4 servings-6

- 1 lb potatoes, cut into chunks
- 3 cups cauliflower florets
- 1 (15.5-oz) can cannellini beans
- ½ cup Kalamata olives, halved
- ½ cup walnuts
- 2 garlic cloves, minced
- ½ cup chopped fresh parsley
- ¼ cup walnut oil
- ¼ cup olive oil
- ¼ cup white wine vinegar
- Salt to taste
- ¼ tsp crushed red pepper

Directions and Total Time: 25 minutes

Cook the potatoes for 15 minutes in salted water. Add in the cauliflower and cook another 5 minutes until the veggies are tender. Drain and remove to a bowl. Stir in beans, olives, and half of the walnuts.

In a food processor, mix the remaining walnuts, garlic, parsley, walnut oil, olive oil, vinegar, salt, sugar, and red pepper. Blitz until well blended. Pour the dressing over the salad and toss to combine. Serve.

Hot Lentil Tacos with Guacamole

Ingredients for 4 servings

- ½ cup red lentils, rinsed and drained
- 2 tbsp olive oil
- ½ cup minced onion
- 1 potato, peeled and shredded
- ½ cup roasted cashews
- ¼ cup chickpea flour
- 1 tbsp minced fresh parsley
- 2 tsp hot powder
- Salt to taste
- 4 corn tortillas, warmed and halved
- Shredded romaine lettuce
- Guacamole

Directions and Total Time: 35 minutes

Place the lentils in a pot and cover with cold water. Bring to a boil and simmer for 15-20 minutes. Heat the oil over medium heat. Place in onion and potato and cook for 5 minutes. Set aside.

In a blender, mince cashews, add in cooked lentils and onion mixture. Pulse to blend. Transfer to a bowl and stir in flour, parsley, hot powder, and salt. Mix to combine. Mold 8 patties out of the mixture.

Heat the remaining oil in a skillet over medium heat. Brown the patties for 10 minutes on both sides. To assemble, put one cake in each tortilla, top with shredded lettuce and guacamole.

Curried Indian Rolls

Ingredients for 4 servings

3 tbsp tahini	3 tbsp water	½ cup fresh cilantro, chopped
Zest and juice of 1 lime	1 (14-oz) can chickpeas, drained	4 large whole-grain wraps
1 tbsp curry powder	1 cup diced peaches	2 cups shredded Iceberg lettuce
Sea salt to taste	1 red bell pepper, diced small	

Directions and Total Time: 15 minutes

In a bowl, beat tahini, lime zest, lime juice, curry powder, 3-4 tbsp of water, and salt until creamy. In another bowl, combine the chickpeas, peaches, bell pepper, cilantro, and tahini dressing. Divide the mixture between the wraps and top with lettuce. Roll up and serve.

Dijon Faro & Walnut Salad

Ingredients for 4 servings

1 cup faro	1 tbsp Dijon mustard	½ cup chopped red bell peppers
1 red onion, sliced	¼ cup olive oil	1/3 cup chopped toasted walnuts
1 garlic clove, minced	½ tsp dried oregano	2 tbsp minced fresh parsley
2 tbsp white wine vinegar	Salt and black pepper to taste	

Directions and Total Time: 50 minutes

Cook faro in salted water for 25 minutes. Drain and set aside to cool. In a bowl, put the onion, garlic, vinegar, mustard, oil, oregano, salt, and pepper. Mix to combine.

To the cooled faro, add bell peppers, walnuts, and parsley; stir. Transfer to a serving plate, drizzle with the onion mixture, and serve.

Awesome Barley Jambalaya

Ingredients for 4 servings

2 tbsp olive oil	2 garlic cloves, minced	1 tsp dried rosemary
1 onion, chopped	1 cup pearl barley	2 ½ cups vegetable broth
2 celery stalks, chopped	2 (15.5-oz) cans kidney beans	1 tbsp chopped fresh parsley
1 green bell pepper, chopped	1 (14.5-oz) can diced tomatoes	Sriracha sauce

Directions and Total Time: 25 minutes

Heat the oil in a pot over medium heat. Place in onion, celery, bell pepper, and garlic. Sauté for 5 minutes. Add in barley, beans, tomatoes, rosemary, salt, and pepper. Stir in broth and simmer for 15 minutes. Top with parsley and drizzle with sriracha sauce to serve.

Baked Mustard Beans ✓

Ingredients for 4 servings

2 tbsp olive oil	1 (14.5-oz) can crushed tomatoes	¼ tsp ground cayenne pepper
1 onion, minced	½ cup pure date syrup	Salt and black pepper to taste
2 garlic cloves, minced	1 ½ tsp dry mustard	2 (15.5-oz) cans Great Northern beans

Directions and Total Time: 25 minutes

Preheat oven to 350 F.

Heat the oil in a pot over medium heat. Place in onion and garlic and sauté for 3 minutes. Add in tomatoes, date syrup, mustard, cayenne pepper, salt, and pepper. Cook for 5 minutes. Pour the beans in a baking dish and stir in the sauce to coat. Bake for 10 minutes. Serve warm.

Hot Bean Salad

Ingredients for 4 servings

1 cup pinto beans, soaked overnight
4 tomatoes, halved and sliced
2 celery stalks, sliced

2 hot chilies, seeded and minced
1/3 cup chopped green onions
1 tbsp chopped fresh parsley

2 tbsp olive oil
2 tbsp balsamic vinegar
Salt and black pepper to taste

Directions and Total Time: 45 minutes

Cook pinto beans in salted water for 40 minutes. Drain and remove to a bowl. Let cool for a few minutes. Stir in tomatoes, celery, chilies, and green onions. In another bowl, mix olive oil, vinegar, salt, and pepper.

Add the dressing to the bean bowl and toss to coat. Transfer to a serving plate. Top with parsley and serve.

Rice, Lentil & Spinach Pilaf

Ingredients for 4 servings

½ cup wild rice
1 (15.5-oz) can lentils, drained

1 (14.5-oz) can diced tomatoes
1 tsp dried thyme

Salt and black pepper to taste
3 cups fresh baby spinach

Directions and Total Time: 25 minutes

In a pot over medium heat, bring the rice and 1 ½ cups of salted water to a boil. Reduce the heat, cover, and simmer for 20 minutes.

Add in lentils, tomatoes, thyme, salt, and pepper. Stir and cook until heated through. Mix in the spinach, cook for 2 minutes until the spinach wilts. Serve warm.

Parsley Bean & Olives Salad

Ingredients for 4 servings

1 cup green olives, pitted and sliced
2 (15.5-oz) cans black beans
½ cup chopped red bell pepper

¼ cup red onions, sliced
2 garlic cloves, crushed
¼ cup chopped fresh parsley

Salt and black pepper to taste
2 tbsp fresh lime juice
¼ cup olive oil

Directions and Total Time: 15 minutes

Combine the olives, beans, bell pepper, and onion in a bowl. Set aside. In a food processor, put garlic, lime juice, 2 tbsp water, olive oil, parsley, salt, and pepper. Pulse until blended. Add to the salad bowl and mix to combine. Serve immediately.

Habanero Pinto Beans with Bell Pepper Pot

Ingredients for 6 servings

1 tsp olive oil
2 red bell peppers, diced
1 habanero pepper, minced

2 (14.5-oz) cans pinto beans
½ cup vegetable broth
1 tsp ground cumin

1 tsp chili powder
Salt and black pepper to taste

Directions and Total Time: 20 minutes

Heat the oil in a pot over medium heat. Place in bell and habanero peppers, sauté for 5 minutes until tender. Add in beans, broth, cumin, chili powder, salt, and pepper. Bring to a boil, then lower the heat and simmer for 10 minutes. Serve.

Cucumber & Carrot Pizza with Pesto

Ingredients for 2 servings

1 prebaked pizza crust
½ cup vegan pesto

1 tomato, sliced
1 carrot, grated

1 red onion, sliced
1 cucumber, sliced

Directions and Total Time: 30 minutes

Preheat oven to 390 F.

Spread half of the pesto over the pizza crust and top with tomato slices. Combine the grated carrot with salt, toss to coat. Put the carrot over the tomato and top with onion.

Transfer to a baking tray and put it in the oven. Bake for 15-20 minutes until golden. Serve topped with cucumber slices.

DINNER

Black-Eyed Pea Oat Bake

Ingredients for 4 servings

1 carrot, shredded
1 onion, chopped
2 garlic cloves, minced
1 (15.5-oz) can black-eyed peas

¾ cup whole-wheat flour
¾ cup quick-cooking oats
½ cup breadcrumbs
¼ cup minced fresh parsley

1 tbsp soy sauce
½ tsp dried sage
Salt and black pepper to taste

Directions and Total Time: 25 minutes

Preheat oven to 360 F.

Combine the carrot, onion, garlic, and peas and pulse until creamy and smooth in a blender. Add in flour, oats, breadcrumbs, parsley, soy sauce, sage, salt, and pepper. Blend until ingredients are evenly mixed. Spoon the mixture into a greased loaf pan. Bake for 40 minutes until golden. Allow it to cool down for a few minutes before slicing. Serve immediately.

Paprika Fava Bean Patties

Ingredients for 4 servings

4 tbsp olive oil
1 minced onion
1 garlic clove, minced
1 (15.5-oz) can fava beans

1 tbsp minced fresh parsley
½ cup breadcrumbs
¼ cup almond flour
1 tsp smoked paprika

½ tsp dried thyme
4 burger buns, toasted
4 lettuce leaves
1 ripe tomato, sliced

Directions and Total Time: 15 minutes

In a blender, add onion, garlic, beans, parsley, breadcrumbs, flour, paprika, thyme, salt, and pepper. Pulse until uniform but not smooth. Shape 4 patties out of the mixture. Refrigerate for 15 minutes.

Heat olive oil in a skillet over medium heat. Fry the patties for 10 minutes on both sides until golden brown. Serve in toasted buns with lettuce and tomato slices.

Walnut Lentil Burgers

Ingredients for 4 servings

2 tbsp olive oil
1 cup dry lentils, rinsed
2 carrots, grated

1 onion, diced
½ cup walnuts
1 tbsp tomato puree

¾ cup almond flour
2 tsp curry powder
4 whole-grain buns

Directions and Total Time: 70 minutes

Place lentils in a pot and cover with water. Bring to a boil and simmer for 15-20 minutes.

Meanwhile, combine the carrots, walnuts, onion, tomato puree, flour, curry powder, salt, and pepper in a bowl. Toss to coat. Once the lentils are ready, drain and transfer into the veggie bowl. Mash the mixture until sticky. Shape the mixture into balls; flatten to make patties.

Heat the oil in a skillet over medium heat. Brown the patties for 8 minutes on both sides. To assemble, put the cakes on the buns and top with your desired toppings.

Couscous & Quinoa Burgers

Ingredients for 4 servings

2 tbsp olive oil
¼ cup couscous
¼ cup boiling water
2 cups cooker quinoa

2 tbsp balsamic vinegar
3 tbsp chopped olives
½ tsp garlic powder
Salt to taste

4 burger buns
Lettuce leaves, for serving
Tomato slices, for serving

Directions and Total Time: 20 minutes

Preheat oven to 350 F.

In a bowl, place the couscous with boiling water. Let sit covered for 5 minutes. Once the liquid is absorbed, fluff with a fork. Add in quinoa and mash them to form a chunky texture. Stir in vinegar, olive oil, olives, garlic powder, and salt.

Shape the mixture into 4 patties. Arrange them on a greased tray and bake for 25-30 minutes. To assemble, place the patties on the buns and top with lettuce and tomato slices. Serve.

Bean & Pecan Sandwiches

Ingredients for 4 servings

- 1 onion, chopped
- 1 garlic clove, crushed
- ¾ cup pecans, chopped
- ¾ cup canned black beans
- ¾ cup almond flour
- 2 tbsp minced fresh parsley
- 1 tbsp soy sauce
- 1 tsp Dijon mustard + to serve
- Salt and black pepper to taste
- ½ tsp ground sage
- ½ tsp sweet paprika
- 2 tbsp olive oil
- Bread slices *(coconut wrap)*
- Lettuce leaves and sliced tomatoes

Directions and Total Time: 20 minutes

Put the onion, garlic, and pecans in a blender and pulse until roughly ground. Add in the beans and pulse until everything is well combined. Transfer to a large mixing bowl and stir in the flour, parsley, soy sauce, mustard, salt, sage, paprika, and pepper. Mold patties out of the mixture.

Heat the oil in a skillet over medium heat. Brown the patties for 10 minutes on both sides. To assemble, lay patties on the bread slices and top with mustard, lettuce, and tomato slices.

Homemade Kitchari

Ingredients for 5 servings

- 4 cups chopped cauliflower and broccoli florets
- ½ cup split peas
- ½ cup brown rice
- 1 red onion, chopped
- 1 (14.5-oz) can diced tomatoes
- 3 garlic cloves, minced
- 1 jalapeño pepper, seeded
- ½ tsp ground ginger
- 1 tsp ground turmeric
- 1 tsp olive oil
- 1 tsp fennel seeds
- Juice of 1 large lemon
- Salt and black pepper to taste

Directions and Total Time: 40 minutes

In a food processor, place the onion, tomatoes with juices, garlic, jalapeño pepper, ginger, turmeric, and 2 tbsp of water. Pulse until ingredients are evenly mixed.

Heat the oil in a pot over medium heat. Cook the cumin and fennel seeds for 2-3 minutes, stirring often. Pour in the puréed mixture, split peas, rice, and 3 cups of water. Bring to a boil, then lower the heat and simmer for 10 minutes. Stir in cauliflower, broccoli, and cook for another 10 minutes. Mix in lemon juice and adjust seasoning.

Picante Green Rice

Ingredients for 4 servings

- 1 roasted bell pepper, chopped
- 3 small hot green chilies, chopped
- 2 ½ cups vegetable broth
- ½ cup chopped fresh parsley
- 1 onion, chopped
- 2 garlic cloves, chopped
- Salt and black pepper to taste
- ½ tsp dried oregano
- 3 tbsp canola oil
- 1 cup long-grain brown rice
- 1 ½ cups cooked black beans
- 2 tbsp minced fresh cilantro

Directions and Total Time: 35 minutes

In a food processor, place bell pepper, chilies, 1 cup of broth, parsley, onion, garlic, pepper, oregano, salt, and pepper and blend until smooth. Heat oil in a skillet over medium heat. Add in rice and veggie mixture. Cook for 5 minutes, stirring often. Add in the remaining broth and bring to a boil, lower the heat, and simmer for 15 minutes. Mix in beans and cook for another 5 minutes. Serve with cilantro.

Asian Quinoa Sauté

Ingredients for 4 servings

- 1 cup quinoa
- Salt to taste
- 1 head cauliflower, break into florets
- 2 tsp untoasted sesame oil
- 1 cup snow peas, cut in half
- 1 cup frozen peas
- 2 cups chopped Swiss chard
- 2 scallions, chopped
- 2 tbsp water
- 1 tsp toasted sesame oil
- 1 tbsp soy sauce
- 2 tbsp sesame seeds

Directions and Total Time: 30 minutes

Place quinoa with 2 cups of water and salt in a bowl. Bring to a boil, lower the heat and simmer for 15 minutes. Do not stir.

Heat the oil in a skillet over medium heat and sauté the cauliflower for 4-5 minutes. Add in snow peas and stir well. Stir in Swiss chard, scallions, and 2 tbsp of water; cook until wilted, about 5 minutes. Season with salt.

Drizzle with sesame oil and soy sauce and cook for 1 minute. Divide the quinoa in bowls and top with the cauliflower mixture. Garnish with sesame seeds and soy sauce to serve.

Faro & Black Bean Loaf

Ingredients for 6 servings

3 tbsp olive oil
1 onion, minced
1 cup faro

2 (15.5-oz) cans black beans, mashed
½ cup quick-cooking oats
1/3 cup whole-wheat flour

2 tbsp nutritional yeast
1 ½ tsp dried thyme
½ tsp dried oregano

Directions and Total Time: 50 minutes

Heat the oil in a pot over medium heat. Place in onion and sauté for 3 minutes. Add in faro, 2 cups of water, salt, and pepper. Bring to a boil, lower the heat and simmer for 20 minutes. Remove to a bowl.

Preheat oven to 350 F.

Add the mashed beans, oats, flour, yeast, thyme, and oregano to the faro bowl. Toss to combine. Taste and adjust the seasoning. Shape the mixture into a greased loaf. Bake for 20 minutes. Let cool for a few minutes. Slice and serve.

Cuban-Style Millet

Ingredients for 4 servings

2 tbsp olive oil
1 onion, chopped
2 zucchinis, chopped

2 garlic cloves, minced
1 tsp dried thyme
½ tsp ground cumin

1 (15.5-oz) can black-eyed peas
1 cup millet
2 tbsp chopped fresh cilantro

Directions and Total Time: 40 minutes

Heat the oil in a pot over medium heat. Place in onion and sauté for 3 minutes until translucent. Add in zucchinis, garlic, thyme, and cumin and cook for 10 minutes. Put in peas, millet, and 2 ½ cups of hot water. Bring to a boil, then lower the heat and simmer for 20 minutes. Fluff the millet using a fork. Serve garnished with cilantro.

Traditional Cilantro Pilaf

Ingredients for 6 servings

3 tbsp olive oil
1 onion, minced
1 carrot, chopped

2 garlic cloves, minced
1 cup wild rice
1 ½ tsp ground fennel seeds

½ tsp ground cumin
Salt and black pepper to taste
3 tbsp minced fresh cilantro

Directions and Total Time: 30 minutes

Heat the oil in a pot over medium heat. Place in onion, carrot, and garlic and sauté for 5 minutes. Stir in rice, fennel seeds, cumin, and 2 cups water. Bring to a boil, then lower the heat and simmer for 20 minutes. Remove to a bowl and fluff using a fork. Serve topped with cilantro and black pepper.

Oriental Bulgur & White Beans

Ingredients for 4 servings

2 tbsp olive oil
3 green onions, chopped
1 cup bulgur

1 cups water
1 tbsp soy sauce
Salt to taste

1 ½ cups cooked white beans
1 tbsp nutritional yeast
1 tbsp dried parsley

Directions and Total Time: 55 minutes

Heat the oil in a pot over medium heat. Place in green onions and sauté for 3 minutes. Stir in bulgur, water, soy sauce, and salt. Bring to a boil, then lower the heat and simmer for 20-22 minutes. Mix in beans and yeast. Cook for 5 minutes. Serve topped with parsley.

One-Pot Red Lentils with Mushrooms

Ingredients for 4 servings

2 tsp olive oil
2 cloves garlic, minced
2 tsp grated fresh ginger

½ tsp ground cumin
½ tsp fennel seeds
1 cup mushrooms, chopped

1 large tomato, chopped
1 cup dried red lentils
2 tbsp lemon juice

Directions and Total Time: 25 minutes

Heat the oil in a pot over medium heat. Place in the garlic and ginger and cook for 3 minutes. Stir in cumin, fennel, mushrooms, tomato, lentils, and 2 ¼ cups of water. Bring to a boil, then lower the heat and simmer for 15 minutes. Mix in lemon juice and serve.

Sherry Shallot Beans

Ingredients for 4 servings

2 tsp olive oil
4 shallots, chopped
1 tsp ground cumin
1 (14.5-oz) cans black beans
1 cup vegetable broth
2 tbsp sherry vinegar

Directions and Total Time: 25 minutes

Heat the oil in a pot over medium heat. Place in shallots and cumin and cook for 3 minutes until soft. Stir in beans and broth. Bring to a boil, then lower the heat and simmer for 10 minutes. Add in sherry vinegar, increase the heat and cook for an additional 3 minutes. Serve warm.

Celery Buckwheat Croquettes

Ingredients for 6 servings

¾ cup cooked buckwheat groats
½ cup cooked brown rice
3 tbsp olive oil
¼ cup minced onion
1 celery stalk, chopped
¼ cup shredded carrots
1/3 cup whole-wheat flour
¼ cup chopped fresh parsley
Salt and black pepper to taste

Directions and Total Time: 25 minutes

Combine the groats and rice in a bowl. Set aside. Heat 1 tbsp of oil in a skillet over medium heat. Place in onion, celery, and carrot and cook for 5 minutes. Transfer to the rice bowl.

Mix in flour, parsley, salt, and pepper. Place in the fridge for 20 minutes. Mold the mixture into cylinder-shaped balls. Heat the remaining oil in a skillet over medium heat. Fry the croquettes for 8 minutes, turning occasionally until golden.

Oregano Chickpeas

Ingredients for 6 servings

1 tsp olive oil
1 onion, cut into half-moon slices
2 (14.5-oz) cans chickpeas
½ cup vegetable broth
2 tsp dried oregano
Salt and black pepper to taste

Directions and Total Time: 5 minutes

Heat the oil in a skillet over medium heat. Cook the onion for 3 minutes. Stir in chickpeas, broth, oregano, salt, and pepper. Bring to a boil, then lower the heat and simmer for 10 minutes. Serve.

Matcha-Infused Tofu Rice

Ingredients for 4 servings

4 matcha tea bags
1 ½ cups brown rice
2 tbsp canola oil
8 oz extra-firm tofu, chopped
3 green onions, minced
2 cups snow peas, cut diagonally
1 tbsp fresh lemon juice
1 tsp grated lemon zest
Salt and black pepper to taste

Directions and Total Time: 35 minutes

Boil 3 cups water in a pot. Place in the tea bags and turn the heat off. Let sit for 7 minutes. Discard the bags. Wash the rice and put it into the tea. Cook for 20 minutes over medium heat. Drain and set aside.

Heat the oil in a skillet over medium heat. Fry the tofu for 5 minutes until golden. Stir in green onions and snow peas and cook for another 3 minutes. Mix in lemon juice and lemon zest. Place the rice in a serving bowl and mix in the tofu mixture. Adjust the seasoning with salt and pepper. Serve right away.

Chinese Fried Rice

Ingredients for 4 servings

2 tbsp canola oil
1 onion, chopped
1 large carrot, chopped
1 head broccoli, cut into florets
2 garlic cloves, minced
2 tsp grated fresh ginger
3 green onions, minced
3 ½ cups cooked brown rice
1 cup frozen peas, thawed
3 tbsp soy sauce
2 tsp dry white wine
1 tbsp toasted sesame oil

Directions and Total Time: 20 minutes

Heat the oil in a skillet over medium heat. Place in onion, carrot, and broccoli, sauté for 5 minutes until tender. Add in garlic, ginger, and green onions and sauté for another 3 minutes. Stir in rice, peas, soy sauce, and white wine and cook for 5 minutes. Add in sesame oil, toss to combine. Serve right away.

Savory Seitan & Bell Pepper Rice

Ingredients for 4 servings

2 cups water
1 cup long-grain brown rice
2 tbsp olive oil
1 onion, chopped

2 garlic cloves, minced
8 oz seitan, chopped
1 green bell pepper, chopped
1 tsp dried basil

½ tsp ground fennel seeds
¼ tsp crushed red pepper
Salt and black pepper to taste

Directions and Total Time: 35 minutes

Bring water to a boil in a pot. Place in rice and lower the heat. Simmer for 20 minutes.

Heat the oil in a skillet over medium heat. Sauté the onion for 3 minutes until translucent. Add in the seitan and bell pepper and cook for another 5 minutes. Stir in basil, fennel, red pepper, salt, and black pepper. Once the rice is ready, remove it to a bowl. Add in seitan mixture and toss to combine. Serve.

Asparagus & Mushrooms with Mashed Potatoes

Ingredients for 4 servings

5 large portobello mushrooms, stems removed
6 potatoes, chopped
4 garlic cloves, minced
2 tsp olive oil

½ cup non-dairy milk
2 tbsp nutritional yeast
Sea salt to taste

7 cups asparagus, chopped
3 tsp coconut oil
2 tbsp nutritional yeast

Directions and Total Time: 60 minutes

Place the chopped potatoes in a pot and cover with salted water. Cook for 20 minutes.

Heat oil in a skillet and sauté garlic for 1 minute. Once the potatoes are ready, drain them and reserve the water. Transfer to a bowl and mash them with some hot water, garlic, milk, yeast, and salt.

Preheat your grill to medium. Grease the mushrooms with cooking spray and season with salt. Arrange the mushrooms face down and grill for 10 minutes. After, grill the asparagus for about 10 minutes, turning often. Arrange the veggies in a serving platter. Add in the potato mash and serve.

Green Pea & Lemon Couscous

Ingredients for 6 servings

1 cup green peas
2 ¾ cups vegetable stock

Juice and zest of 1 lemon
2 tbsp chopped fresh thyme

1 ½ cups couscous
¼ cup chopped fresh parsley

Directions and Total Time: 15 minutes

Pour the vegetable stock, lemon juice, thyme, salt, and pepper in a pot. Bring to a boil, then add in green peas and couscous. Turn the heat off and let sit covered for 5 minutes, until the liquid has absorbed. Fluff the couscous using a fork and mix in the lemon and parsley. Serve immediately.

Chimichurri Fusili with Navy Beans

Ingredients for 4 servings

8 oz whole-wheat fusilli
1 ½ cups canned navy beans

½ cup chimichurri salsa
1 cup chopped tomatoes

1 red onion, chopped
½ cup chopped pitted black olives

Directions and Total Time: 25 minutes

In a large pot over medium heat, pour 8 cups of salted water. Bring to a boil and add in the pasta. Cook for 8-10 minutes, drain and let cool. Combine the pasta, beans, and chimichurri in a bowl. Toss to coat. Stir in tomato, red onion, and olives.

Quinoa & Chickpea Pot

Ingredients for 2 servings

2 tsp olive oil
1 cup cooked quinoa

1 (15-oz) can chickpeas
1 bunch arugula chopped

1 tbsp soy
Sea salt and black pepper to taste

Directions and Total Time: 15 minutes

Heat the oil in a skillet over medium heat. Stir in quinoa, chickpeas, and arugula and cook for 3-5 minutes until the arugula wilts. Pour in soy sauce, salt, and pepper. Toss to coat. Serve immediately.

Buckwheat Pilaf with Pine Nuts

Ingredients for 4 servings

1 cup buckwheat groats
2 cups vegetable stock

¼ cup pine nuts
2 tbsp olive oil

½ onion, chopped
⅓ cup chopped fresh parsley

Directions and Total Time: 25 minutes

Put the groats and vegetable stock in a pot. Bring to a boil, then lower the heat and simmer for 15 minutes. Heat a skillet over medium heat. Place in the pine nuts and toast for 2-3 minutes, shaking often. Heat the oil in the same skillet and sauté the onion for 3 minutes until translucent.

Once the groats are ready, fluff them using a fork. Mix in pine nuts, onion, and parsley. Sprinkle with salt and pepper. Serve.

Italian Holiday Stuffing

Ingredients for 4 servings

¼ cup plant butter
1 onion, chopped
2 celery stalks, sliced
1 cup button mushrooms, sliced

3 garlic cloves, minced
½ cup vegetable broth
½ cup raisins
½ cup chopped walnuts

2 cups cooked quinoa
1 tsp Italian seasoning
Sea salt to taste
Chopped fresh parsley

Directions and Total Time: 25 minutes

In a skillet over medium heat, melt the butter. Sauté the onion, garlic, celery, and mushrooms for 5 minutes until tender, stirring occasionally. Pour in broth, raisins, and walnuts. Bring to a boil, then lower the heat and simmer for 5 minutes. Stir in quinoa, Italian seasoning, and salt. Cook for another 4 minutes. Serve garnished with parsley.

Pressure Cooker Green Lentils

Ingredients for 6 servings

3 tbsp coconut oil
2 tbsp curry powder
1 tsp ground ginger

1 onion, chopped
2 garlic cloves, sliced
1 cup dried green lentils

3 cups water
Salt and black pepper to taste

Directions and Total Time: 30 minutes

Set your IP to Sauté. Add in coconut oil, curry powder, ginger, onion, and garlic. Cook for 3 minutes. Stir in green lentils. Pour in water. Lock the lid and set the time to 10 minutes on High. Once ready, perform a natural pressure release for 10 minutes. Unlock the lid and season with salt and pepper. Serve.

Cherry & Pistachio Bulgur

Ingredients for 4 servings

1 tbsp plant butter
1 white onion, chopped
1 carrot, chopped

1 celery stalk, chopped
1 cup chopped mushrooms
1 ½ cups bulgur

4 cups vegetable broth
1 cup chopped dried cherries, soaked
½ cup chopped pistachios

Directions and Total Time: 45 minutes

Preheat oven to 375 F.

Melt butter in a skillet over medium heat. Sauté the onion, carrot, and celery for 5 minutes until tender. Add in mushrooms and cook for 3 more minutes. Pour in bulgur and broth. Transfer to a casserole and bake covered for 30 minutes. Once ready, uncover and stir in cherries. Top with pistachios to serve.

Mushroom Fried Rice

Ingredients for 6 servings

2 tbsp sesame oil
1 onion, chopped
1 carrot, chopped

1 cup okra, chopped
1 cup sliced shiitake mushrooms
2 garlic cloves, minced

¼ cup soy sauce
1 cups cooked brown rice
2 green onions, chopped

Directions and Total Time: 25 minutes

Heat the oil in a skillet over medium heat. Place in onion and carrot and cook for 3 minutes. Add in okra and mushrooms, cook for 5-7 minutes. Stir in garlic and cook for 30 seconds. Put in soy sauce and rice. Cook until hot. Add in green onions and stir. Serve warm.

Bean & Brown Rice with Artichokes

Ingredients for 4 servings

2 tbsp olive oil
3 garlic cloves, minced
1 cup artichokes hearts, chopped
1 tsp dried basil
1 ½ cups cooked navy beans
1 ½ cups long-grain brown rice
3 cups vegetable broth
Salt and black pepper to taste
2 ripe grape tomatoes, quartered
2 tbsp minced fresh parsley

Directions and Total Time: 35 minutes

Heat the oil in a pot over medium heat. Sauté the garlic for 1 minute. Stir in artichokes, basil, navy beans, rice, and broth. Sprinkle with salt and pepper. Lower the heat and simmer for 20-25 minutes. Remove to a bowl and mix in tomatoes and parsley. Using a fork, fluff the rice and serve right away.

Pressure Cooker Celery & Spinach Chickpeas

Ingredients for 5 servings

1 cup chickpeas, soaked overnight
1 onion, chopped
2 garlic cloves, minced
1 celery stalk, chopped
2 tbsp olive oil
3 tsp ground cinnamon
½ tsp ground nutmeg
1 tbsp coconut oil
1 cup spinach, chopped

Directions and Total Time: 50 minutes

Place chickpeas in your IP with the onion, garlic, celery, olive oil, 2 cups water, cinnamon, and nutmeg.
Lock the lid in place; set the time to 30 minutes on High. Once ready, perform a natural pressure release for 10 minutes. Unlock the lid and drain the excess water. Put back the chickpeas and stir in coconut oil and spinach. Set the pot to Sauté and cook for another 5 minutes.

Veggie Paella with Lentils

Ingredients for 4 servings

2 tbsp olive oil
1 onion, chopped
1 green bell pepper, chopped
2 garlic cloves, minced
1 (14.5-oz) can diced tomatoes
1 tbsp capers
¼ tsp crushed red pepper
1 ½ cups long-grain brown rice
3 cups vegetable broth
1 ½ cups cooked lentils, drained
¼ cup sliced pitted black olives
2 tbsp minced fresh parsley

Directions and Total Time: 50 minutes

Heat oil in a pot over medium heat and sauté onion, bell pepper, and garlic for 5 minutes. Stir in tomatoes, capers, red pepper, and salt. Cook for 5 minutes. Pour in the rice and broth. Bring to a boil, then lower the heat. Simmer for 20 minutes. Turn the heat off and mix in lentils. Serve garnished with olives and parsley.

Curry Bean with Artichokes

Ingredients for 4 servings

1 (14.5-oz) can artichoke hearts, drained and quartered
1 tsp olive oil
1 small onion, diced
2 garlic cloves, minced
1 (14.5-oz) can cannellini beans
2 tsp curry powder
½ tsp ground coriander
1 (5.4-oz) can coconut milk
Salt and black pepper to taste

Directions and Total Time: 25 minutes

Heat the oil in a skillet over medium heat. Sauté the onion and garlic for 3 minutes until translucent. Stir in beans, artichoke, curry powder, and coriander. Add in coconut milk. Bring to a boil, then lower the heat and simmer for 10 minutes. Serve.

Endive Slaw with Olives

Ingredients for 6 servings

1 lb curly endive, chopped
⅓ cup vegan mayonnaise
¼ cup rice vinegar
2 tbsp vegan yogurt
1 tbsp pure date sugar
10 black olives for garnish
¼ tsp freshly ground black pepper
¼ tsp smoked paprika
¼ tsp chipotle powder

Directions and Total Time: 10 minutes

In a bowl, mix the mayonnaise, vinegar, yogurt, sugar, salt, pepper, paprika, and chipotle powder. Gently add in the curly endive and mix with a wooden spatula to coat. Top with black olives and serve.

Paprika Cauliflower Tacos

Ingredients for 6 servings

1 head cauliflower, cut into pieces
2 tbsp olive oil
2 tbsp whole-wheat flour
2 tbsp nutritional yeast
2 tsp paprika

1 tsp cayenne pepper
Salt to taste
1 cups shredded watercress
2 cups cherry tomatoes, halved
2 carrots, grated

½ cup mango salsa
½ cup guacamole
8 small corn tortillas, warm
1 lime, cut into wedges

Directions and Total Time: 40 minutes

Preheat oven to 350 F.

Brush the cauliflower with oil in a bowl. In another bowl, mix the flour, yeast, paprika, cayenne pepper, and salt. Pour into the cauliflower bowl and toss to coat. Spread the cauliflower on a greased baking sheet. Bake for 20-30 minutes.

In a bowl, combine the watercress, cherry tomatoes, carrots, mango salsa, and guacamole. Once the cauliflower is ready, divide it between the tortillas, add the mango mixture, roll up and serve with lime wedges on the side.

Simple Pesto Millet

Ingredients for 4 servings

1 cup millet

2 ½ cups vegetable broth

½ cup vegan basil pesto

Directions and Total Time: 50 minutes

Place the millet and broth in a pot. Bring to a boil, then lower the heat and simmer for 25 minutes. Let cool for 5 minutes and fluff the millet. Mix in the pesto and serve.

Peppered Pinto Beans

Ingredients for 6 servings

1 serrano pepper, cut into strips
1 red bell pepper, cut into strips
1 green bell pepper, cut into strips

1 onion, chopped
2 carrots, chopped
2 garlic cloves, minced

3 (15-oz) cans pinto beans
18-ounce bottle barbecue sauce
½ tsp chipotle powder

Directions and Total Time: 30 minutes

In a blender, place the serrano and bell peppers, onion, carrot, and garlic. Pulse until well mixed.

Place the mixture in a pot with the beans, BBQ sauce, and chipotle powder. Cook for 15 minutes. Season with salt and pepper. Serve warm.

Black-Eyed Peas with Sun-Dried Tomatoes

Ingredients for 4 servings

1 cup black-eyed peas, soaked overnight
¼ cup sun-dried tomatoes, chopped
2 tbsp olive oil

2 tsp ground chipotle pepper
1 ½ tsp ground cumin
1 ½ tsp onion powder

1 tsp dried oregano
¾ tsp garlic powder
½ tsp smoked paprika

Directions and Total Time: 35 minutes

Place the black-eyed peas in a pot and add 2 cups of water, olive oil, chipotle pepper, cumin, onion powder, oregano, garlic powder, salt, and paprika. Cook for 20 minutes over medium heat. Mix in sun-dried tomatoes, let sit for a few minutes and serve.

Vegetarian Quinoa Curry

Ingredients for 4 servings

4 tsp olive oil
1 onion, chopped
2 tbsp curry powder

1 ½ cups quinoa
1 cup canned diced tomatoes
4 cups chopped spinach

½ cup non-dairy milk
2 tbsp soy sauce
Salt to taste

Directions and Total Time: 35 minutes

Heat the oil in a pot over medium heat. Sauté the onion and ginger for 3 minutes until tender. Pour in curry powder, quinoa, and 3 cups of water. Bring to a boil, then lower the heat and simmer for 15-20 minutes. Mix in tomatoes, spinach, milk, soy sauce, and salt. Simmer for an additional 3 minutes.

Alfredo Rice with Green Beans

Ingredients for 3 servings

1 cup Alfredo arugula vegan pesto
1 cup frozen green beans, thawed
2 cups brown rice

Directions and Total Time: 25 minutes

Cook the rice in salted water in a pot over medium heat for 20 minutes. Drain and let it cool completely. Place the Alfredo sauce and beans in a skillet. Cook over low heat for 3-5 minutes. Stir in the rice to coat. Serve immediately.

Korean-Style Millet

Ingredients for 4 servings

1 cup dried millet, drained
1 tsp gochugaru flakes
Salt and black pepper to taste

Directions and Total Time: 30 minutes

Place the millet and gochugaru flakes in a pot. Cover with enough water and bring to a boil. Lower the heat and simmer for 20 minutes. Drain and let cool. Transfer to a serving bowl and season with salt and pepper. Serve.

Lemony Chickpeas with Kale

Ingredients for 4 servings

4 tbsp olive oil
1 (15-oz) can chickpeas
1 onion, chopped
2 garlic cloves, minced
1 tbsp Italian seasoning
2 cups kale, chopped
Sea salt and black pepper to taste
Juice and zest of 1 lemon

Directions and Total Time: 20 minutes

Heat the oil in a skillet over medium heat. Place in chickpeas and cook for 5 minutes. Add in onion, garlic, Italian seasoning, and kale and cook for 5 minutes until the kale wilts. Stir in salt, lemon juice, lemon zest, and pepper. Serve warm.

Dinner Rice & Lentils

Ingredients for 4 servings

2 tbsp olive oil
4 scallions, chopped
1 carrot, diced
1 celery stalk, chopped
2 (15-oz) cans lentils, drained
1 (15-oz) can diced tomatoes
1 tbsp dried rosemary
1 tsp ground coriander
1 tbsp garlic powder
2 cups cooked brown rice
Sea salt and black pepper to taste

Directions and Total Time: 25 minutes

Heat the oil in a pot over medium heat. Place in scallions, carrot, and celery and cook for 5 minutes until tender. Stir in lentils, tomatoes, rosemary, coriander, and garlic powder. Lower the heat and simmer for 5-7 minutes. Mix in rice, salt, and pepper and cook another 2-3 minutes. Serve.

Sesame Kale Slaw

Ingredients for 4 servings

¼ cup tahini
2 tbsp white miso paste
1 tbsp rice vinegar
1 tbsp toasted sesame oil
2 tsp soy sauce
1 (12-oz) bag kale slaw
2 scallions, minced
¼ cup toasted sesame seeds

Directions and Total Time: 15 minutes

In a bowl, combine the tahini, miso, vinegar, oil, and soy sauce. Stir in kale slaw, scallions, and sesame seeds. Let sit for 20 minutes. Serve immediately.

Spicy Steamed Broccoli

Ingredients for 6 servings

1 large head broccoli, into florets
Salt to taste
1 tsp red pepper flakes

Directions and Total Time: 15 minutes

Boil 1 cup water in a pot over medium heat. Place in a steamer basket and put in the florets. Steam covered for 5-7 minutes. In a bowl, toss the broccoli with red pepper flakes and salt. Serve.

Garlic Roasted Carrots

Ingredients for 4 servings

2 lb carrots, chopped into ¾ inch cubes
2 tsp olive oil
½ tsp chili powder
½ tsp smoked paprika
½ tsp dried oregano
½ tsp dried thyme
½ tsp garlic powder
Salt to taste

Directions and Total Time: 35 minutes

Preheat oven to 400 F. Line with parchment paper a baking sheet. Rinse the carrots and pat dry. Chop into ¾ inch cubes. Place in a bowl and toss with olive oil.

In a bowl, mix chili powder, paprika, oregano, thyme, olive oil, salt, and garlic powder. Pour over the carrots and toss to coat. Transfer to a greased baking sheet and bake for 30 minutes, turn once by half.

Eggplant & Hummus Pizza

Ingredients for 2 servings

½ eggplant, sliced
½ red onion, sliced
1 cup cherry tomatoes, halved
3 tbsp chopped black olives
Salt to taste
Drizzle olive oil
2 prebaked pizza crusts
½ cup hummus
2 tbsp oregano

Directions and Total Time: 25 minutes

Preheat oven to 390 F.

In a bowl, combine the eggplant, onion, tomatoes, olives, and salt. Toss to coat. Sprinkle with some olive oil. Arrange the crusts on a baking sheet and spread the hummus on each pizza. Top with the eggplant mixture. Bake for 20-30 minutes. Serve warm.

Miso Green Cabbage

Ingredients for 4 servings

1 lb green cabbage, halved
2 tsp olive
3 tsp miso paste
1 tsp dried oregano
½ tsp dried rosemary
1 tbsp balsamic vinegar

Directions and Total Time: 50 minutes

Preheat oven to 390 F. Line with parchment paper a baking sheet.

Put the green cabbage in a bowl. Coat with olive oil, miso, oregano, rosemary, salt, and pepper. Remove to the baking sheet and bake for 35-40 minutes, shaking every 5 minutes until tender. Remove from the oven to a plate. Drizzle with balsamic vinegar and serve.

Steamed Broccoli with Hazelnuts

Ingredients for 4 servings

1 lb broccoli, cut into florets
2 tbsp olive oil
3 garlic cloves, minced
1 cup sliced white mushrooms
¼ cup dry white wine
2 tbsp minced fresh parsley
Salt and black pepper to taste
½ cup slivered toasted hazelnuts

Directions and Total Time: 20 minutes

Steam the broccoli for 8 minutes or until tender. Remove and set aside.

Heat 1 tbsp of oil in a skillet over medium heat. Add in garlic and mushrooms and sauté for 5 minutes until tender. Pour in the wine and cook for 1 minute. Stir in broccoli, parsley, salt, and pepper. Cook for 3 minutes, until the liquid has reduced. Remove to a bowl and add in the remaining oil and hazelnuts and toss to coat. Serve warm.

Cilantro Okra

Ingredients for 4 servings

2 tbsp olive oil
4 cups okra, halved
Sea salt and black pepper to taste
3 tbsp chopped fresh cilantro

Directions and Total Time: 10 minutes

Heat the oil in a skillet over medium heat. Place in the okra, cook for 5 minutes. Turn the heat off and mix in salt, pepper, and cilantro. Serve immediately.

Citrus Asparagus

Ingredients for 4 servings

- 1 onion, minced
- 2 tsp lemon zest
- 1/3 cup fresh lemon juice
- 1 tbsp olive oil
- Salt and black pepper to taste
- 1 lb asparagus, trimmed

Directions and Total Time: 15 minutes

Combine the onion, lemon zest, lemon juice, and oil in a bowl. Sprinkle with salt and pepper. Let sit for 5-10 minutes.

Insert a steamer basket and 1 cup of water in a pot over medium heat. Place the asparagus on the basket and steam for 4-5 minutes until tender but crispy. Leave to cool for 10 minutes, then arrange on a plate. Serve drizzled with the dressing.

Japanese-Style Tofu with Haricots Vert

Ingredients for 4 servings

- 1 cup haricots vert
- 1 tbsp grapeseed oil
- 1 onion, minced
- 5 shiitake mushroom caps, sliced
- 1 tsp grated fresh ginger
- 3 green onions, minced
- 8 oz firm tofu, crumbled
- 2 tbsp soy sauce
- 3 cups hot cooked rice
- 1 tbsp toasted sesame oil
- 1 tbsp toasted sesame seeds

Directions and Total Time: 25 minutes

Place the haricots in boiled salted water and cook for 10 minutes until tender. Drain and set aside.

Heat the oil in a skillet over medium heat. Place in onion and cook for 3 minutes until translucent. Add in mushrooms, ginger, green onions, tofu, and soy sauce. Cook for 10 minutes. Share into 4 bowls and top with haricot and tofu mixture. Sprinkle with sesame oil. Serve garnished with sesame seeds.

Raisin & Orzo Stuffed Tomatoes

Ingredients for 4 servings

- 2 cups cooked orzo
- Salt and black pepper to taste
- 3 green onions, minced
- 1/3 cup golden raisins
- 1 tsp orange zest
- 4 large ripe tomatoes
- 1/3 cup toasted pine nuts
- ¼ cup minced fresh parsley
- 2 tsp olive oil

Directions and Total Time: 40 minutes

Preheat oven to 380 F.

Mix the orzo, green onions, raisins, and orange zest in a bowl. Set aside. Slice the top of the tomato by ½-inch and take out the pulp. Cut the pulp and place it in a bowl. Stir in orzo mixture, pine nuts, parsley, salt, and pepper.

Spoon the mixture into the tomatoes and arrange on a greased baking tray. Sprinkle with oil and cover with foil. Bake for 15 minutes. Uncover and bake for another 5 minutes until golden.

Rosemary Baked Potatoes with Cherry Tomatoes

Ingredients for 5 servings

- 5 russet potatoes, sliced
- ½ cup cherry tomatoes, halved
- 2 tbsp rosemary
- 2 tbsp olive oil
- Salt and black pepper to taste

Directions and Total Time: 65 minutes

Preheat oven to 390 F. Make several incisions with a fork in each potato. Rub each potato and cherry tomatoes with olive oil and sprinkle with salt, rosemary, and pepper. Arrange on a baking dish and bake for 50-60 minutes. Once ready, transfer to a rack and allow to completely cool before serving.

Parsley Carrots & Parsnips

Ingredients for 4 servings

- 2 tbsp plant butter
- ½ lb carrots, cut lengthways
- ½ lb parsnips, cut lengthways
- Salt and black pepper to taste
- ½ cup Port wine
- ¼ cup chopped fresh parsley

Directions and Total Time: 25 minutes

Melt the butter in a skillet over medium heat. Place in carrots and parsnips and cook for 5 minutes, stirring occasionally. Sprinkle with salt and pepper. Pour in Port wine and ¼ cup water. Lower the heat and simmer for 15 minutes. Uncover and increase the heat. Cook until a syrupy sauce forms. Remove to a bowl and serve garnished with parsley.

Sesame Roasted Broccoli with Brown Rice

Ingredients for 4 servings

1 head broccoli, cut into florets
2 tbsp olive oil
¾ cup pure date sugar
⅔ cup water
⅓ cup apple cider vinegar
1 tbsp ketchup
¼ cup soy sauce
2 tbsp cornstarch
4 cups cooked brown rice
2 scallions, chopped
Sesame seeds

Directions and Total Time: 30 minutes

Preheat oven to 420 F. Line with parchment paper a baking sheet. Coat the broccoli with oil in a bowl. Spread on the baking sheet and roast for 20 minutes, turning once.

Add the sugar, water, vinegar, and ketchup in a skillet and bring to a boil. Lower the heat and simmer for 5 minutes. In a bowl, whisk the soy sauce with cornstarch and pour it into the skillet. Stir for 2-4 minutes. Once the broccoli is ready, transfer into the skillet and toss to combine. Share the rice into 4 bowls and top with the broccoli. Serve garnished with scallions and sesame seeds.

Date Caramelized Vegetables

Ingredients for 4 servings

1 tbsp olive oil
2 garlic cloves, minced
4 medium shallots, halved
3 sweet potatoes, cut into chunks
2 large carrots, cut into chunks
2 large parsnips, cut into chunks
2 small turnips, cut into chunks
½ cup pure date sugar
¼ cup water
¼ cup sherry vinegar
Salt and black pepper to taste

Directions and Total Time: 30 minutes

Heat oil in a skillet over medium heat. Place in garlic and shallots and sauté for 3 minutes. Stir in sweet potatoes, carrots, parsnips, and turnips; cook for 5 minutes until tender. Pour in the sugar and 2 tbsp of water, cook for 5 minutes until the sugar dissolves. Stir in the remaining water and vinegar, simmer for 2-3 minutes. Season with salt and pepper. Lower the heat and cook for 25 minutes, stirring often.

Squash & Zucchini Stir-Fry

Ingredients for 4 servings

2 tbsp olive oil
1 red onion, sliced
3 garlic cloves, sliced
2 green zucchinis, sliced half-moons
2 yellow squashes, sliced half-moons
1 tsp herbs de Provence

Directions and Total Time: 20 minutes

Heat oil in a skillet over medium heat. Sauté the onion and garlic for 3 minutes. Mix in zucchini, squashes, herbs de Provence, salt, and pepper. Cook for 4-6 minutes, stirring often. Serve.

Sweet Potatoes with Curry Glaze

Ingredients for 6 servings

1 lb sweet potatoes, sliced
2 tbsp olive oil
2 tbsp curry powder
2 tbsp pure date syrup
Juice of ½ lemon
Sea salt and black pepper to taste

Directions and Total Time: 20 minutes

Cook the sweet potatoes covered with salted water for 10 minutes. Drain and return the potatoes to the pot. Lower the heat. Add in oil, curry powder, date syrup, and lemon juice. Cook for 5 minutes. Season with salt and pepper. Serve warm.

Spaghetti Squash in Tahini Sauce

Ingredients for 4 servings

1 (3-pound) spaghetti squash, halved lengthwise
1 tbsp rice vinegar
1 tbsp tahini
Salt and black pepper to taste

Directions and Total Time: 50 minutes

Preheat oven to 390 F. Line with wax paper a baking sheet. Slice the squash half lengthwise and arrange on the baking sheet skin-side up. Bake for 35-40 minutes. Let cool before scraping the flesh to make "noodles." Place the spaghetti in a bowl. In another bowl, whisk 1 tbsp hot water, vinegar, tahini, salt, and pepper. Add into the spaghetti bowl and toss to coat. Serve.

Cumin Red & White Cabbage with Apples

Ingredients for 6 servings

2 tbsp olive oil
1 onion, sliced
1 head red cabbage, shredded

1 head white cabbage, shredded
2 apples, sliced
2 tbsp pure date sugar

¼ cup cider vinegar
1 tsp cumin seeds, crushed
Salt and black pepper to taste

Directions and Total Time: 30 minutes

Heat the oil in a pot over medium heat. Place in onion, shredded cabbages, and apples and sauté for 5 minutes until tender. Stir in date sugar, 1 cup water, vinegar, cumin seeds, salt, and pepper. Lower the heat and simmer for 20 minutes. Serve right away.

Basil Beet Pasta

Ingredients for 4 servings

1 tsp olive oil
1 garlic clove, minced

4 medium beets, spiralized
½ tsp dried basil

½ tsp dried oregano
½ tsp red pepper flakes

Directions and Total Time: 20 minutes

Heat the oil in a skillet over medium heat. Place in garlic, beets, basil, oregano, pepper flakes, salt, and pepper. Cook for 15 minutes. Serve.

Sherry Eggplants with Cherry Tomatoes

Ingredients for 4 servings

1 garlic cloves, minced
2 tbsp tamari sauce
1 tbsp dry sherry

1 tsp toasted sesame oil
½ tsp pure date sugar
1 tbsp canola oil

2 eggplants, unpeeled and sliced
2 green onions, minced
10 pitted black olives, chopped

Directions and Total Time: 20 minutes

Combine the garlic, tamari, sherry, sesame oil, and sugar in a bowl. Set aside.

Heat the oil in a skillet over medium heat. Place in the eggplant slices, fry for 4 minutes per side. Spread the tamari sauce on the eggplants. Pour in ¼ cup water and cook for 15 minutes. Remove to a plate and sprinkle with green onions and black olives. Serve right away.

Tofu Eggplant Pizza

Ingredients for 4 servings

2 eggplants, sliced lengthwise
1/3 cup melted plant butter
2 garlic cloves, minced

1 red onion
12 oz crumbled tofu
7 oz tomato sauce

½ tsp cinnamon powder
1 cup grated plant-based Parmesan
¼ cup chopped fresh oregano

Directions and Total Time: 45 minutes

Preheat oven to 400 F and line a baking sheet with parchment paper. Brush eggplants with some plant butter. Transfer to the baking sheet and bake until lightly browned, about 20 minutes.

Heat the remaining butter in a skillet and sauté the garlic and onion until fragrant and soft, about 3 minutes. Stir in the tofu and cook for 3 minutes. Add the tomato sauce and season with salt and black pepper. Simmer for 10 minutes.

Remove the eggplant from the oven and spread the tofu sauce on top. Sprinkle with the plant-based Parmesan cheese and oregano. Bake further for 10 minutes or until the cheese has melted. Serve.

Maple Green Cabbage Hash

Ingredients for 4 servings

3 tbsp olive oil
2 shallots, thinly sliced

1 ½ lb green cabbage, shredded
3 tbsp apple cider vinegar

1 tbsp pure maple syrup
½ tsp sriracha sauce

Directions and Total Time: 25 minutes

Heat the oil in a skillet over medium heat. Place in shallots and cabbage and cook for 10 minutes until tender. Pour in vinegar and scrape any bits from the bottom. Mix in maple syrup and sriracha sauce. Cook for 3-5 minutes, until the liquid absorbs. Sprinkle with salt and pepper. Serve right away.

Raisin & Pine Nut Zucchini Rolls

Ingredients for 4 servings

4 zucchinis, sliced lengthwise
Salt and black pepper to taste
2 tbsp olive oil
1 garlic cloves, minced

4 green onions, chopped
¼ cup ground pine nuts
2 tbsp chopped sun-dried tomatoes
3 tbsp golden raisins

3 tbsp plant-based Parmesan
1 tbsp minced fresh parsley
2 cups marinara sauce

Directions and Total Time: 50 minutes

Preheat oven to 360 F. Arrange the zucchini slices on a greased baking sheet. Season with salt and pepper and bake for 15 minutes. Set aside.

Heat the oil in a skillet over medium heat. Place in garlic, green onions, and pine nuts and cook for 1 minute. Stir in tomatoes, raisins, Parmesan cheese, parsley, salt, and pepper. Spread the mixture onto the zucchini slices. Roll up and transfer to the baking dish. Top with marinara sauce. Cover with foil and bake for 30 minutes. Serve hot.

Almond & Chickpea Patties

Ingredients for 6 servings

1 roasted red bell pepper, chopped
1 (19-oz) can chickpeas
1 cup ground almonds

2 tsp Dijon mustard
2 tsp date syrup
1 garlic clove, pressed

Juice of ½ lemon
1 cup kale, chopped
1 ½ cups rolled oats

Directions and Total Time: 50 minutes

Preheat oven to 360 F. Line with parchment paper a baking sheet.

In a blender, place the chickpeas, almonds, bell pepper, mustard, date syrup, garlic, lemon juice, and kale. Pulse until ingredients are finely chopped but not over blended. Add in the oats. Pulse until everything is well combined. Shape the mixture into 12 patties and arrange on the baking sheet. Bake for 30 minutes until light brown. Serve.

Korean-Style Buckwheat

Ingredients for 4 servings

2 cups water
1 cup buckwheat groats, rinsed

¼ cup unseasoned rice vinegar
¼ cup Mirin wine

Directions and Total Time: 25 minutes

Boil water in a pot. Put in the buckwheat groats, lower the heat, and simmer covered for 15-20 minutes, until the liquid absorbs. Let cool for a few minutes. Using a fork, fluff the groats and stir in vinegar and Mirin wine. Serve.

Basil Bell Pepper & Mushroom Medley

Ingredients for 4 servings

3 tbsp olive oil
1 cup mushrooms, sliced
1 red bell pepper, sliced

1 orange bell pepper, sliced
1 yellow bell pepper, sliced
1 green bell pepper, sliced

2 garlic cloves, minced
3 tbsp red wine vinegar
2 tbsp chopped fresh basil

Directions and Total Time: 25 minutes

Heat the oil in a skillet over medium heat. Place in mushrooms, garlic, and bell peppers and sauté for 7-10 minutes. Pour in vinegar and scrape any bit from the bottom. Cook for 2-3 minutes until the vinegar is reduced. Sprinkle with salt and pepper. Serve topped with basil.

Peanut Quinoa & Chickpea Pilaf

Ingredients for 4 servings

1 tbsp olive oil
1 medium red onion, minced
1 ½ cups quinoa, rinsed

3 cups vegetable broth
2 (15.5-oz) cans chickpeas
¼ tsp ground cayenne

1 tbsp minced fresh chives
1 tangerine, chopped
½ cup peanuts

Directions and Total Time: 30 minutes

Heat the oil in a pot over medium heat. Place the onion and cook for 3 minutes until softened. Add in quinoa and broth. Bring to a boil, then lower the heat and sprinkle with salt. Simmer for 20 minutes. Stir in chickpeas, cayenne pepper, chives, tangerine, and peanuts. Serve warm.

Spicy Vegetable Paella

Ingredients for 4 servings

2 tbsp olive oil	3 garlic cloves, chopped	½ tsp crushed red pepper
2 medium carrots, sliced	8 oz green peas	½ tsp ground fennel seed
1 celery stalk, sliced	1 cup Spanish brown rice	¼ tsp saffron
1 medium yellow onion, chopped	1 (14.5-oz) can diced tomatoes	2 cups oyster mushrooms
1 medium red bell pepper, diced	2 ½ cups vegetable broth	1 cup asparagus, chopped

Directions and Total Time: 35 minutes

Heat the oil in a pot over medium heat. Place in carrots, celery, onion, bell pepper, and garlic. Cook for 5 minutes until tender. Stir in green peas, rice, tomatoes, broth, salt, red pepper, fennel seeds, and saffron. Cook for 20 minutes. Mix in mushrooms and asparagus. Cook covered another 10 minutes.

Baked Potatoes & Asparagus & Pine Nuts

Ingredients for 4 servings

1 bunch of asparagus, sliced	Salt and black pepper to taste	½ cup vegetable broth
2 tbsp olive oil	1 tsp dried basil	2 tbsp nutritional yeast
2 garlic cloves, minced	½ tsp dried thyme	½ cup ground pine nuts
5 cups fresh baby spinach	2 potatoes, sliced	

Directions and Total Time: 50 minutes

Preheat oven to 370 F.

Heat half of the oil in a skillet over medium heat. Place in garlic, spinach, salt, and pepper and cook for 4 minutes until the spinach wilts. Add in basil and thyme. Set aside.

Arrange half of the potato slices on a greased casserole and season with salt and pepper. Top with the asparagus slices and finish with the spinach mixture. Cover with the remaining potato slices.

Whisk the broth with nutritional yeast in a bowl. Pour over the vegetables. Sprinkle with remaining oil and pine nuts. Cover with foil and bake for 40 minutes. Uncover and bake for another 10 minutes until golden brown. Serve warm.

Italian Potato & Swiss Chard Au Gratin

Ingredients for 4 servings

3 tbsp olive oil	1 cup Swiss chard, chopped	1 tsp Italian seasoning
1 medium yellow onion, minced	Salt and black pepper to taste	2 tbsp plant-based Parmesan
3 garlic cloves, minced	2 lb new potatoes, unpeeled, sliced	

Directions and Total Time: 1 hour 15 minutes

Preheat oven to 360 F.

Warm half of the oil in a skillet over medium heat. Place in onion and garlic and sauté for 3 minutes until translucent. Add in Swiss chard to wilt for 3-4 minutes. Season with salt and pepper. Set aside.

Arrange half of the potato slices on a greased baking dish. Sprinkle with Italian seasoning, salt, and pepper. Sprinkle with the remaining olive oil. Top with Swiss chard mixture and cover with the remaining potatoes. Cover with foil and bake for 1 hour. Scatter Parmesan cheese over and bake another 10 minutes. Serve immediately.

Bean & Pecan Stuffed Mushrooms

Ingredients for 4 servings

4 mushroom caps	2 garlic cloves, minced	1 cup finely chopped pecans
2 tbsp olive oil	1 carrot, chopped	2 tbsp minced fresh parsley
1 onion, minced	1 (15.5-oz) can white beans, mashed	½ cup dry breadcrumbs

Directions and Total Time: 45 minutes

Preheat oven to 360 F.

Heat the oil in a skillet over medium heat. Place the onion, garlic, and carrot and sauté for 5 minutes until tender. Stir in beans, pecans, parsley, and half of the breadcrumbs. Sprinkle with salt and pepper.

Stuff the mushrooms with the mixture and arrange on a greased baking dish. Cover with foil and bake for 20 minutes. Uncover and scatter with the remaining breadcrumbs. Bake another 10 minutes until golden brown. Serve warm.

Sautéed Veggies with Rice

Ingredients for 4 servings

- 1 ½ cups brown rice, rinsed
- 2 tbsp olive oil
- 4 shallots, chopped
- 1 medium red bell pepper, chopped
- 1 medium zucchini, chopped
- 2 cups cooked shelled edamame
- 2 cups corn kernels
- 2 tomatoes, chopped
- 3 tbsp chopped parsley

Directions and Total Time: 40 minutes

Boil 3 cups of salted water in a pot over high heat. Place in rice, lower the heat, and cook for 20 minutes. Set aside.

Heat the oil in a skillet over medium heat. Add in shallots, zucchini, and bell pepper and sauté for 5 minutes until tender. Mix in edamame, corn, tomatoes, salt, and pepper. Cook for 5 minutes, stirring often. Put in cooked rice and parsley, toss to combine. Serve warm.

French Vegetable Byaldi

Ingredients for 6 servings

- 2 potatoes, sliced
- 2 eggplants, sliced diagonally
- 3 tbsp olive oil
- 1 onion, chopped
- 3 garlic cloves, minced
- 3 cups spinach, chopped
- 2 cups kale, chopped
- 2 cups collard greens, chopped
- 1 cup loosely packed basil leaves
- 6 ripe plum tomatoes, sliced
- ¾ cup breadcrumbs
- 3 tbsp plant-based Parmesan

Directions and Total Time: 75 minutes

Preheat oven to 390 F.

Arrange the potato slices on a greased baking sheet and the eggplant slices in a separate baking sheet. Sprinkle the vegetables with oil, salt, and pepper. Bake the eggplants for 10 minutes and the potato for 20 minutes. Set aside.

Heat oil in a skillet over medium heat. Place in onion and garlic and sauté for 3 minutes until soft. Add in spinach, kale, collard greens, salt, and pepper. Cook for 7 minutes until the greens wilt. Remove the mixture to a blender. Add in basil and remaining oil, salt, and pepper and blend until smooth.

On a grease baking dish, arrange half of the potato slices and cover with some greens mixture. Then add a layer of eggplant slices and cover with more greens mixture. Then add a layer of tomato slices and cover with more greens mixture. Repeat the process until any ingredients left. Sprinkle each layer with salt and pepper. Finally, scatter with breadcrumbs and Parmesan cheese. Sprinkle the remaining oil. Bake for another 10 minutes. Serve warm.

Roasted Sweet Potato Porridge

Ingredients for 4 servings

- 2 sweet potatoes, chopped
- 2 tbsp olive oil
- 1 onion, finely chopped
- 1 cup buckwheat groats
- 2 cups vegetable broth
- 1 cup green beans, chopped

Directions and Total Time: 25 minutes

Preheat oven to 420 F.

Arrange the sweet potatoes on a greased baking dish and coat with half of the oil. Sprinkle with salt and pepper. Roast for 25 minutes, turning once. Set aside.

Heat the remaining oil in a skillet over medium heat. Place the onion and sauté for 3 minutes, stirring often. Stir in buckwheat groats and broth. Bring to a boil, then lower the heat and simmer for 15 minutes. Mix in green beans, sweet potatoes, salt, and pepper. Serve right away.

Balsamic Artichoke Hearts

Ingredients for 4 servings

- 1 ½ lb artichoke hearts
- 2 tbsp olive oil
- Sea salt and black pepper to taste
- ⅓ cup balsamic vinegar
- Juice and zest of 1 lemon

Directions and Total Time: 35 minutes

Preheat oven to 360 F. Brush the artichoke hearts with olive oil, salt, and pepper. Arrange on a baking sheet. Roast for 20-25 minutes, turning once.

Meanwhile, put the vinegar in a skillet over medium heat and bring to a boil. Lower the heat and simmer for 8 minutes until it gets a syrupy texture. Once the artichokes are ready, coat them with lemon juice and lemon zest. Serve topped with balsamic reduction.

Melon & Cucumber Gazpacho

Ingredients for 4 servings

- 2 large tomatoes
- 1 jalapeño pepper, seeded
- 4 cups cubed fresh melon, divided
- 2 tsp rice vinegar
- ¼ cup extra-virgin olive oil
- 1 large cucumber, peeled, chopped
- 1 small red onion, chopped
- 1 small red bell pepper, chopped
- ¼ cup minced fresh dill

Directions and Total Time: 10 minutes

Put the tomatoes, jalapeño pepper, vinegar, olive oil, and half of the melon in a food processor and blitz. Place in cucumber, onion, bell pepper, and dill and blend until uniform and smooth. Adjust seasoning with salt and pepper. Place the remaining melon in a bowl and top with the gazpacho.

Artichoke & Tomato Tart with Peanuts

Ingredients for 4 servings

- 1 (10-oz) package artichoke hearts
- 1 frozen puff pastry sheet, thawed
- ½ cup toasted peanuts
- 8 oz extra-firm tofu, crumbled
- 3 green onions, minced
- 2 tsp fresh lemon juice
- 2 tbsp minced fresh parsley
- 1 tbsp minced fresh marjoram
- 2 tomatoes, sliced

Directions and Total Time: 55 minutes

Preheat oven to 390 F.

Boil salted water in a pot over high heat. Place in artichoke hearts and cook for 12 minutes. Drain and set aside. Lay the pastry on a floured flat surface and roll out. Transfer to a tart dish and trim the edges. Bake for 10 minutes. Set aside.

Cut finely 2 artichoke hearts and set aside. In a blender, place the remaining hearts, half of the peanuts, tofu, and green onions and pulse until finely chopped. Add in lemon juice, parsley, marjoram, salt, and pepper. Blitz until smooth. Remove to a bowl and mix in remaining peanuts and reserved artichokes.

Spread the mixture over the tart pastry and top with tomato slices. Sprinkle with salt and pepper. Bake for 25 minutes until golden brown. Let cool 10-15 minutes before slicing.

Chili Broccoli & Beans with Almonds

Ingredients for 4 servings

- 1 ½ lb potatoes
- 4 cups broccoli florets
- 3 tbsp olive oil
- 3 garlic cloves, minced
- ¾ cup chopped almonds
- ¼ tsp crushed red pepper
- 1 (15.5-oz) can white beans
- 1 tsp dried thyme
- 1 tbsp fresh lemon juice

Directions and Total Time: 40 minutes

Place the potatoes in water and cook for 20 minutes. Set aside. Place the broccoli in water and steam for 7 minutes.

Heat 2 tbsp of oil in a skillet over medium heat. Place in garlic, almonds, and red pepper and cook for 1 minute. Add in potatoes, broccoli, beans, thyme, salt, and pepper. Cook for 5 minutes. Drizzle with lemon juice and remaining oil. Serve.

Dilly Potatoes

Ingredients for 4 servings

- 1 ½ lb baby red potatoes, halved
- 2 tbsp plant butter
- 3 garlic cloves, minced
- 1 tbsp minced fresh dill
- Sea salt to taste

Directions and Total Time: 35 minutes

Preheat oven to 430 F. Line with parchment paper a baking sheet. Mix in the potatoes, butter, garlic, dill, and salt and spread evenly. Bake for 30 minutes until golden brown. Serve.

Orange Kale Stir-Fry

Ingredients for 4 servings

- 2 tbsp olive oil
- 1 shallot, chopped
- 2 garlic cloves, minced
- 10 oz kale
- Zest and juice of 1 orange
- Sea salt and black pepper to taste

Directions and Total Time: 20 minutes

Heat the oil in a skillet over medium heat. Place the shallot and garlic and sauté for 3 minutes until translucent. Stir in kale, orange juice, and orange zest. Cook for 2-3 minutes until the kale wilts. Sprinkle with salt and pepper. Serve immediately.

Parsley Faro & Bean Casserole

Ingredients for 6 servings

2 ¾ cups water
1 cup faro
3 tbsp olive oil
1 medium yellow onion, chopped
1 medium red bell pepper, chopped

2 garlic cloves, minced
3 cups chopped Swiss chard
Salt and black pepper to taste
1 (15.5-oz) can Great Northern beans
1 cup cherry tomatoes, quartered

2 tbsp fresh lemon juice
¼ cup nutritional yeast
2 tbsp minced fresh dill weed
2 tbsp minced fresh parsley
1/3 cup dry breadcrumbs

Directions and Total Time: 50 minutes

Boil salted water in a pot over high heat. Place in faro, the lower the heat and simmer for 30 minutes. Set aside. Preheat oven to 360 F.

Heat the oil in a skillet over medium heat. Add in onion and bell pepper and sauté for 5 minutes. Stir in garlic, Swiss chard, salt, and pepper. Cook for 5 minutes until the chard wilts. Remove to the faro pot. Put in beans, tomatoes, lemon juice, yeast, dill weed, and parsley; stir.

Transfer into a greased baking pan and scatter breadcrumbs over. Bake for 10-15 minutes. Serve immediately.

Sicilian Spaghetti Squash

Ingredients for 4 servings

1 (4-pound) spaghetti squash, halved and seeded
3 tbsp olive oil
1 onion, chopped
2 cups chopped artichoke hearts
½ cup pitted and sliced green olives

1 cup halved cherry tomatoes
3 garlic cloves, minced
1 ½ tsp Italian seasoning
Sea salt and black pepper to taste

Pine nuts
Plant-based Parmesan cheese
Red pepper flakes

Directions and Total Time: 50 minutes

Preheat oven to 390 F. Line with parchment paper a baking sheet. Rub each squash half with some oil on all sides. Arrange on the sheet cut-sides down and bake for 40-45 minutes until tender. Let cool.

Meanwhile, heat the olive oil in a skillet over medium heat. Place in onion, garlic, and artichoke and cook for 5 minutes. Add in olives and tomatoes and cook for another 3-5 minutes. Set aside.

Take out the squash flesh, using a fork, and separate into strands. Transfer to the veggie skillet. Season with Italian seasoning, salt, and pepper; toss to combine. Share into bowls and serve garnished with pine nuts, Parmesan cheese, and pepper flakes.

Sesame Tempeh Sauté

Ingredients for 4 servings

8 oz tempeh
Salt and black pepper to taste
2 tsp cornstarch
3 cups cauliflower florets
2 tbsp canola oil

3 tbsp soy sauce
2 tbsp water
1 tbsp Mirin wine
½ tsp crushed red pepper
2 tsp toasted sesame oil

1 medium red bell pepper, sliced
8 oz white mushrooms, sliced
2 garlic cloves, minced
3 tbsp minced green onions
1 tsp grated fresh ginger

Directions and Total Time: 50 minutes

Combine the soy sauce, water, Mirin wine, red pepper, and sesame oil in a bowl. Boil water in a pot and place in tempeh. Simmer for 30 minutes. Drain and let cool. Chop tempeh into cubes. Transfer to a bowl and sprinkle with salt, pepper, and cornstarch. Set aside.

Steam the cauliflower for 5 minutes; reserve. Heat the canola oil in a skillet over medium heat. Place in tempeh and fry for 5 minutes. Remove to a plate.

Add bell pepper, mushrooms, garlic, green onions, and ginger to the same skillet and sauté for 5 minutes. Stir in cauliflower and tempeh and stir-fry for 1 minute. Pour in the Mirin wine mixture and stir to coat. Serve warm.

Bell Pepper & Spinach with Walnuts

Ingredients for 4 servings

2 lb spinach, chopped
3 tbsp olive oil
1 onion, chopped

2 red bell peppers, cut into strips
2 garlic cloves, minced
¼ tsp red pepper flakes

Sea salt and black pepper to taste
¼ cup toasted walnuts for garnish

Directions and Total Time: 15 minutes

Place the spinach in a steamer basket and cook for 5 minutes until tender. Set aside.

Warm the olive oil in a skillet over medium heat. Add in onion, garlic, and bell peppers and sauté for 5 minutes. Turn the heat off and mix in spinach, pepper flakes, salt, and pepper. Serve topped with walnuts.

Creamy Bell Pepper Goulash

Ingredients for 4 servings

2 tbsp olive oil	1 lb bell peppers, chopped	1 tsp caraway seeds
1 onion, chopped	1 tbsp tomato paste	1 ½ cups sauerkraut, drained
2 garlic cloves, minced	½ cup dry white wine	1 ½ cups vegetable broth
1 potato, chopped	1 ½ tbsp sweet paprika	½ cup vegan sour cream

Directions and Total Time: 50 minutes

Heat the oil in a pot over medium heat. Place in onion, garlic, bell peppers, and potato and sauté for 8-10 minutes. Mix in tomato paste, wine, paprika, caraway seeds, sauerkraut, and broth. Bring to a boil, then lower the heat and sprinkle with salt and pepper. Simmer for 30 minutes.

Whisk 1 cup of cooking liquid with sour cream in a bowl. Pour into the pot and adjust the seasonings if needed. Serve hot.

Thyme Black Bean Loaf with Artichokes

Ingredients for 6 servings

1 potato, chopped	¼ cup vegetable broth	½ cup nutritional yeast
1 (10-oz) package artichoke hearts	2 tbsp tahini	1 tsp dried thyme
¼ cup olive oil	1 ½ tbsp soy sauce	Salt and black pepper to taste
1 onion, chopped	1 ½ tbsp fresh lemon juice	½ cup chopped sun-dried tomatoes
1 (15.5-oz) can black beans	1 cup whole-wheat flour	¼ cup minced fresh parsley

Directions and Total Time: 60 minutes

Preheat oven to 360 F. Place the potatoes and artichokes in hot water and steam for 15 minutes. Drain and set aside. Cut 2 artichoke hearts and set aside.

Heat the oil in a skillet. Place onion and sauté for 3 minutes. Add in potatoes and artichokes. Remove to a blender and add beans, broth, tahini, soy sauce, and lemon juice. Pulse until smooth.

In a bowl, combine the flour, yeast, thyme, salt, and pepper. Pour the potato mixture into the flour mixture. Add in sun-dried tomatoes, parsley, and reserved artichokes. Toss to coat. Shape the mixture into a loaf and place in a greased loaf pan to bake for 40 minutes until golden brown. Leave to cool for 15 minutes. Slice and serve.

Pomegranate Bell Peppers & Eggplants

Ingredients for 4 servings

½ cup olive oil	1 yellow bell pepper, chopped	½ cup orange juice
1 onion, chopped	2 garlic cloves, minced	2 tsp pure date sugar
3 eggplants, cut into chunks	1 hot chili, seeded and minced	1 ripe peach, chopped
1 red pepper, chopped	2 tbsp pomegranate molasses	½ cup finely chopped fresh cilantro

Directions and Total Time: 40 minutes

Heat the oil in a skillet over medium heat. Place the onion and sauté for 5 minutes. Add in eggplants, bell peppers, garlic, and chili. Cook for 10 minutes. Stir in pomegranate molasses, orange juice, sugar, salt, and pepper. Bring to a boil, then lower the heat and simmer for 20 minutes until the liquid reduces. Top with peach and cilantro and serve right away.

Lemony Arugula with Pine Nuts

Ingredients for 4 servings

2 bunches arugula, chopped	3 garlic cloves, minced	Zest of 1 lemon
3 tbsp olive oil	1 tsp cayenne pepper	¼ cup toasted pine nuts for garnish

Directions and Total Time: 20 minutes

Steam the arugula in a pot over medium heat for 2-3 minutes. Drain and set aside. Heat the oil in a skillet over medium heat. Add in garlic and cook for 30 seconds. Mix in arugula, cayenne pepper, lemon zest, salt, pepper. Serve garnished with toasted pine nuts.

Leek & Mushroom Stroganoff

Ingredients for 6 servings

2 tbsp plant butter
1 leek, chopped
1 cup button mushrooms, sliced
3 garlic cloves, minced

1 red bell pepper, chopped
¼ cup vegetable broth
1 tsp paprika
Sea salt and black pepper to taste

¼ cup vegan sour cream
2 tbsp chopped parsley
1 lb pasta, cooked

Directions and Total Time: 15 minutes

In a skillet over medium heat, melt the butter. Place in leek, mushrooms, garlic, and bell pepper and cook for 5 minutes until tender. Stir in broth, paprika, salt, and pepper and cook for another 5 minutes. Turn the heat off and mix in sour cream and pasta. Share into 6 bowls and serve topped with parsley.

Couscous & Lentil Curry

Ingredients for 4 servings

2 tbsp olive oil
3 green onions, chopped
1 eggplant, diced
Salt to taste

1-inch piece fresh ginger, minced
1 (15-oz) can green lentils, drained
1 tomato, chopped
1 ½ cups couscous

2 ¼ cups boiling water
6 tbsp curry sauce
Chopped cilantro

Directions and Total Time: 20 minutes

Place the couscous in a bowl with hot water. Cover and let sit until the liquid absorbs. Warm the oil in a skillet over medium heat. Place in green onion, eggplant, ginger, lentils, tomato, and salt. Cook for 8-10 minutes.

Mix the curry sauce with the vegetables. Using a fork, fluff the couscous and divide between 4 bowls. Top with the lentil mixture. Garnish with cilantro and serve.

Lentil & Sweet Potato Tortillas

Ingredients for 2 servings

2 tsp olive oil
¼ onion, chopped
1 cooked sweet potato

½ cup canned lentils, drained
1 tsp chili powder
1 tsp lime juice

2 corn tortillas
¼ cup grated plant-based mozzarella
1 tbsp cilantro, chopped for serving

Directions and Total Time: 20 minutes

Warm the oil in a skillet over medium heat. Place the onion and cook for 5 minutes until softened. Remove to a bowl. Add in sweet potato, lentils, chili powder, lime juice, and salt and mash well. Divide the mixture between the tortillas, top with plant-based mozzarella cheese and fold them. Heat the oil in the skillet and put it in the tortillas. Cook for 4 minutes on both sides until golden brown. Cut in thirds and top with cilantro. Serve immediately.

Cayenne Kale

Ingredients for 4 servings

Sea salt and black pepper to taste
2 Bunches kale, chopped

3 tbsp olive oil
3 garlic cloves, minced

1 tsp cayenne pepper
Zest of 1 lemon

Directions and Total Time: 20 minutes

Boil 8 cups of water in a pot. Add salt and kale. Cook for 2 minutes. Drain and reserve. Heat the oil in a skillet over medium heat. Place in garlic and sauté for 30 seconds. Stir in kale, cayenne pepper, lemon zest, salt, and pepper. Serve right away.

Cinnamon-Brandy Acorn Squash

Ingredients for 4 servings

1 acorn squash, sliced
½ cup brandy

⅓ cup pure date syrup
¼ cup plant butter

¼ tsp ground cinnamon
Sea salt to taste

Directions and Total Time: 40 minutes

Preheat oven to 430 F. Line with wax paper a baking sheet. Arrange the squash slices on the sheet and bake for 20 minutes.

In the meantime, pour the brandy, date syrup, and butter in a pot over medium heat. Cook for 2-3 minutes. Turn the squash slices over and sprinkle the brandy mixture on top. Season with cinnamon and salt. Bake another 8-10 minutes, until the squash is tender and caramelized on top.

Mustard Tofu & Cauliflower

Ingredients for 6 servings

4 cups cauliflower florets
1 ½ cups almond milk
¼ cup soft tofu
Juice of ½ lemon

1 tbsp English mustard
1 ½ tsp onion powder
Sea salt and black pepper to taste
1 tsp garlic powder

1 lb whole-wheat macaroni, cooked
Plant-based Parmesan cheese
Chopped fresh parsley

Directions and Total Time: 20 minutes

Steam the cauliflower for 10 minutes. Remove to a blender. Put in milk, tofu, lemon juice, mustard, onion powder, salt, garlic powder, and pepper. Pulse until smooth. Remove to a bowl and add in the pasta; toss to coat. Sprinkle with plant-based Parmesan cheese, parsley, and pepper to serve.

Eggplant with Tofu

Ingredients for 2 servings

½ cup non-dairy milk
½ cup breadcrumbs
2 tbsp nutritional yeast

Salt to taste
2 eggplants, sliced
2 tbsp olive oil

4 tbsp tomato sauce
½ cup tofu, crumbled

Directions and Total Time: 25 minutes

Pour the milk in a bowl. In another bowl, mix the breadcrumbs, yeast, and salt. Dip the eggplant slices in the milk, then coat in the breadcrumbs. Remove to a plate. In a skillet over medium heat, warm the oil. Fry the eggplant slices for 10 minutes on both sides. Remove to a baking sheet. Top with tomato sauce and tofu. Place the sheet under the broiler for 6 minutes until the tofu begins to brown. Serve.

Lentil Stuffed Avocados

Ingredients for 4 servings

2 avocados, halved and pitted
1 (15-oz) can lentils, drained
1 cup corn kernels

½ cup diced tomato
Juice of ½ lime
1 tbsp maple syrup

1 tsp olive oil
Sea salt and black pepper to taste
1 tbsp chopped fresh cilantro

Directions and Total Time: 10 minutes

Take out the avocado flesh, leaving ½-inch of flesh in the shell.

Place the avocado flesh in a bowl and stir the lentils, corn, tomato, lime juice, maple syrup, oil, salt, pepper, and cilantro. Scoop the mixture into the shells and serve immediately.

Spicy Broccoli in Pecan Pesto

Ingredients for 4 servings

1 lb broccoli florets
2 cups chopped fresh basil

¼ cup olive oil
4 garlic cloves

½ cup pecans
1 tsp chili powder

Directions and Total Time: 15 minutes

Place water in a pot and add the broccoli. Bring to a boil and steam for 5 minutes. In a blender, put basil, olive oil, garlic, pecans, and chili powder. Pulse until everything is blended. Drain the broccoli and toss in the basil sauce. Serve.

Bulgur & Bean Bowls with Tortilla Chips

Ingredients for 4 servings

Juice of 2 limes
1 tbsp olive oil
1 tbsp maple syrup
2 cups cooked bulgur

1 tbsp Taco seasoning
2 heads romaine lettuce, chopped
1 (15-oz) can black beans
1 cup cherry tomatoes, halved

1 cup corn kernels
1 avocado, peeled, pitted, and diced
4 scallions, thinly sliced
12 tortilla chips, crushed

Directions and Total Time: 15 minutes

Mix the lime juice, olive oil, maple syrup, and salt in a bowl. Set aside. In a bowl, combine the bulgur and taco seasoning. In another bowl, mix the lettuce with the vinaigrette. Separate into 4 bowls and add on each bowl the bulgur, beans, tomatoes, corn, avocado, scallions, and tortilla chips. Serve.

SNACKS & SIDES

Kentucky Cauliflower with Mashed Parsnips

Ingredients for 6 servings

½ cup unsweetened almond milk
¼ cup coconut flour
¼ tsp cayenne pepper
½ cup whole-grain breadcrumbs

½ cup grated plant-based mozzarella
30 oz cauliflower florets
1 lb parsnips, peeled and quartered
3 tbsp melted plant butter

A pinch of nutmeg
1 tsp cumin powder
1 cup coconut cream
2 tbsp sesame oil

Directions and Total Time: 35 minutes

Preheat oven to 425 F and line a baking sheet with parchment paper.

In a small bowl, combine almond milk, coconut flour, and cayenne pepper. In another bowl, mix salt, breadcrumbs, and plant-based mozzarella cheese. Dip each cauliflower floret into the milk mixture, coating properly, and then into the cheese mixture. Place the breaded cauliflower on the baking sheet and bake in the oven for 30 minutes, turning once after 15 minutes.

Make slightly salted water in a saucepan and add the parsnips. Bring to boil over medium heat for 15 minutes or until the parsnips are fork-tender. Drain and transfer to a bowl. Add in melted plant butter, cumin powder, nutmeg, and coconut cream. Puree the ingredients using an immersion blender until smooth. Spoon the parsnip mash into serving plates and drizzle with some sesame oil. Serve with the baked cauliflower when ready.

Spinach Chips with Guacamole Hummus

Ingredients for 4 servings

½ cup baby spinach
1 tbsp olive oil
½ tsp plain vinegar
3 large avocados, chopped

½ cup chopped parsley + for garnish
½ cup melted plant butter
¼ cup pumpkin seeds
¼ cup sesame paste

Juice from ½ lemon
1 garlic clove, minced
½ tsp coriander powder
Salt and black pepper to taste

Directions and Total Time: 30 minutes

Preheat oven to 300 F. Put spinach in a bowl and toss with olive oil, vinegar, and salt. Place in a parchment paper-lined baking sheet and bake until the leaves are crispy but not burned, about 15 minutes.

Place avocado into the bowl of a food processor. Add in parsley, plant butter, pumpkin seeds, sesame paste, lemon juice, garlic, coriander powder, salt, and black pepper. Puree until smooth. Spoon the hummus into a bowl and garnish with parsley. Serve with the spinach chips.

Buttered Carrot Noodles with Kale

Ingredients for 4 servings

2 large carrots
¼ cup vegetable broth

4 tbsp plant butter
1 garlic clove, minced

1 cup chopped kale
Salt and black pepper to taste

Directions and Total Time: 15 minutes

Peel the carrots with a slicer and run both through a spiralizer to form noodles.

Pour the vegetable broth into a saucepan and add the carrot noodles. Simmer (over low heat) the carrots for 3 minutes. Strain through a colander and set the vegetables aside.

Place a large skillet over medium heat and melt the plant butter. Add the garlic and sauté until softened and put in the kale; cook until wilted. Pour the carrots into the pan, season with the salt and black pepper, and stir-fry for 3 to 4 minutes. Spoon the vegetables into a bowl and serve with pan-grilled tofu.

Parsley Pumpkin Noodles

Ingredients for 4 servings

¼ cup plant butter
½ cup chopped onion

1 lb pumpkin, spiralized
1 bunch kale, sliced

¼ cup chopped fresh parsley
Salt and black pepper to taste

Directions and Total Time: 15 minutes

Mel butter in a skillet over medium heat. Place the onion and cook for 3 minutes. Add in pumpkin and cook for another 7-8 minutes. Stir in kale and cook for another 2 minutes, until the kale wilts. Sprinkle with parsley, salt, and pepper and serve.

Curry Cauli Rice with Mushrooms

Ingredients for 4 servings

8 oz baby Bella mushrooms, stemmed and sliced
2 large heads cauliflower
2 tbsp toasted sesame oil, divided
1 onion, chopped
3 garlic cloves, minced
Salt and black pepper to taste
½ tsp curry powder
1 tsp freshly chopped parsley
2 scallions, thinly sliced

Directions and Total Time: 15 minutes

Use a knife to cut the entire cauliflower head into 6 pieces and transfer to a food processor. With the grater attachment, shred the cauliflower into a rice-like consistency.

Heat half of the sesame oil in a large skillet over medium heat and then add the onion and mushrooms. Sauté for 5 minutes or until the mushrooms are soft.

Add the garlic and sauté for 2 minutes or until fragrant. Pour in the cauliflower and cook until the rice has slightly softened, about 10 minutes.

Season with salt, black pepper, and curry powder; then, mix the ingredients to be well combined. After, turn the heat off and stir in the parsley and scallions. Dish the cauli rice into serving plates and serve warm.

Mixed Seed Crackers

Ingredients for 6 servings

1/3 cup sesame seed flour
1/3 cup pumpkin seeds
1/3 cup sunflower seeds
1/3 cup sesame seeds
1/3 cup chia seeds
1 tbsp psyllium husk powder
1 tsp salt
¼ cup plant butter, melted
1 cup boiling water

Directions and Total Time: 57 minutes

Preheat oven to 300 F.

Combine the sesame seed flour with the pumpkin seeds, sunflower seeds, sesame seeds, chia seeds, psyllium husk powder, and salt. Pour in the plant butter and hot water and mix the ingredients until a dough forms with a gel-like consistency.

Line a baking sheet with parchment paper and place the dough on the sheet. Cover the dough with another parchment paper and, with a rolling pin, flatten the dough into the baking sheet. Remove the parchment paper on top.

Tuck the baking sheet in the oven and bake for 45 minutes. Allow the crackers to cool and dry in the oven, about 10 minutes. After, remove the sheet and break the crackers into small pieces. Serve.

Grilled Tofu Mayo Sandwiches

Ingredients for 2 servings

¼ cup tofu mayonnaise
2 slices whole-grain bread
¼ cucumber, sliced
½ cup lettuce, chopped
½ tomato, sliced
1 tsp olive oil, divided

Directions and Total Time: 15 minutes

Spread the vegan mayonnaise over a bread slice, top with the cucumber, lettuce, and tomato, and finish with the other slice. Heat the oil in a skillet over medium heat. Place the sandwich and grill for 3 minutes, then flip over and cook for a further 3 minutes. Cut the sandwich in half and serve.

Mushroom Broccoli Faux Risotto

Ingredients for 4 servings

4 oz plant butter
1 cup cremini mushrooms, chopped
2 garlic cloves, minced
1 small red onion, finely chopped
1 large head broccoli, grated
¾ cup white wine
1 cup coconut whipping cream
¾ cup grated plant-based Parmesan
Freshly chopped thyme

Directions and Total Time: 25 minutes

Place a pot over medium heat, add, and melt the plant butter. Sauté the mushrooms in the pot until golden, about 5 minutes. Add the garlic and onions and cook for 3 minutes or until fragrant and soft. Mix in the broccoli, 1 cup water, and half of the white wine. Season with salt and black pepper and simmer the ingredients (uncovered) for 8 to 10 minutes or until the broccoli is soft.

Mix in the coconut whipping cream and simmer until most of the cream has evaporated. Turn the heat off and stir in the parmesan cheese and thyme until well incorporated. Dish the risotto and serve warm as itself or with grilled tofu.

Baked Spicy Eggplant

Ingredients for 4 servings

2 large eggplants
Salt and black pepper to taste

2 tbsp plant butter
1 tsp red chili flakes

4 oz raw ground almonds

Directions and Total Time: 30 minutes

Preheat oven to 400 F.

Cut off the head of the eggplants and slice the body into 2-inch rounds. Season with salt and black pepper and arrange on a parchment paper-lined baking sheet.

Drop thin slices of the plant butter on each eggplant slice, sprinkle with red chili flakes, and bake in the oven for 20 minutes.

Slide the baking sheet out and sprinkle with the almonds. Roast further for 5 minutes or until golden brown. Dish the eggplants and serve with arugula salad.

Mashed Broccoli with Roasted Garlic

Ingredients for 4 servings

½ head garlic
2 tbsp olive oil + for garnish
1 head broccoli, cut into florets

1 tsp salt
4 oz plant butter
¼ tsp dried thyme

Juice and zest of half a lemon
4 tbsp coconut cream

Directions and Total Time: 45 minutes

Preheat oven to 400 F.

Use a knife to cut a ¼ inch off the top of the garlic cloves, drizzle with olive oil, and wrap in aluminum foil. Place on a baking sheet and roast for 30 minutes. Remove and set aside when ready.

Pour the broccoli into a pot, add 3 cups of water, and 1 teaspoon of salt. Bring to a boil until tender, about 7 minutes. Drain and transfer the broccoli to a bowl. Add the plant butter, thyme, lemon juice and zest, coconut cream, and olive oil. Use an immersion blender to puree the ingredients until smooth and nice. Spoon the mash into serving bowls and garnish with some olive oil. Serve.

Spicy Pistachio Dip

Ingredients for 4 servings

3 oz toasted pistachios + for garnish
3 tbsp coconut cream
¼ cup water

Juice of half a lemon
½ tsp smoked paprika
Cayenne pepper to taste

½ tsp salt
½ cup olive oil

Directions and Total Time: 10 minutes

Pour the pistachios, coconut cream, water, lemon juice, paprika, cayenne pepper, and salt. Puree the ingredients on high speed until smooth. Add the olive oil and puree a little further. Manage the consistency of the dip by adding more oil or water. Spoon the dip into little bowls, garnish with some pistachios, and serve with julienned celery and carrots.

Paprika Roasted Nuts

Ingredients for 4 servings

8 oz walnuts and pecans
1 tsp salt

1 tbsp coconut oil
1 tsp cumin powder

1 tsp paprika powder

Directions and Total Time: 10 minutes

In a bowl, mix walnuts, pecans, salt, coconut oil, cumin powder, and paprika powder until the nuts are well coated with spice and oil. Pour the mixture into a pan and toast while stirring continually. Once the nuts are fragrant and brown, transfer to a bowl. Allow cooling and serve with a chilled berry juice.

Mixed Vegetables with Basil

Ingredients for 4 servings

2 medium zucchinis, chopped
2 medium yellow squash, chopped
1 red onion, cut into 1-inch wedges
1 red bell pepper, diced

1 cup cherry tomatoes, halved
4 tbsp olive oil
Salt and black pepper to taste
3 garlic cloves, minced

2/3 cup whole-wheat breadcrumbs
1 lemon, zested
¼ cup chopped fresh basil

Directions and Total Time: 40 minutes

Preheat the oven to 450 F. Lightly grease a large baking sheet with cooking spray.

In a medium bowl, add the zucchini, yellow squash, red onion, bell pepper, tomatoes, olive oil, salt, black pepper, and garlic. Toss well and spread the mixture on the baking sheet. Roast in the oven for 25 to 30 minutes or until the vegetables are tender while stirring every 5 minutes.

Meanwhile, heat the olive oil in a medium skillet and sauté the garlic until fragrant. Mix in the breadcrumbs, lemon zest, and basil. Cook for 2 to 3 minutes. Remove the vegetables from the oven and toss in the breadcrumb's mixture. Serve.

Onion Rings & Kale Dip

Ingredients for 4 servings

1 onion, sliced into rings
1 tbsp flaxseed meal + 3 tbsp water
1 cup almond flour
½ cup grated plant-based Parmesan
2 tsp garlic powder

½ tbsp sweet paprika powder
2 oz chopped kale
2 tbsp olive oil
2 tbsp dried cilantro
1 tbsp dried oregano

Salt and black pepper to taste
1 cup tofu mayonnaise
4 tbsp coconut cream
Juice of ½ a lemon

Directions and Total Time: 35 minutes

Preheat oven to 400 F. In a bowl, mix the flaxseed meal and water and leave the mixture to thicken and fully absorb for 5 minutes. In another bowl, combine almond flour, plant-based Parmesan cheese, half of the garlic powder, sweet paprika, and salt. Line a baking sheet with parchment paper in readiness for the rings. When the vegan "flax egg" is ready, dip in the onion rings one after another, and then into the almond flour mixture. Place the rings on the baking sheet and grease with cooking spray. Bake for 15-20 minutes or until golden brown and crispy. Remove the onion rings into a serving bowl.

Put kale in a food processor. Add in olive oil, cilantro, oregano, remaining garlic powder, salt, black pepper, tofu mayonnaise, coconut cream, and lemon juice; puree until nice and smooth. Allow the dip to sit for about 10 minutes for the flavors to develop. After, serve the dip with the crispy onion rings.

Soy Chorizo Stuffed Cabbage Rolls

Ingredients for 4 servings

¼ cup coconut oil, divided
1 large white onion, chopped
3 cloves garlic, minced, divided

1 cup crumbled soy chorizo
1 cup cauliflower rice
1 can tomato sauce

1 tsp dried oregano
1 tsp dried basil
8 full green cabbage leaves

Directions and Total Time: 35 minutes

Heat half of the coconut oil in a saucepan over medium heat.

Add half of the onion, half of the garlic, and all of the soy chorizo. Sauté for 5 minutes or until the chorizo has browned further, and the onion softened. Stir in the cauli rice, season with salt and black pepper, and cook for 3 to 4 minutes. Turn the heat off and set the pot aside.

Heat the remaining oil in a saucepan over medium heat, add, and sauté the remaining onion and garlic until fragrant and soft. Pour in the tomato sauce, and season with salt, black pepper, oregano, and basil. Add ¼ cup water and simmer the sauce for 10 minutes.

While the sauce cooks, lay the cabbage leaves on a flat surface and spoon the soy chorizo mixture into the middle of each leaf. Roll the leaves to secure the filling. Place the cabbage rolls in the tomato sauce and cook further for 10 minutes. When ready, serve the cabbage rolls with sauce over mashed broccoli or with mixed seed bread.

Sesame Cabbage Sauté

Ingredients for 4 servings

2 tbsp soy sauce
1 tbsp toasted sesame oil
1 tbsp hot sauce
½ tbsp pure date sugar

½ tbsp olive oil
1 head green cabbage, shredded
2 carrots, julienned
3 green onions, thinly sliced

2 garlic cloves, minced
1 tbsp fresh grated ginger
Salt and black pepper to taste
1 tbsp sesame seeds

Directions and Total Time: 15 minutes

In a small bowl, mix the soy sauce, sesame oil, hot sauce, and date sugar.

Heat the olive oil in a large skillet and sauté the cabbage, carrots, green onion, garlic, and ginger until softened, 5 minutes. Mix in the prepared sauce and toss well. Cook for 1 to 2 minutes. Dish the food and garnish with the sesame seeds.

Tomatoes Stuffed with Chickpeas & Quinoa

Ingredients for 4 servings

8 medium tomatoes
¾ cup quinoa, rinsed and drained
1 ½ cups water

1 tbsp olive oil
1 small onion, diced
3 garlic cloves, minced

1 cup chopped spinach
1 (7 oz) can chickpeas, drained
½ cup chopped fresh basil

Directions and Total Time: 50 minutes

Preheat the oven to 400 F.

Cut off the heads of tomatoes and use a paring knife to scoop the inner pulp of the tomatoes. Season with some olive oil, salt, and black pepper. Add the quinoa and water to a medium pot, season with salt, and cook until the quinoa is tender and the water absorbs, 10 to 15 minutes. Fluff and set aside.

Heat the remaining olive oil in a skillet and sauté the onion and garlic for 30 seconds. Mix in the spinach and cook until wilted, 2 minutes. Stir in the basil, chickpeas, and quinoa; allow warming from 2 minutes.

Spoon the mixture into the tomatoes, place the tomatoes into the baking dish and bake in the oven for 20 minutes or until the tomatoes soften. Remove the tomatoes from the oven and dish the food.

Herbed Vegetable Traybake

Ingredients for 4 servings

2 tbsp plant butter
1 large onion, diced
1 cup celery, diced

½ cup carrots, diced
½ tsp dried marjoram
2 cups chopped cremini mushrooms

1 cup vegetable broth
¼ cup chopped fresh parsley
1 whole-grain bread loaf, cubed

Directions and Total Time: 85 minutes

Melt the butter in a large skillet and sauté onion, celery, mushrooms, and carrots for 5 minutes. Mix in marjoram, salt, and pepper. Pour in the vegetable broth and mix in parsley and bread. Cook until the broth reduces by half, 10 minutes. Pour the mixture into a baking dish and cover with foil. Bake in the oven at 375 F for 30 minutes. Uncover and bake further for 30 minutes or until golden brown on top, and the liquid absorbs. Remove the dish from the oven and serve the stuffing.

Louisiana-Style Sweet Potato Chips

Ingredients for 4 servings

2 sweet potatoes, peeled and sliced
2 tbsp melted plant butter
1 tbsp Cajun seasoning

Directions and Total Time: 55 minutes

Preheat the oven to 400 F and line a baking sheet with parchment paper.

In a medium bowl, add the sweet potatoes, salt, plant butter, and Cajun seasoning. Toss well. Spread the chips on the baking sheet, making sure not to overlap, and bake in the oven for 50 minutes to 1 hour or until crispy. Remove the sheet and pour the chips into a large bowl. Allow cooling and enjoy.

Bell Pepper & Seitan Balls

Ingredients for 4 servings

1 tbsp flaxseed powder
1 lb seitan, crumbled
¼ cup chopped mixed bell peppers

Salt and black pepper to taste
1 tbsp almond flour
1 tsp garlic powder

1 tsp onion powder
1 tsp tofu mayonnaise
Olive oil for brushing

Directions and Total Time: 25 minutes

Preheat the oven to 400 F and line a baking sheet with parchment paper.

In a bowl, mix flaxseed powder with 3 tbsp water and allow thicken for 5 minutes. Add in seitan, bell peppers, salt, pepper, almond flour, garlic powder, onion powder, and tofu mayonnaise. Mix and form 1-inch balls from the mixture. Arrange on the baking sheet, brush with cooking spray, and bake in the oven for 15 to 20 minutes or until brown and compacted. Remove from the oven and serve.

Parmesan Broccoli Tots

Ingredients for 4 servings

1 tbsp flaxseed powder
1 head broccoli, cut into florets

2/3 cup toasted almond flour
2 garlic cloves, minced

2 cups grated plant-based Parmesan
Salt to taste

Directions and Total Time: 30 minutes

Preheat the oven to 350 F and line a baking sheet with parchment paper.

In a small bowl, mix the flaxseed powder with the 3 tbsp water and allow thicken for 5 minutes to make the vegan "flax egg". Place the broccoli in a safe microwave bowl, sprinkle with 2 tbsp of water, and steam in the microwave for 1 minute or until softened. Transfer the broccoli to a food processor and add the vegan "flax egg," almond flour, garlic, plant cheese, and salt. Blend until coarsely smooth.

Pour the mixture into a bowl and form 2-inch oblong balls from the mixture. Place the tots on the baking sheet and bake in the oven for 15 to 20 minutes or until firm and compacted. Remove the tots from the oven and serve warm with tomato dipping sauce.

Chocolate Bars with Walnuts

Ingredients for 4 servings

1 cup walnuts
3 tbsp sunflower seeds
2 tbsp unsweetened chocolate chips
1 tbsp unsweetened cocoa powder
1 ½ tsp vanilla extract
¼ tsp cinnamon powder
2 tbsp melted coconut oil
2 tbsp toasted almond meal
2 tsp pure maple syrup

Directions and Total Time: 60 minutes

In a food processor, add the walnuts, sunflower seeds, chocolate chips, cocoa powder, vanilla extract, cinnamon powder, coconut oil, almond meal, maple syrup, and blitz a few times until combined.

Line a flat baking sheet with plastic wrap, pour the mixture onto the sheet and place another plastic wrap on top. Use a rolling pin to flatten the batter and then remove the top plastic wrap. Freeze the snack until firm, 1 hour. Remove from the freezer, cut into 1 ½-inch sized bars and enjoy immediately.

Dijon Roasted Asparagus

Ingredients for 4 servings

2 tbsp plant butter
1 lb asparagus, hard part trimmed
2 garlic cloves, minced
1 tsp Dijon mustard
1 tbsp freshly squeezed lemon juice

Directions and Total Time: 35 minutes

Melt the butter in a large skillet and sauté the asparagus until softened with some crunch, 7 minutes. Mix in the garlic and cook until fragrant, 30 seconds.

Meanwhile, in a small bowl, quickly whisk the mustard, lemon juice and pour the mixture over the asparagus. Cook for 2 minutes. Plate the asparagus. Serve warm.

Paprika Tofu & Zucchini Skewers

Ingredients for 4 servings

1 (14 oz) block tofu, pressed cubed
1 medium zucchini, cut into rounds
1 tbsp olive oil
2 tbsp freshly squeezed lemon juice
1 tsp smoked paprika
1 tsp cumin powder
1 tsp garlic powder
Salt and black pepper to taste

Directions and Total Time: 10 minutes

Preheat a grill to medium heat.

Meanwhile, thread the tofu and zucchini alternately on the wooden skewers.

In a small bowl, whisk the olive oil, lemon juice, paprika, cumin powder, and garlic powder. Brush the skewers all around with the mixture and place on the grill grate. Cook on both sides until golden brown, 5 minutes. Season with salt and pepper and serve afterward.

Strawberries Stuffed with Banana Cream

Ingredients for 4 servings

12 strawberries, heads removed
¼ cup cashew cream
¼ tsp banana extract
1 tbsp unsweetened coconut flakes

Directions and Total Time: 10 minutes

Use a teaspoon to scoop out some of the strawberries pulp to create a hole within. In a small bowl, mix the cashew cream, banana extract, and maple syrup. Spoon the mixture into the strawberries and garnish with the coconut flakes. Serve.

Rolls

Ingredients for 4 servings rolls

2 tbsp almond butter
2 tbsp tamari sauce
4 standard nori sheets
1 green bell pepper, sliced
1 tbsp pickled ginger
½ cup grated carrots

Directions and Total Time: 15 minutes

Preheat oven to 350 F.

Whisk the almond butter and tamari until smooth and thick.

Place a nori sheet on a flat surface with the rough side facing up. Spoon a bit of the tamari mixture at the other side of the nori sheet, and spread on all sides. Put bell pepper slices, carrots, and ginger in a layer at the other end of the sheet. Fold up in the tahini direction to seal. Repeat the process with the remaining sheets. Arrange on a baking tray and bake for about 10 minutes, until browned and crispy. Allow cooling for a few minutes before slicing into 4 pieces.

Cinnamon-Maple Popcorn

Ingredients for 4 servings

½ cup popcorn kernels
¼ tsp cinnamon powder
½ tsp pure maple syrup
1 tsp plant butter, melted
Salt to taste

Directions and Total Time: 15 minutes

Pour the popcorn kernels in a large pot and set over medium heat. Cover the lid and let the kernels pop completely. Shake the pot a few times to ensure even popping, 10 minutes.

In a small bowl, mix the cinnamon powder, maple syrup, butter, and salt. When the popcorn is ready, turn the heat off, and toss in the cinnamon mixture until well distributed. Pour the popcorn into serving bowls, allow cooling, and enjoy.

Mediterranean Tahini Beans

Ingredients for 4 servings

1 tbsp sesame oil
1 cup string beans, trimmed
Salt to taste
2 tbsp pure tahini
2 tbsp coarsely chopped mint leaves
¼ tsp red chili flakes for topping

Directions and Total Time: 10 minutes

Pour the string beans into a medium safe microwave dish, sprinkle with 1 tbsp of water, and steam in the microwave until softened, 1 minute.

Heat the sesame oil in a large skillet and toss in the string beans until well coated in the butter. Season with salt and mix in the tahini and mint leaves. Cook for 1 to 2 minutes and turn the heat off. Serve.

Hot Crunchy Nuts

Ingredients for 4 servings

1 cup mixed nuts
1 tbsp plant butter, melted
¼ tsp hot sauce
¼ tsp garlic powder
¼ tsp onion powder

Directions and Total Time: 35 minutes

Preheat the oven to 350 F and line a baking sheet with baking paper.

In a medium bowl, mix the nuts, butter, hot sauce, garlic powder, and onion powder. Spread the mixture on the baking sheet and toast in the oven for 10 minutes. Remove the sheet, allow complete cooling, and serve.

Beet & Carrot Stir-Fry

Ingredients for 4 servings

2 beets, peeled and cut into wedges
3 small carrots, cut crosswise
2 tbsp plant butter
1 red onion, cut into wedges
½ tsp dried oregano
1/8 tsp salt

Directions and Total Time: 20 minutes

Steam the beets and carrots in a medium safe microwave bowl until softened, 6 minutes.

Meanwhile, melt the butter in a large skillet and sauté the onion until softened, 3 minutes. Stir in the carrots, beets, oregano, and salt. Mix well and cook for 5 minutes. Serve warm.

Mustard Tofu-Avocado Wraps

Ingredients for 4 servings

6 tbsp olive oil
1 lb extra-firm tofu, cut into strips
1 tbsp soy sauce
¼ cup apple cider vinegar

1 tsp yellow mustard
3 cups shredded romaine lettuce
3 ripe Roma tomatoes, chopped
1 large carrot, shredded

1 medium avocado, chopped
⅓ cup minced red onion
¼ cup sliced pitted green olives
4 whole-grain flour tortillas

Directions and Total Time: 25 minutes

Heat 2 tbsp of olive oil in a skillet over medium heat. Place the tofu, cook for 10 minutes until golden brown. Drizzle with soy sauce. Let cool.

In a bowl, whisk the vinegar, mustard, salt, pepper, and the remaining oil. In another bowl, mix the lettuce, tomatoes, carrot, avocado, onion, and olives. Pour the dressing over the salad and toss to coat. Lay out a tortilla on a clean flat surface and spoon ¼ of the salad, some tofu, and then roll-up. Cut in half. Repeat the process with the remaining tortillas. Serve.

Maple-Glazed Butternut Squash

Ingredients for 4 servings

1 butternut squash, cubed
2 tbsp olive oil

4 garlic cloves, minced
¼ cup pure maple syrup

1 tsp red chili flakes
1 tsp coriander seeds

Directions and Total Time: 40 minutes

Preheat the oven to 375 F.

In a medium bowl, toss the squash with the olive oil, garlic, maple syrup, salt, black pepper, red chili flakes, and coriander seeds. Spread the mixture on a baking sheet and roast in the oven for 25 to 30 minutes or until the potatoes soften and golden brown. Remove from the oven, plate, and serve.

Tofu & Tomato Sandwiches

Ingredients for 4 servings

1 lb extra-firm tofu, crumbled
1 medium carrot, chopped
1 celery stalk, chopped

3 green onions, minced
¼ cup shelled sunflower seeds
½ cup tofu mayonnaise

8 slices whole-grain bread
4 slices ripe tomato
4 lettuce leaves

Directions and Total Time: 15 minutes

Place the tofu in a bowl. Stir in carrot, celery, green onions, and sunflower seeds. Mix in mayonnaise, salt, and pepper. Toast the bread slices. Spread the tofu mixture onto 4 bread slices. Layer a tomato slice and lettuce leaf. Top each sandwich with a bread slice and cut diagonally. Serve immediately.

Parmesan Baby Potatoes

Ingredients for 4 servings

4 tbsp plant butter, melted
4 garlic cloves, minced

3 tbsp chopped chives
Salt and black pepper to taste

2 tbsp grated plant-based Parmesan
1 ½ lb baby potatoes

Directions and Total Time: 40 minutes

Preheat the oven to 400 F.

In a bowl, mix butter, garlic, chives, salt, pepper, and plant Parmesan cheese. Toss the potatoes in the butter mixture until coated. Spread the mixture into a baking sheet, cover with foil, and roast for 30 minutes. Remove the potatoes from the oven and toss in the remaining butter mixture. Serve.

Guacamole with Daikon

Ingredients for 4 servings

Juice of 1 lime
1 avocado, cubed

½ red onion, sliced
1 garlic clove, minced

¼ cup chopped cilantro
1 daikon, cut into matchsticks

Directions and Total Time: 15 minutes

Place the avocado in a bowl and squeeze the lime juice. Sprinkle with salt. Mash the avocado using a fork, stir in onion, garlic, and cilantro. Serve with daikon slices.

Tofu Stuffed Peppers

Ingredients for 4 servings

1 cup red and yellow bell peppers	1 cup cashew cream cheese	2 tbsp melted plant butter
1 oz tofu, chopped into small bits	1 tbsp chili paste, mild	1 cup grated plant-based Parmesan

Directions and Total Time: 25 minutes

Preheat oven to 400 F. Use a knife to cut the bell peppers into two (lengthwise) and remove the core.

In a bowl, mix tofu, cashew cream cheese, chili paste, and melted butter until smooth. Spoon the cheese mixture into the bell peppers and use the back of the spoon to level the filling in the peppers. Grease a baking sheet with cooking spray and arrange the stuffed peppers on the sheet.

Sprinkle the plant-based Parmesan cheese on top and bake the peppers for 15-20 minutes until the peppers are golden brown and the cheese melted. Remove onto a serving platter and serve warm.

Crispy Squash Nacho Chips

Ingredients for 4 servings

1 large yellow squash	1 ½ cups coconut oil	1 tbsp taco seasoning

Directions and Total Time: 26 minutes

With a mandolin slicer, cut the squash into thin, round slices and place in a colander.

Sprinkle the squash with a lot of salt and allow sitting for 5 minutes. After, press the water out of the squash and pat dry with a paper towel. Pour the coconut oil in a deep skillet and heat the oil over medium heat. Carefully, add the squash slices in the oil, about 20 pieces at a time, and fry until crispy and golden brown. Use a slotted spoon to remove the squash onto a paper towel-lined plate. Sprinkle the slices with taco seasoning and serve.

Pepita Cheese Tomato Chips

Ingredients for 6 servings

5 tomatoes, sliced	½ cup pepitas seeds	Salt and black pepper, to taste
¼ cup olive oil	1 tbsp nutritional yeast	1 tsp garlic puree

Directions and Total Time: 15 minutes

Preheat oven to 400 F. Over the sliced tomatoes, drizzle olive oil. In a food processor, add pepitas seeds, nutritional yeast, garlic, salt, and pepper and pulse until the desired consistency is attained. Toss in tomato slices to coat. Set the tomato slices on a baking pan and bake for 10 minutes.

Baked Brussels Sprouts with Cranberries

Ingredients for 4 servings

1 lb Brussels sprouts, halved	1 medium white onion, chopped	1 lemon, juiced
3 tbsp olive oil	½ cup dried cranberries	1 tbsp chopped fresh basil

Directions and Total Time: 50 minutes

Preheat the oven to 425 F.

Spread the Brussels sprouts on a roasting sheet, drizzle with the olive oil, and season with salt and black pepper. Mix the seasoning onto the vegetables and roast in the oven until light brown and tender, 20 to 25 minutes. Transfer the Brussels sprouts to a large salad bowl and mix in the onion, cranberries, lemon juice, and basil. Serve immediately.

Four-Seed Crackers

Ingredients for 4 servings

1/3 cup coconut flour	1/3 cup sunflower seeds	1/3 cup pumpkin seeds
1/3 cup sesame seeds	1/3 cup chia seeds	¼ cup plant butter, melted

Directions and Total Time: 50 minutes

Preheat an oven to 300 F and line a baking sheet with parchment paper.

In a bowl, mix the coconut flour, sesame seeds, sunflower seeds, chia seeds, pumpkin seeds, and salt. Add the plant butter, 1 cup of boiling water, and mix until well combined. Spread the mixture on the baking sheet and bake in the oven until the batter is firm, 45 minutes. Remove the crackers and allow cooling for 10 minutes. Break the crackers into pieces and serve.

Pecan Tempeh Cakes

Ingredients for 4 servings

8 oz tempeh, chopped
1 chopped onion
2 garlic cloves, minced
¾ cup chopped pecans
½ cup old-fashioned oats
1 tbsp minced fresh parsley
½ tsp dried oregano
½ tsp dried thyme
Salt and black pepper to taste
3 tbsp olive oil
1 tbsp Dijon mustard
4 whole-grain burger buns
Sliced red onion, tomato, lettuce, and avocado

Directions and Total Time: 20 minutes

Place the tempeh in a pot with hot water. Cook for 30 minutes. Drain and let cool.

In a blender, add onion, garlic, tempeh, pecans, oats, parsley, oregano, thyme, salt, and pepper. Pulse until everything is well combined. Form the mixture into 4 balls; flatten to make burgers.

Lemon-Maple Glazed Carrots

Ingredients for 4 servings

1 lb baby carrots
2 tbsp plant butter
2 tbsp pure maple syrup
1 tbsp freshly squeezed lemon juice
½ tsp black pepper
¼ cup chopped fresh parsley

Directions and Total Time: 15 minutes

Boil some water in a medium pot. Add some salt and cook the carrots until tender, 5 to 6 minutes. Drain the carrots. Melt the butter in a large skillet and mix in the maple syrup and lemon juice. Toss in the carrots, season with black pepper, and toss in the parsley. Serve the carrots.

Walnut & Tempeh Ball

Ingredients for 8 servings

8 oz tempeh, cut into ½-inch pieces
1 (2-oz) jar chopped pimientos
¼ cup nutritional yeast
¼ cup tofu mayonnaise
2 tbsp soy sauce
¾ cup chopped walnuts

Directions and Total Time: 35 minutes

Place the tempeh in a pot with boiling water and cook for 30 minutes. Let cool. In a blender, put the tempeh, pimientos, yeast, mayo, and soy sauce. Pulse until smooth. Remove to a bowl and let chill in the fridge for 2 hours.

Heat a skillet over medium heat. Add the walnuts and toast for 5 minutes, shaking constantly. Remove to a large plate and leave to cool. Mold the tempeh mixture into a ball and roll in the walnuts' plate; be sure it's coated through. Serve chilled.

Yummy Vegetarian Burritos

Ingredients for 2 servings

3 tbsp soy sauce
3 tbsp fresh lemon juice
1 ½ tbsp toasted sesame oil
2 portobello mushroom caps, sliced
1 ripe avocado, pitted and peeled
2 whole-grain flour tortillas
2 cups kale, chopped
1 red bell pepper, cut into strips
1 ripe tomato, chopped

Directions and Total Time: 15 minutes

Whisk soy sauce, 2 tbsp of lemon juice, and oil in a bowl. Toss in portobello strips and marinate for 45 minutes. Drain and set aside. Using a fork, mash the avocado with the remaining lemon juice. Spread the avocado mash over tortillas and top with kale, mushrooms, bell pepper strips, and tomato. Sprinkle with salt and pepper. Fold the outside edges over the filling to make burritos. Cut in half and serve.

Roman Balsamic Tomato Bruschetta

Ingredients for 12 servings

3 tomatoes, chopped
¼ cup chopped fresh basil
1 tbsp olive oil
1 whole-wheat baguette, sliced
1 garlic clove, halved
Balsamic vinegar for garnish

Directions and Total Time: 20 minutes

Preheat oven to 420 F.

Mix the tomatoes, basil, olive oil, and salt in a bowl. Set aside. Arrange baguette slices on a baking sheet and toast for 6 minutes on both sides until brown. Spread the garlic over the bread and top with the tomato mixture. Serve right away.

Spicy Nut Burgers

Ingredients for 4 servings

¾ cup chopped walnuts
¾ cup chopped cashews
1 medium carrot, grated
1 small onion, chopped
1 garlic clove, minced
1 serrano pepper, minced
¾ cup old-fashioned oats
¾ cup breadcrumbs
2 tbsp minced fresh cilantro
½ tsp ground coriander
Salt and black pepper to taste
2 tsp fresh lime juice
Canola oil, for frying
4 sandwich rolls
Lettuce leaves for garnish

Directions and Total Time: 20 minutes

Pulse walnuts, cashews, carrot, onion, garlic, serrano pepper, oats, breadcrumbs, cilantro, coriander, lime juice, salt, and pepper in a food processor until well mixed. Remove and form into 4 burgers.

Warm the oil in a skillet over medium heat. Cook the burgers for 5 minutes per side, until golden brown. Serve in sandwich rolls with lettuce and a dressing of your choice.

Soy Chorizo & Avocado Tacos

Ingredients for 4 servings

2 tbsp olive oil
8 oz soy chorizo
4 soft flour tortillas
¼ cup tofu mayonnaise
4 large lettuce leaves
2 ripe avocados, sliced
1 tomato, sliced

Directions and Total Time: 20 minutes

Warm the oil in a skillet over medium heat. Place the soy chorizo and cook for 6 minutes on all sides until browned. Set aside. Spread mayonnaise over tortillas and top with lettuce leaves and tomato slies. Cover with avocado slices and finish with soy chorizo. Roll up the tortillas and serve immediately.

Hazelnut Snack

Ingredients for 1 serving

½ cup raw hazelnuts
2 tbsp tamari sauce
1 tsp toasted sesame oil

Directions and Total Time: 10 minutes

Heat a skillet over medium heat. Place in hazelnuts and toast for 7-8 minutes, moving continually with a spatula. Stir in tamari sauce and sesame oil to coat. Remove from the heat and allow the tamari mixture to dry on the hazelnuts.

Curry Mango-Tofu Pitas

Ingredients for 4 servings

4 pieces of whole-wheat pita bread, halved
1 lb extra-firm tofu, crumbled
½ cup tofu mayonnaise
¼ cup chopped mango chutney
2 tsp Dijon mustard
1 tbsp curry powder
Salt to taste
⅛ tsp ground cayenne
¾ cup shredded carrots
1 fennel bulb, sliced
¼ cup minced red onion
4 lettuce leaves

Directions and Total Time: 15 minutes

In a bowl, place tofu, mayonnaise, chutney, mustard, curry powder, salt, and cayenne pepper and stir to combine. Mix in the carrots, fennel, and onion. Let sit in the fridge for 20 minutes. Cover the pieces of the pita bread with lettuce leaves and scoop some of the tofu mixture in. Serve immediately.

Homemade Seedy Bars

Ingredients for 6 servings

¾ cup pumpkin seeds
½ cup sunflower seeds
½ cup sesame seeds
¼ cup poppy seeds
1 tsp minced garlic
1 tsp tamari sauce
1 tsp vegan Worcestershire sauce
½ tsp ground cayenne pepper
½ tsp dried oregano

Directions and Total Time: 55 minutes

Preheat oven to 320 F. Line with parchment paper a baking sheet. Mix the pumpkin seeds, sunflower seeds, sesame seeds, poppy seeds, garlic, tamari, Worcestershire sauce, cayenne, oregano, and ½ cup water in a bowl. Spread on the baking sheet and bake for 25 minutes. Turn the seeds and bake for another 20-25 minutes. Allow cooling before slicing into bars.

Crispy Mushroom Wontons

Ingredients for 12 servings

12 vegan wonton wrappers
3 tbsp toasted sesame oil
2 tbsp olive oil

12 shiitake mushrooms, sliced
4 green beans, chopped crosswise
1 tsp soy sauce

1 tbsp fresh lime juice
1 medium carrot, shredded
Toasted sesame seeds

Directions and Total Time: 20 minutes

Preheat oven to 360 F.

Coat the wonton with some sesame oil and arrange on a baking sheet. Put in the oven and bake for 5 minutes until golden brown and crispy. Set aside. Warm the olive oil in a skillet over medium heat. Place the mushrooms and stir-fry for 5 minutes until softened. Add in green beans and soy sauce and cook for 2-3 minutes; reserve.

In a bowl, whisk the lime juice and the remaining sesame oil. Stir in carrot and mushroom mixture. Divide the mixture between the wontons and sprinkle with sesame seeds. Serve.

French Mushroom Tarts

Ingredients for 4 servings

12 thin slices whole-grain bread
1 tbsp olive oil + more for brushing
2 spring onions, chopped

2 garlic cloves, minced
12 oz white mushrooms, chopped
¼ cup chopped fresh cilantro

1 tsp dried thyme
1 tbsp soy sauce

Directions and Total Time: 20 minutes

Preheat oven to 390 F.

Using a small round tin, make circles from the bread slices. Coat the circles with oil and press at the bottom of a muffin tin. Bake for 10 minutes, until toasted.

Heat 1 tbsp of oil in a skillet over medium heat. Place in spring onions, garlic, and mushrooms and cook for 5 minutes, until tender. Add in cilantro, thyme, and soy sauce and cook for 2-3 minutes more, until liquid has absorbed. Divide the mixture between the muffin cups and bake for 3-5 minutes. Serve.

Chickpea & Pecan Balls

Ingredients for 6 servings

1 (15.5-oz) can chickpeas
½ cup chopped pecans
¼ cup minced green onions

1 garlic clove, minced
3 tbsp whole-wheat flour
3 tbsp breadcrumbs

4 tbsp hot sauce ¼ tsp salt
⅛ tsp ground cayenne pepper
¼ cup plant butter, melted

Directions and Total Time: 35 minutes

Preheat oven to 350 F.

In a food processor, put the chickpeas, pecans, green onions, garlic, flour, breadcrumbs, 2 tbsp of hot sauce, salt, and cayenne pepper. Pulse until chunky texture is formed.

Shape the mixture into 1-inch balls. Arrange on a greased baking pan and bake for 25-30 minutes, turning halfway through to ensure they cook evenly. In a bowl, whisk the remaining hot sauce with melted plant butter. Remove the balls to a serving plate and pour the hot butter all over and serve.

Maple-Pumpkin Cookies

Ingredients for 12 servings

1 (2-pound) pumpkin, sliced
3 tbsp melted coconut oil, divided

1 tbsp maple syrup
1 cup whole-wheat flour

2 tsp baking powder
Sea salt to taste

Directions and Total Time: 70 minutes

Preheat oven to 360 F.

Place the pumpkin in a greased tray and bake for 45 minutes until tender. Let cool before mashing it. Mix the mashed pumpkin, 1 ½ tbsp of coconut oil, and maple syrup in a bowl.

Combine the flour and baking powder in another bowl. Fold in the pumpkin mixture and whisk with a fork until smooth.

Divide the mixture into balls. Arrange spaced out on a lined with a wax paper baking sheet; flatten the balls until a cookie shape is formed. Brush with the remaining melted coconut oil. Bake for 10 minutes, until they rise and become gold. Serve.

Vegetable & Rice Vermicelli Lettuce Rolls

Ingredients for 4 servings

- 2 green onions
- 2 tbsp sesame oil
- 2 tbsp soy sauce
- 2 tbsp balsamic vinegar
- 1 tsp pure date sugar
- ⅛ tsp crushed red pepper
- 3 oz rice vermicelli
- 6 soft green leaf lettuce leaves
- 1 medium carrot, shredded
- ½ cucumber, sliced lengthwise
- ½ red bell pepper, cut into strips
- 1 cup fresh cilantro leaves

Directions and Total Time: 15 minutes

Separate the white part of the green onions, chop and transfer to a bowl. Stir in soy sauce, balsamic vinegar, date sugar, red pepper, and 3 tbsp water. Set aside. Slice the green part diagonally and set aside.

Submerge the vermicelli in a bowl with hot water for 4 minutes. Drain and mix in the sesame oil. Allow cooling. Put the lettuce leaves on a flat surface.

Divide rice noodles between each leaf, in the middle, add green onion slices, carrot, cucumber, bell pepper, and cilantro. Roll the leaves up from the smaller edges. Arrange the rolls seam facing down in a plate. Serve with the dipping sauce.

Garbanzo Quesadillas with Salsa

Ingredients for 4 servings

- 1 (15.5-oz) can garbanzo beans, mashed
- 2 tbsp canola oil
- 1 tsp chili powder
- 8 whole-wheat flour tortilla wraps
- 1 cup tomato salsa
- ½ cup minced red onion

Directions and Total Time: 15 minutes

Warm the canola oil in a pot over medium heat. Place in mashed garbanzo and chili powder, cook for 5 minutes, stirring often. Set aside.

Heat a pan over medium heat. Put one tortilla in the pan and top with ¼ each of the garbanzo spread, tomato salsa, and onion. Cover with other tortilla and cook for 2 minutes, flip the quesadilla and cook for another 2 minutes until crispy. Repeat the process with the remaining tortillas. Slice and serve.

Coconut & Parsley Wraps

Ingredients for 8 servings

- ½ cup fresh parsley, chopped
- 1 cup sprouts
- 1 garlic clove, pressed
- 2 tbsp ground hazelnuts
- 2 tbsp flaked coconut
- 1 tbsp coconut oil
- 1 tsp cayenne pepper
- Salt and black pepper to taste
- Zest and juice of 1 lime
- 2 tbsp ground flaxseed
- 2 tbsp water
- 2 whole-wheat wraps

Directions and Total Time: 60 minutes

Pulse parsley, sprouts, garlic, hazelnuts, coconut flakes, coconut oil, cayenne, salt, pepper, lime juice, lime zest, flaxseed, and water in a food processor until well blended.

Divide the mixture between the wraps and roll-up. Let chill in the fridge for 30 minutes. Slice into 8 pieces and serve.

Tarragon Potato Chips

Ingredients for 4 servings

- 1 lb potato, peeled and sliced
- 1 tsp smoked paprika
- ½ tsp garlic powder
- 1 tbsp tarragon
- ¼ tsp onion powder
- ¼ tsp chili powder
- ⅛ tsp ground mustard
- 1 tsp canola oil
- ⅛ tsp liquid smoke

Directions and Total Time: 40 minutes

Preheat oven to 390 F.

Combine the paprika, garlic powder, tarragon, onion powder, chili powder, salt, and mustard in a bowl. Mix the potatoes, canola oil, liquid smoke, and tarragon mixture in another bowl; toss to coat. Spread the potatoes on a lined with parchment paper baking tray and bake for 30 minutes, flipping once halfway through cooking until golden. Serve.

Tamari Lentil Dip

Ingredients for 2 servings

- 1 (14-oz) can lentils, drained
- Zest and juice of 1 lime
- 1 tbsp tamari sauce
- ¼ cup fresh cilantro, chopped
- 1 tsp ground cumin
- 1 tsp cayenne pepper

Directions and Total Time: 10 minutes

In a blender, put the lentils, lime zest, lime juice, tamari sauce, and ¼ cup of water. Pulse until smooth. Transfer to a bowl and stir in cilantro, cumin and cayenne pepper. Serve.

Chili Roasted Hazelnuts

Ingredients for 8 servings

1 lb raw hazelnuts	2 tbsp extra-virgin olive oil	2 tsp chili powder
3 tbsp tamari sauce	1 tbsp nutritional yeast	

Directions and Total Time: 20 minutes

Preheat oven to 390 F.

Combine the hazelnuts, tamari, and oil in a bowl. Toss to coat. Spread the mixture on a parchment-lined baking pan and roast for 10-15 minutes, until browned. Let cool for e few minutes. Sprinkle with yeast and chili powder.

Balsamic Roasted Red Pepper & Pecan Crostini

Ingredients for 16 servings

2 jarred roasted red peppers	1 tbsp soy sauce	2 tbsp balsamic vinegar
1 cup unsalted pecans	2 tbsp chopped green onions	2 tbsp olive oil
¼ cup water	¼ cup nutritional yeast	

Directions and Total Time: 15 minutes

Cut 1 red pepper and set aside. Slice the remaining pepper into strips, reserve for garnish. Pulse the pecans in a food processor until a fine powder forms. Pour in water, chopped red pepper, and soy sauce. Pulse until smooth. Put in green onions, yeast, vinegar, and oil. Blend until well mixed. Spread mixture onto toasted bread slices topped with pepper strips.

Paprika Hummus with Mushrooms

Ingredients for 4 servings

1 (15-oz) can chickpeas	3 tbsp olive oil	¼ tsp paprika
Juice of 1 lemon	½ tsp ground cumin	1 lb sautéed mushrooms
¼ cup tahini	1 tbsp water	

Directions and Total Time: 15 minutes

In a blender, put the chickpeas, lemon juice, tahini, 2 tbsp of olive oil, cumin, and water. Pulse for 30 seconds until ingredients are evenly mixed. Remove to a bowl and sprinkle with the remaining olive oil and paprika. Serve with mushrooms.

Bell Peppers Stuffed with Spinach & Tofu

Ingredients for 4 servings

2 tbsp olive oil	1 (14-oz) block tofu, crumbled	Salt and black pepper to taste
1 onion, chopped	1 (5-oz) package baby spinach	4 large bell peppers, top removed
2 garlic cloves, minced	2 tsp Italian seasoning	

Directions and Total Time: 35 minutes

Preheat oven to 450 F.

Heat the oil in a skillet over medium heat. Place onion and garlic and cook for 3 minutes. Put in tofu and spinach and cook for 3 minutes until the spinach wilts. Stir in Italian seasoning, salt, and pepper.

Fill the bell peppers with the spinach mixture and arrange them on a greased baking sheet. Bake in the oven for 25 minutes.

Kale & Hummus Pinwheels

Ingredients for 4 servings

3 whole-grain flour tortillas	¾ cup hummus
1 cup kale, chopped	¾ cup shredded carrots

Directions and Total Time: 10 minutes

Spread hummus over tortillas and top with kale and carrots. Fold the edges over the filling and roll up to make burritos. Cut into pinwheels and serve.

Paprika Baked Beans

Ingredients for 1 serving

1 (14-oz) can white beans
2 tbsp soy sauce
1 tbsp nutritional yeast
1 tsp smoked paprika
1 tsp onion powder
½ tsp garlic powder

Directions and Total Time: 30 minutes

Preheat oven to 390 F.

Mix the beans, soy sauce, yeast, paprika, onion powder, and garlic powder. Arrange on a greased baking sheet and bake for 20-25 minutes, turning once. Lower the heat and bake until dried and crispy.

Heat the oil in a skillet over medium heat. Place the burgers and fry for 10-12 minutes on both sides. Spread a layer of the mustard over each bun half. Top the bottom buns with the lettuce, tomato, onion, avocado, and burgers and cover with the remaining bun half. Serve right away.

Middle Eastern Onion Phyllo

Ingredients for 8 servings

2 tbsp olive oil
2 medium onions, thinly sliced
1 garlic clove, minced
1 tsp chopped fresh rosemary
Salt and black pepper to taste
1 tbsp chopped dill pickles
1 sheet vegan puff pastry, thawed
18 pitted black olives, quartered

Directions and Total Time: 25 minutes

Warm the oil in a skillet over medium heat. Place in onions, garlic, rosemary, salt, and pepper and sauté for 5 minutes. Add in dill pickles, stir and set aside.

Preheat oven to 390 F. Roll out the pastry and, using a small bowl, cut into 3-inch circles. Arrange the circles on a greased baking sheet and top with onion mixture. Scatter the olives over. Bake for 15 minutes until golden brown. Serve warm.

Arugula & Hummus Pitas

Ingredients for 4 servings

4 pieces of whole-wheat pita bread, halved
1 garlic clove, chopped
¾ cup tahini
2 tbsp fresh lemon juice
⅛ tsp ground cayenne
¼ cup water
1 (15.5-oz) can chickpeas
2 medium carrots, grated
1 large ripe tomato, sliced
2 cups arugula

Directions and Total Time: 15 minutes

In a food processor, add in garlic, tahini, lemon juice, salt, cayenne pepper, and water. Pulse until smooth. In a bowl, mash the chickpeas with a fork. Stir in carrots and tahini mixture; reserve. Spread the hummus over the pitas and top with a tomato slice and arugula. Serve immediately.

Authentic Guacamole

Ingredients for 2 servings

2 ripe avocados
2 garlic cloves, pressed
Zest and juice of 1 lime
1 tsp ground cumin
1 tomato, chopped
1 tbsp cilantro, chopped

Directions and Total Time: 10 minutes

Place the avocados in a bowl and mash them. Stir in garlic, lime juice, lime zest, cumin, tomato, cilantro, salt, and pepper. Serve immediately.

Cucumber Stuffed Tomatoes

Ingredients for 6 servings

6 tomatoes, whole
2 cucumbers, chopped
Juice of 1 lemon
½ red bell pepper, minced
2 green onions, finely minced
1 tbsp minced fresh tarragon

Directions and Total Time: 15 minutes

Remove the tops of the tomatoes. Using a tablespoon, scoop out the seeds and pulp. Arrange them on a platter. Combine the cucumbers, lemon juice, bell pepper, scallions, tarragon, and salt in a bowl. Stir to combine. Divide the mixture between the tomatoes and serve.

Minty Berry Cocktail

Ingredients for 4 servings

- 2 tbsp pineapple juice
- 1 tbsp fresh lime juice
- 1 tbsp agave nectar
- 2 tsp minced fresh mint
- 2 cups pitted fresh prunes
- 1 cup fresh blueberries
- 1 cup fresh strawberries, halved
- ½ cup fresh raspberries

Directions and Total Time: 15 minutes

Whisk the pineapple juice, lime juice, agave nectar, and mint in a bowl. Set aside.

In another bowl, combine the prunes, blueberries, strawberries, and raspberries. Pour over the dressing and toss to coat. Serve right away.

Swiss Chard & Pecan Stuffed Mushrooms

Ingredients for 4 servings

- 8 oz white mushrooms, stems chopped and reserved
- 2 tbsp olive oil
- 1 garlic clove, minced
- 1 cup cooked Swiss chard
- 1 cup finely chopped pecans
- ½ cup breadcrumbs
- Salt and black pepper to taste

Directions and Total Time: 20 minutes

Preheat oven to 390 F.

Warm oil in a skillet over medium heat, add the mushroom stems and garlic and sauté for 3 minutes. Mix in chard, pecans, breadcrumbs, salt, and pepper. Cook for another 2 minutes, stirring occasionally.

Divide the resulting mixture between the mushroom caps and arrange on a greased baking dish. Bake for 15 minutes, until golden. Serve immediately.

Green Salsa

Ingredients for 4 servings

- 3 large heirloom tomatoes, chopped
- 1 green onion, finely chopped
- ½ bunch parsley, chopped
- 2 garlic cloves, minced
- 1 Jalapeño pepper, minced
- Juice of 1 lime
- ¼ cup olive oil Salt to taste
- Whole-grain tortilla chips

Directions and Total Time: 15 minutes

Combine the tomatoes, green onion, parsley, garlic, jalapeño pepper, lime juice, olive oil, and salt in a bowl. Let it rest for 10 minutes at room temperature. Serve with tortilla chips.

Primavera Lettuce Rolls

Ingredients for 4 servings

- 1 tbsp olive oil
- 2 oz rice noodles
- 2 tbsp Thai basil, chopped
- 2 tbsp cilantro, chopped
- 1 garlic clove, minced
- 1 tbsp minced fresh ginger
- Juice of ½ lime
- 2 tbsp soy sauce
- 1 avocado, sliced
- 2 carrots, peeled and julienned
- 8 leaves butter lettuce

Directions and Total Time: 20 minutes

In a bowl, place the noodles in hot water and let them sit for 4 minutes. Drain and mix with the olive oil. Allow cooling.

Combine the basil, cilantro, garlic, ginger, lime juice, and soy sauce in another bowl. Add in cooked noodles, avocado, and carrots. Divide the mixture between the lettuce leaves. Fold in and secure with toothpicks. Serve right away.

Citrus-Parsley Mushrooms

Ingredients for 4 servings

- 3 tbsp plant butter
- 3 tbsp fresh lime juice
- 2 garlic cloves, crushed
- 1 tsp dried marjoram
- ½ tsp ground fennel seed
- Salt and black pepper to taste
- 8 oz white mushrooms, stemmed
- 1 tbsp minced fresh parsley

Directions and Total Time: 15 minutes

Mix the butter, lime juice, garlic, marjoram, fennel seed, salt, and pepper in a bowl. Stir in mushrooms and parsley to coat. Marinate covered in the fridge for at least 2 hours. Stir to serve.

Mustard Mac & Cheese

Ingredients for 4 servings

8 oz elbow macaroni
2 tbsp olive oil
½ tsp dry mustard powder

2 cups almond milk
2 cups plant-based cheddar, grated
Salt and black pepper to taste

¼ cup flour
2 tbsp parsley, chopped

Directions and Total Time: 35 minutes

Cook elbow macaroni in boiling water for 8-10 minutes until al dente. Drain.

Heat olive oil in a skillet over medium heat. Place flour, mustard powder, salt, and pepper and stir for about 3-5 minutes. Gradually pour in almond milk while stirring constantly with a spatula for another 5 minutes until the mixture is smooth. Turn off the heat and mix in cheddar cheese. When the cheese is melted, fold in macaroni and toss to coat. Sprinkle with parsley to serve.

Grilled Vegetables with Romesco Dip

Ingredients for 4 servings

1 (12-oz) jar roasted peppers, drained
½ cup toasted almonds
1 garlic clove, minced
1 tbsp red wine vinegar
1 tsp crushed red chili flakes

2 slices toasted bread, chopped
½ tsp sweet paprika
1 tbsp tomato paste
½ cup olive oil + 2 tbsp for brushing
Salt and black pepper to taste

1 green bell pepper, julienned
1 yellow bell pepper, julienned
1 bunch of asparagus, trimmed

Directions and Total Time: 35 minutes

In a food processor, place roasted peppers, almonds, garlic, vinegar, toasted bread, paprika, and tomato paste; pulse, pouring slowly ½ cup of olive oil until the desired consistency is reached. Season with salt and black pepper and set aside.

Heat a grill pan over medium heat. Toss the vegetables in the remaining olive oil, season with salt and pepper, and cook in the pan for 3-5 minutes per side. Serve with the dip.

Cacao Nut Bites

Ingredients for 4 servings

3 ½ oz dairy-free dark chocolate
½ cup mixed nuts

2 tbsp roasted coconut chips
1 tbsp sunflower seeds

Sea salt

Directions and Total Time: 5 minutes

Pour the chocolate into a safe microwave bowl and melt in the microwave for 1 to 2 minutes.

Into 10 small cupcake liners (2-inches in diameters), share the chocolate. Drop in the nuts, coconut chips, sunflower seeds, and sprinkle with some salt. Chill in the refrigerator until firm.

Berries, Nuts & Cream Bowl

Ingredients for 6 servings

5 tbsp flaxseed powder
1 cup dairy-free dark chocolate
1 cup plant butter

2 tsp vanilla extract
2 cups fresh blueberries
4 tbsp lemon juice

2 cups coconut cream
4 oz walnuts, chopped
½ cup roasted coconut chips

Directions and Total Time: 30 minutes

Preheat oven to 320 F. Grease a springform pan with cooking spray and line with parchment paper. In a bowl, mix the flaxseed powder with 2/3 cup water and allow thicken for 5 minutes. Break the chocolate and butter into a bowl and melt in the microwave for 1-2 minutes.

Share the vegan "flax egg" into two bowls; whisk 1 pinch of salt into one portion and then 1 teaspoon of vanilla into the other. Pour the chocolate mixture into the vanilla mixture and combine well. Fold into the other vegan "flax egg" mixture. Pour the batter into the springform pan and bake for 15-20 minutes. When ready, slice the cake into squares and share it into serving bowls. Set aside.

Pour blueberries, lemon juice, and the remaining vanilla into a bowl. Break blueberries and allow sitting for a few minutes. Whip the coconut cream with a whisk until a soft peak forms. Spoon the cream on the cakes, top with the blueberry mixture, and sprinkle with walnuts and coconut flakes. Serve.

DESSERTS & SWEET TREATS

Vanilla Brownies

Ingredients for 4 servings

2 tbsp flaxseed powder
¼ cup cocoa powder
½ cup almond flour

½ tsp baking powder
½ cup erythritol
10 tablespoons plant butter

2 oz dairy-free dark chocolate
½ teaspoon vanilla extract

Directions and Total Time: 30 minutes + chilling time

Preheat oven to 375 F and line a baking sheet with parchment paper. Mix the flaxseed powder with 6 tbsp water in a bowl and allow thicken for 5 minutes. In a separate bowl, mix cocoa powder, almond flour, baking powder, and erythritol until no lumps. In another bowl, add the plant butter and dark chocolate and melt both in the microwave for 30 seconds to 1 minute.

Whisk the vegan "flax egg" and vanilla into the chocolate mixture, then pour the mixture into the dry ingredients. Combine evenly. Pour the batter onto the paper-lined baking sheet and bake for 20 minutes. Cool completely and refrigerate for 2 hours. When ready, slice into squares and serve.

Vegan Cheesecake with Blueberries

Ingredients for 6 servings

2 oz plant butter
1 ¼ cups almond flour
3 tbsp Swerve sugar

1 tsp vanilla extract
3 tbsp flaxseed powder
2 cups cashew cream cheese

½ cup coconut cream
1 tsp lemon zest
2 oz fresh blueberries

Directions and Total Time: 1 hour 30 minutes + chilling time

Preheat oven to 350 F and grease a springform pan with cooking spray. Line with parchment paper.

To make the crust, melt the plant butter in a skillet over low heat until nutty in flavor. Turn the heat off and stir in almond flour, 2 tbsp of Swerve sugar, and half of the vanilla until a dough forms. Press the mixture into the springform pan and bake for 8 minutes.

Mix flaxseed powder with 9 tbsp water and allow sitting for 5 minutes to thicken. In a bowl, combine cashew cream cheese, coconut cream, remaining Swerve sugar, lemon zest, remaining vanilla extract, and vegan "flax egg." Remove the crust from the oven and pour the mixture on top. Use a spatula to layer evenly. Bake the cake for 15 minutes at 400 F. Then, reduce the heat to 230 F and bake for 45-60 minutes. Remove to cool completely. Refrigerate overnight and scatter the blueberries on top. Serve.

Lime Avocado Ice Cream

Ingredients for 4 servings

2 large avocados, pitted
Juice and zest of 3 limes

1/3 cup erythritol
1 ¾ cups coconut cream

¼ tsp vanilla extract

Directions and Total Time: 10 minutes

In a blender, combine the avocado pulp, lime juice and zest, erythritol, coconut cream, and vanilla extract. Process until the mixture is smooth. Pour the mixture into your ice cream maker and freeze based on the manufacturer's instructions. When ready, remove and scoop the ice cream into bowls. Serve immediately.

Walnut Chocolate Squares

Ingredients for 6 servings

3½ oz dairy-free dark chocolate
4 tbsp plant butter

1 pinch salt
¼ cup walnut butter

½ tsp vanilla extract
¼ cup chopped walnuts to garnish

Directions and Total Time: 10 minutes

Pour the chocolate and plant butter in a safe microwave bowl and melt in the microwave for about 1 to 2 minutes. Remove the bowl from the microwave and mix in the salt, walnut butter, and vanilla.

Grease a small baking sheet with cooking spray and line with parchment paper. Pour in the batter and use a spatula to spread out into a 4 x 6-inch rectangle. Top with the chopped walnuts and chill in the refrigerator. Once set, cut into 1 x 1-inch squares. Serve while firming.

Vanilla White Chocolate Pudding

Ingredients for 4 servings

3 tbsp flaxseed + 9 tbsp water
3 tbsp cornstarch
1 cup cashew cream

2 ½ cups almond milk
½ pure date sugar
1 tbsp vanilla caviar

6 oz white chocolate chips
Whipped coconut cream
Sliced bananas and raspberries

Directions and Total Time: 20 minutes+ cooling time

In a small bowl, mix the flaxseed powder with water and allow thicken for 5 minutes to make the vegan "flax egg." In a large bowl, whisk the cornstarch and cashew cream until smooth. Beat in the vegan "flax egg" until well combined.

Pour the almond milk into a pot and whisk in the date sugar. Cook over medium heat while frequently stirring until the sugar dissolves. Reduce the heat to low and simmer until steamy and bubbly around the edges.

Pour half of the almond milk mixture into the vegan "flax egg" mix, whisk well and pour this mixture into the remaining milk content in the pot. Whisk continuously until well combined. Bring the new mixture to a boil over medium heat while still frequently stirring and scraping all the pot's corners, 2 minutes.

Turn the heat off, stir in the vanilla caviar, then the white chocolate chips until melted. Spoon the mixture into a bowl, allow cooling for 2 minutes, cover with plastic wraps, making sure to press the plastic onto the surface of the pudding, and refrigerate for 4 hours. Remove the pudding from the fridge, take off the plastic wrap, and whip for about a minute. Spoon the dessert into serving cups, swirl some coconut whipping cream on top, and top with the bananas and raspberries. Enjoy.

Aunt's Apricot Tarte Tatin

Ingredients for 4 servings

4 tbsp flaxseed powder
¼ cup almond flour
3 tbsp whole-wheat flour
½ tsp salt
¼ cup cold plant butter, crumbled

3 tbsp pure maple syrup
4 tbsp melted plant butter
3 tsp pure maple syrup
1 tsp vanilla extract
1 lemon, juiced

12 apricots, halved and pitted
½ cup coconut cream
4 fresh basil leaves

Directions and Total Time: 30 minutes+ cooling time

Preheat the oven to 350 F and grease a large pie pan with cooking spray.

In a medium bowl, mix the flaxseed powder with 12 tbsp water and allow thicken for 5 minutes.

In a large bowl, combine the flours and salt. Add the plant butter and using an electric hand mixer, whisk until crumbly. Pour in the vegan "flax egg" and maple syrup and mix until smooth dough forms. Flatten the dough on a flat surface, cover with plastic wrap, and refrigerate for 1 hour.

Dust a working surface with almond flour, remove the dough onto the surface, and using a rolling pin, flatten the dough into a 1-inch diameter circle. Set aside. In a large bowl, mix the plant butter, maple syrup, vanilla, and lemon juice. Add the apricots to the mixture and coat well.

Arrange the apricots (open side down) in the pie pan and lay the dough on top. Press to fit and cut off the dough hanging on the edges. Brush the top with more plant butter and bake in the oven for 35 to 40 minutes or until golden brown and puffed up.

Remove the pie pan from the oven, allow cooling for 5 minutes, and run a butter knife around the edges of the pastry. Invert the dessert onto a large plate, spread the coconut cream on top, and garnish with the basil leaves. Slice and serve.

Southern Apple Cobbler with Raspberries

Ingredients for 4 servings

3 apples, chopped
2 tbsp pure date sugar
1 cup fresh raspberries

2 tbsp unsalted plant butter
½ cup whole-wheat flour
1 cup toasted rolled oats

2 tbsp pure date sugar
1 tsp cinnamon powder

Directions and Total Time: 50 minutes

Preheat the oven to 350 F and grease a baking dish with some plant butter.

Add apples, date sugar, and 3 tbsp of water to a pot. Cook over low heat until the date sugar melts and then mix in the raspberries. Cook until the fruits soften, 10 minutes. Pour and spread the fruit mixture into the baking dish and set aside.

In a blender, add the plant butter, flour, oats, date sugar, and cinnamon powder. Pulse a few times until crumbly. Spoon and spread the mixture on the fruit mix until evenly layered. Bake in the oven for 25 to 30 minutes or until golden brown on top. Remove the dessert, allow cooling for 2 minutes, and serve.

Chocolate Peppermint Mousse

Ingredients for 4 servings

¼ cup Swerve sugar, divided
4 oz cashew cream cheese, softened
3 tbsp cocoa powder
¾ tsp peppermint extract
½ tsp vanilla extract
1/3 cup coconut cream

Directions and Total Time: 10 minutes + chilling time

Put 2 tablespoons of Swerve sugar, cashew cream cheese, and cocoa powder in a blender. Add the peppermint extract, ¼ cup warm water, and process until smooth. In a bowl, whip vanilla extract, coconut cream, and the remaining Swerve sugar using a whisk. Fetch out 5-6 tablespoons for garnishing. Fold in the cocoa mixture until thoroughly combined. Spoon the mousse into serving cups and chill in the fridge for 30 minutes. Garnish with the reserved whipped cream and serve.

Raspberries Turmeric Panna Cotta

Ingredients for 6 servings

½ tbsp powdered vegetarian gelatin
2 cups coconut cream
¼ tsp vanilla extract
1 pinch turmeric powder
1 tbsp erythritol
1 tbsp chopped toasted pecans
12 fresh raspberries

Directions and Total Time: 10 minutes + chilling time

Mix gelatin and ½ tsp water and allow sitting to dissolve. Pour coconut cream, vanilla extract, turmeric, and erythritol into a saucepan and bring to a boil over medium heat, then simmer for 2 minutes. Turn the heat off. Stir in the gelatin until dissolved. Pour the mixture into 6 glasses, cover with a plastic wrap, and refrigerate for 2 hours or more. Top with the pecans and raspberries and serve.

Summer Banana Pudding

Ingredients for 4 servings

1 cup unsweetened almond milk
2 cups cashew cream
¾ cup + 1 tbsp pure date sugar
¼ tsp salt
3 tbsp cornstarch
2 tbsp plant butter, cut into 4 pieces
1 tsp vanilla extract
2 banana, sliced

Directions and Total Time: 25 minutes + cooling time

In a medium pot, mix almond milk, cashew cream, date sugar, and salt. Cook over medium heat until slightly thickened, 10-15 minutes. Stir in the cornstarch, plant butter, vanilla extract, and banana extract. Cook further for 1 to 2 minutes or until the pudding thickens. Dish the pudding into 4 serving bowls and chill in the refrigerator for at least 1 hour. To serve, top with the bananas and enjoy!

Baked Apples Filled with Nuts

Ingredients for 4 servings

4 gala apples
3 tbsp pure maple syrup
4 tbsp almond flour
6 tbsp pure date sugar
6 tbsp plant butter, cold and cubed
1 cup chopped mixed nuts

Directions and Total Time: 35 minutes + cooling time

Preheat the oven the 400 F.

Slice off the top of the apples and use a melon baller or spoon to scoop out the cores of the apples. In a bowl, mix the maple syrup, almond flour, date sugar, butter, and nuts. Spoon the mixture into the apples and then bake in the oven for 25 minutes or until the nuts are golden brown on top and the apples soft. Remove the apples from the oven, allow cooling, and serve.

Mint Ice Cream

Ingredients for 4 servings

2 avocados, pitted
1 ¼ cups coconut cream
½ tsp vanilla extract
2 tbsp erythritol
2 tsp chopped mint leaves

Directions and Total Time: 10 minutes + chilling time

Into a blender, spoon the avocado pulps, pour in the coconut cream, vanilla extract, erythritol, and mint leaves. Process until smooth. Pour the mixture into your ice cream maker and freeze according to the manufacturer's instructions. When ready, remove and scoop the ice cream into bowls. Serve.

Cardamom Coconut Fat Bombs

Ingredients for 6 servings

½ cup grated coconut
3 oz plant butter, softened
¼ tsp green cardamom powder
½ tsp vanilla extract
¼ tsp cinnamon powder

Directions and Total Time: 10 minutes

Pour the grated coconut into a skillet and roast until lightly brown. Set aside to cool. In a bowl, combine butter, half of the coconut, cardamom, vanilla, and cinnamon. Form balls from the mixture and roll each one in the remaining coconut. Refrigerate until ready to serve.

Cinnamon Faux Rice Pudding

Ingredients for 6 servings

1 ¼ cups coconut cream
1 tsp vanilla extract
1 tsp cinnamon powder
1 cup mashed tofu
2 oz fresh strawberries

Directions and Total Time: 25 minutes

Pour the coconut cream into a bowl and whisk until a soft peak forms. Mix in the vanilla and cinnamon. Lightly fold in the vegan cottage cheese and refrigerate for 10 to 15 minutes to set. Spoon into serving glasses, top with the strawberries and serve immediately.

White Chocolate Fudge

Ingredients for 6 servings

2 cups coconut cream
1 tsp vanilla extract
3 oz plant butter
3 oz vegan white chocolate
Swerve sugar for sprinkling

Directions and Total Time: 20 minutes + chilling time

Pour coconut cream and vanilla into a saucepan and bring to a boil over medium heat, then simmer until reduced by half, 15 minutes. Stir in plant butter until the batter is smooth. Chop white chocolate into bits and stir in the cream until melted. Pour the mixture into a baking sheet; chill in the fridge for 3 hours. Cut into squares, sprinkle with swerve sugar, and serve.

Macedonia Salad with Coconut & Pecans

Ingredients for 4 servings

1 cup pure coconut cream
½ tsp vanilla extract
2 bananas, cut into chunks
1 ½ cups coconut flakes
4 tbsp toasted pecans, chopped
1 cup pineapple tidbits, drained
1 (11-oz) can mandarin oranges
¾ cup maraschino cherries, stems removed

Directions and Total Time: 15 minutes + cooling time

In a medium bowl, mix the coconut cream and vanilla extract until well combined.

In a larger bowl, combine the bananas, coconut flakes, pecans, pineapple, oranges, and cherries until evenly distributed. Pour on the coconut cream mixture and fold well into the salad. Chill in the refrigerator for 1 hour and serve afterward.

Berry Hazelnut Trifle

Ingredients for 4 servings

1 ½ ripe avocados
¾ cup coconut cream
Zest and juice of ½ a lemon
1 tbsp vanilla extract
3 oz fresh strawberries
2 oz toasted hazelnuts

Directions and Total Time: 10 minutes

In a bowl, add avocado pulp, coconut cream, lemon zest and juice, and half of the vanilla extract. Mix with an immersion blender. Put the strawberries and remaining vanilla in another bowl and use a fork to mash the fruits. In a tall glass, alternate layering the cream and strawberry mixtures. Drop a few hazelnuts on each and serve the dessert immediately.

Avocado Truffles with Chocolate Coating

Ingredients for 6 servings

1 ripe avocado, pitted
½ tsp vanilla extract
½ tsp lemon zest
5 oz dairy-free dark chocolate
1 tbsp coconut oil
1 tbsp unsweetened cocoa powder

Directions and Total Time: 5 minutes

Scoop the pulp of the avocado into a bowl and mix with the vanilla using an immersion blender. Stir in the lemon zest and a pinch of salt. Pour the chocolate and coconut oil into a safe microwave bowl and melt in the microwave for 1 minute. Add to the avocado mixture and stir. Allow cooling to firm up a bit. Form balls out of the mix. Roll each ball in the cocoa powder and serve immediately.

Vanilla Berry Tarts

Ingredients for 4 servings

4 tbsp flaxseed powder
1/3 cup whole-wheat flour
½ tsp salt

¼ cup plant butter, crumbled
3 tbsp pure malt syrup
6 oz cashew cream

6 tbsp pure date sugar
¾ tsp vanilla extract
1 cup mixed frozen berries

Directions and Total Time: 35 minutes + cooling time

Preheat oven to 350 F and grease mini pie pans with cooking spray. In a bowl, mix flaxseed powder with 12 tbsp water and allow soaking for 5 minutes. In a large bowl, combine flour and salt. Add in butter and whisk until crumbly. Pour in the vegan "flax egg" and malt syrup and mix until smooth dough forms. Flatten the dough on a flat surface, cover with plastic wrap, and refrigerate for 1 hour.

Dust a working surface with some flour, remove the dough onto the surface, and using a rolling pin, flatten the dough into a 1-inch diameter circle. Use a large cookie cutter, cut out rounds of the dough and fit into the pie pans. Use a knife to trim the edges of the pan. Lay a parchment paper on the dough cups, pour on some baking beans, and bake in the oven until golden brown, 15-20 minutes. Remove the pans from the oven, pour out the baking beans, and allow cooling. In a bowl, mix cashew cream, date sugar, and vanilla extract. Divide the mixture into the tart cups and top with berries. Serve.

Chocolate Fudge with Nuts

Ingredients for 4 servings

3 cups chocolate chips
¼ cup thick coconut milk

1 ½ tsp vanilla extract
A pinch salt

1 cup chopped mixed nuts

Directions and Total Time: 10 minutes + cooling time

Line a square pan with baking paper. Melt the chocolate chips, coconut milk, and vanilla in a medium pot over low heat. Mix in the salt and nuts until well distributed and pour the mixture into the square pan. Refrigerate for at least 2 hours. Remove from the fridge, cut into squares, and serve.

Chocolate & Peanut Butter Cookies

Ingredients for 4 servings

1 tbsp flaxseed powder
1 cup pure date sugar + for dusting
½ cup vega butter, softened

½ cup creamy peanut butter
1 tsp vanilla extract
1 ¾ cup whole-wheat flour

1 tsp baking soda
¼ tsp salt
¼ cup unsweetened chocolate chips

Directions and Total Time: 15 minutes + cooling time

In a small bowl, mix the flaxseed powder with 3 tbsp water and allow thicken for 5 minutes to make the vegan "flax egg." In a medium bowl, whisk the date sugar, plant butter, and peanut butter until light and fluffy. Mix in the flax egg and vanilla until combined. Add in flour, baking soda, salt, and whisk well again. Fold in chocolate chips, cover the bowl with a plastic wrap, and refrigerate for 1 hour.

Preheat oven to 375 F and line a baking sheet with parchment paper. Use a cookie sheet to scoop mounds of the batter onto the sheet with 1-inch intervals. Bake for 10 minutes. Remove the cookies from the oven, cool for 3 minutes, roll in some date sugar, and serve.

Mixed Berry Yogurt Ice Pops

Ingredients for 6 servings

2/3 cup avocado, halved and pitted
2/3 cup frozen berries, thawed

1 cup dairy-free yogurt
½ cup coconut cream

1 tsp vanilla extract

Directions and Total Time: 5 minutes + chilling time

Pour the avocado pulp, berries, dairy-free yogurt, coconut cream, and vanilla extract. Process until smooth. Pour into ice pop sleeves and freeze for 8 or more hours. Enjoy the ice pops when ready.

Holiday Pecan Tart

Ingredients for 4 servings

- 4 tbsp flaxseed powder
- 1/3 cup whole-wheat flour
- ½ tsp salt
- ¼ cup cold plant butter, crumbled
- 3 tbsp pure malt syrup

For the filling:

- 3 tbsp flaxseed powder + 9 tbsp water
- 2 cups toasted pecans, chopped
- 1 cup light corn syrup
- ½ cup pure date sugar
- 1 tbsp pure pomegranate molasses
- 4 tbsp plant butter, melted
- ½ tsp salt
- 2 tsp vanilla extract

Directions and Total Time: 50 minutes + cooling time

Preheat oven to 350 F. In a bowl, mix the flaxseed powder with 12 tbsp water and allow thicken for 5 minutes. Do this for the filling's vegan "flax egg" too in a separate bowl. In a bowl, combine flour and salt. Add in plant butter and whisk until crumbly. Pour in the crust's vegan "flax egg" and maple syrup and mix until smooth dough forms. Flatten the dough on a flat surface, cover with plastic wrap, and refrigerate for 1 hour. Dust a working surface with flour, remove the dough onto the surface, and using a rolling pin, flatten the dough into a 1-inch diameter circle. Lay the dough on a greased pie pan and press to fit the shape of the pan. Trim the edges of the pan. Lay a parchment paper on the dough, pour on some baking beans and bake for 20 minutes. Remove, pour out baking beans, and allow cooling.

In a bowl, mix the filling's vegan "flax egg," pecans, corn syrup, date sugar, pomegranate molasses, plant butter, salt, and vanilla. Pour and spread the mixture on the piecrust. Bake for 20 minutes or until the filling sets. Remove from the oven, decorate with more pecans, slice, and cool. Slice and serve.

Coconut Chocolate Barks

Ingredients for 4 servings

- 1/3 cup coconut oil, melted
- ¼ cup almond butter, melted
- 2 tbsp unsweetened coconut flakes.
- 1 tsp pure maple syrup
- A pinch ground rock salt
- ¼ cup unsweetened cocoa nibs

Directions and Total Time: 35 minutes

Line a baking tray with baking paper and set aside. In a medium bowl, mix the coconut oil, almond butter, coconut flakes, maple syrup, and fold in the rock salt and cocoa nibs. Pour and spread the mixture on the baking sheet, chill in the refrigerator for 20 minutes or until firm. Remove the dessert, break into shards, and enjoy. Preserve extras in the refrigerator.

Nutty Date Cake

Ingredients for 4 servings

- ½ cup cold plant butter, cut in pieces
- 1 tbsp flaxseed powder
- ½ cup whole-wheat flour
- ¼ cup chopped pecans and walnuts
- 1 tsp baking powder
- 1 tsp baking soda
- 1 tsp cinnamon powder
- 1 tsp salt
- 1/3 cup pitted dates, chopped
- ½ cup pure date sugar
- 1 tsp vanilla extract
- ¼ cup pure date syrup for drizzling.

Directions and Total Time: 1 hour 30 minutes

Preheat oven to 350 F and lightly grease a baking dish with some plant butter. In a small bowl, mix the flaxseed powder with 3 tbsp water and allow thicken for 5 minutes to make the vegan "flax egg."

In a food processor, add the flour, nuts, baking powder, baking soda, cinnamon powder, and salt. Blend until well combined. Add 1/3 cup of water, dates, date sugar, and vanilla. Process until smooth with tiny pieces of dates evident.

Pour the batter into the baking dish and bake in the oven for 1 hour and 10 minutes or until a toothpick inserted comes out clean. Remove the dish from the oven, invert the cake onto a serving platter to cool, drizzle with the date syrup, slice, and serve.

Berry Cupcakes with Cashew Cheese Icing

Ingredients for 4 servings

- 2 cups whole-wheat flour
- ¼ cup cornstarch
- 2 ½ tsp baking powder
- 1 ½ cups pure date sugar
- ½ tsp salt
- ¾ cup plant butter, softened
- 3 tsp vanilla extract
- 1 cup strawberries, pureed
- 1 cup oat milk, room temperature
- ¾ cup cashew cream
- 2 tbsp coconut oil, melted
- 3 tbsp pure maple syrup
- 1 tsp vanilla extract
- 1 tsp freshly squeezed lemon juice

Directions and Total Time: 35 minutes + cooling time

Preheat the oven to 350 F and line a 12-holed muffin tray with cupcake liners. Set aside.

In a bowl, mix flour, cornstarch, baking powder, date sugar, and salt. Whisk in plant butter, vanilla extract, strawberries, and oat milk until well combined. Divide the mixture into the muffin cups two-thirds way up and bake for 20-25 minutes. Allow cooling while you make the frosting.

In a blender, add cashew cream, coconut oil, maple syrup, vanilla, and lemon juice. Process until smooth. Pour the frosting into a medium bowl and chill for 30 minutes. Transfer the mixture into a piping bag and swirl mounds of the frosting onto the cupcakes. Serve immediately.

Coconut & Chocolate Cake

Ingredients for 4 servings

2/3 cup toasted almond flour
¼ cup unsalted plant butter, melted

2 cups chocolate bars, cubed
2 ½ cups coconut cream

Fresh berries for topping

Directions and Total Time: 40 minutes + cooling time

Lightly grease a 9-inch springform pan with some plant butter and set aside.

Mix the almond flour and plant butter in a medium bowl and pour the mixture into the springform pan. Use the spoon to spread and press the mixture into the bottom of the pan. Place in the refrigerator to firm for 30 minutes.

Meanwhile, pour the chocolate in a safe microwave bowl and melt for 1 minute stirring every 30 seconds. Remove from the microwave and mix in the coconut cream and maple syrup.

Remove the cake pan from the oven, pour the chocolate mixture on top, and shake the pan and even the layer. Chill further for 4 to 6 hours. Take out the pan from the fridge, release the cake and garnish with the raspberries or strawberries. Slice and serve.

Berry Macedonia with Mint

Ingredients for 4 servings

¼ cup lemon juice
4 tsp agave syrup

2 cups chopped pears
2 cups chopped strawberries

3 cups mixed berries
8 fresh mint leaves

Directions and Total Time: 20 minutes

Chop half of the mint leaves; reserve.

In a large bowl, combine together pears, strawberries, raspberries, blackberries, and half of the mint leaves. Divide the Macedonia salad between 4 small cups. Top with lemon juice, agave syrup, and mint leaves and serve chilled.

Cinnamon Pumpkin Pie

Ingredients for 4 servings

For the piecrust:

4 tbsp flaxseed powder
1/3 cup whole-wheat flour

½ tsp salt
¼ cup cold plant butter, crumbled

3 tbsp pure malt syrup

For the filling:

2 tbsp flaxseed powder + 6 tbsp water
4 tbsp plant butter
¼ cup pure maple syrup

¼ cup pure date sugar
1 tsp cinnamon powder
½ tsp ginger powder

1/8 tsp cloves powder
1 (15 oz) can pumpkin purée
1 cup almond milk

Directions and Total Time: 1 hr 10 min + cooling time

Preheat oven to 350 F. In a bowl, mix flaxseed powder with 12 tbsp water and allow thicken for 5 minutes. Do this for the filling's vegan "flax egg" too in another bowl. In a bowl, combine flour and salt. Add in plant butter and whisk until crumbly. Pour in crust's vegan "flax egg," maple syrup, vanilla, and mix until smooth dough forms. Flatten, cover with plastic wrap, and refrigerate for 1 hour.

Dust a working surface with flour, remove the dough onto the surface and flatten it into a 1-inch diameter circle. Lay the dough on a greased pie pan and press to fit the shape of the pan. Use a knife to trim the edges of the pan. Lay a parchment paper on the dough, pour on some baking beans and bake for 15-20 minutes. Remove, pour out the baking beans, and allow cooling. In a bowl, whisk filling's flaxseed, butter, maple syrup, date sugar, cinnamon powder, ginger powder, cloves powder, pumpkin puree, and almond milk. Pour the mixture onto the piecrust and bake for 35-40 minutes.

Party Matcha & Hazelnut Cheesecake

Ingredients for 4 servings

2/3 cup toasted rolled oats
¼ cup plant butter, melted
3 tbsp pure date sugar

6 oz cashew cream cheese
¼ cup almond milk
1 tbsp matcha powder

¼ cup just-boiled water
3 tsp agar agar powder
2 tbsp toasted hazelnuts, chopped

Directions and Total Time: 20 minutes + cooling time

Process the oats, butter, and date sugar in a blender until smooth.

Pour the mixture into a greased 9-inch springform pan and press the mixture onto the bottom of the pan. Refrigerate for 30 minutes until firm while you make the filling.

In a large bowl, using an electric mixer, whisk the cashew cream cheese until smooth. Beat in the almond milk and mix in the matcha powder until smooth.

Mix the boiled water and agar agar until dissolved and whisk this mixture into the creamy mix. Fold in the hazelnuts until well distributed. Remove the cake pan from the fridge and pour in the cream mixture. Shake the pan to ensure a smooth layering on top. Refrigerate further for at least 3 hours. Take out the cake pan, release the cake, slice, and serve.

Pistachios & Chocolate Popsicles

Ingredients for 4 servings

½ cup chocolate chips, melted
1 ½ cups oat milk

1 tbsp unsweetened cocoa powder
3 tbsp pure date syrup

1 tsp vanilla extract
A handful pistachios, chopped

Directions and Total Time: 5 minutes + cooling time

In a blender, add chocolate, oat milk, cocoa powder, date syrup, vanilla, pistachios, and process until smooth. Divide the mixture into popsicle molds and freeze for 3 hours. Dip the popsicle molds in warm water to loosen the popsicles and pull out the popsicles.

Oatmeal Cookies with Hazelnuts

Ingredients for 2 servings

1 ½ cups whole-grain flour
1 tsp baking powder
⅛ tsp salt
1 tsp ground cinnamon

¼ tsp ground nutmeg
1 ½ cups old-fashioned oats
1 cup chopped hazelnuts
½ cup plant butter, melted

½ cup pure maple syrup
¼ cup pure date sugar
2 tsp pure vanilla extract

Directions and Total Time: 15 minutes

Preheat oven to 360 F.

Combine the flour, baking powder, salt, cinnamon, and nutmeg in a bowl. Add in oats and hazelnuts. In another bowl, whisk the butter, maple syrup, sugar, and vanilla. Pour over the flour mixture. Mix well. Spoon a small ball of cookie dough on a baking sheet and press down with a fork. Bake for 10-12 minutes, until browned. Let completely cool on a rack.

Coconut Chocolate Truffles

Ingredients for 12 truffles

1 cup raw cashews, soaked overnight
¾ cup pitted cherries

2 tbsp coconut oil
1 cup shredded coconut

2 tbsp cocoa powder

Directions and Total Time: 1 hour 15 minutes

Line a baking sheet with parchment paper and set aside.

Blend cashews, cherries, coconut oil, half of the shredded coconut, and cocoa powder in a food processor until ingredients are evenly mixed. Spread the remaining shredded coconut on a dish. Mold the mixture into 12 truffle shapes. Roll the truffles in the coconut dish, shaking off any excess, then arrange on the prepared baking sheet. Refrigerate for 1 hour.

Layered Raspberry & Tofu Cups

Ingredients for 4 servings

½ cup unsalted raw cashews
3 tbsp pure date sugar
½ cup soy milk

¾ cup firm silken tofu, drained
1 tsp vanilla extract
2 cups sliced raspberries

1 tsp fresh lemon juice
Fresh mint leaves

Directions and Total Time: 60 minutes

Grind the cashews and 3 tbsp of date sugar in a blender until a fine powder is obtained. Pour in soy milk and blend smooth. Add in tofu and vanilla and pulse until creamy. Remove to a bowl and refrigerate covered for 30 minutes.

In a bowl, mix the raspberries, lemon juice, and remaining date sugar. Let sit for 20 minutes. Assemble by alternating in small cups, one layer of raspberries and one layer of cashew cream, ending with the cashew cream. Serve garnished with mint leaves.

Cashew & Cranberry Truffles

Ingredients for 4 servings

2 cups fresh cranberries
2 tbsp pure date syrup
1 tsp vanilla extract
16 oz cashew cream
4 tbsp plant butter
3 tbsp unsweetened cocoa powder
2 tbsp pure date sugar

Directions and Total Time: 15 minutes

Set a silicone egg tray aside. Puree the cranberries, date syrup, and vanilla in a blender until smooth.

Add the cashew cream and plant butter to a medium pot. Heat over medium heat until the mixture is well combined. Turn the heat off. Mix in the cranberry mixture and divide the mixture into the muffin holes. Refrigerate for 40 minutes or until firm. Remove the tray and pop out the truffles.

Meanwhile, mix the cocoa powder and date sugar on a plate. Roll the truffles in the mixture until well dusted and serve.

Coconut Peach Tart

Ingredients for 8 servings

½ cup rolled oats
1 cup cashews
1 cup soft pitted dates
1 cup canned coconut milk
2 large peaches, chopped
½ cup shredded coconut

Directions and Total Time: 10 minutes

In a food processor, pulse the oats, cashews, and dates until a dough-like mixture forms. Press down into a greased baking pan.

Pulse the coconut milk, ½ cup water, peaches, and shredded coconut in the food processor until smooth. Pour this mixture over the crust and spread evenly. Freeze for 30 minutes. Soften 15 minutes before serving. Top with whipped coconut cream and shredded coconut.

Mango Muffins with Chocolate Chips

Ingredients for 12 servings

2 medium mangoes, chopped
1 cup non-dairy milk
2 tbsp almond butter
1 tsp apple cider vinegar
1 tsp pure vanilla extract
1 ¼ cups whole-wheat flour
½ cup rolled oats
¼ cup coconut sugar
1 tsp baking powder
½ tsp baking soda
½ cup unsweetened cocoa powder
¼ cup sesame seeds
A pinch of salt
¼ cup dark chocolate chips

Directions and Total Time: 40 minutes

Preheat oven to 360 F.

In a food processor, put the mangoes, milk, almond butter, vinegar, and vanilla. Blend until smooth.

In a bowl, combine the flour, oats, sugar, baking powder, baking soda, cocoa powder, sesame seeds, salt, and chocolate chips. Pour into the mango mixture and mix. Scoop into greased muffin cups and bake for 20-25 minutes. Let cool completely before removing from the cups.

Easy Maple Rice Pudding

Ingredients for 4 servings

1 cup short-grain brown rice
1 ¾ cups non-dairy milk
4 tbsp pure maple syrup
1 tsp vanilla extract
A pinch of salt
¼ cup dates, pitted and chopped

Directions and Total Time: 30 minutes

In a pot over medium heat, place the rice, milk, 1 ½ cups water, maple, vanilla, and salt. Bring to a boil, then reduce the heat. Cook for 20 minutes, stirring occasionally. Mix in dates and cook another 5 minutes. Serve chilled in cups.

...with Poppy Seeds

(partial - top of recipe obscured)

1 tsp pure vanilla extract
2 tbsp pure maple syrup
2 cups whole-grain flour
¾ cup poppy seeds, lightly toasted

...5 minutes

...bowl until creamy and fluffy. Add in vanilla, and maple syrup, blend. Stir in flour and poppy ...gn in a cylinder and cover it with plastic foil. Let chill in the fridge.

...ven to 330 F. Cut the dough into thin circles and arrange on a baking sheet. Bake for 12 minutes, until light brown. ...completely cool before serving.

Kiwi & Peanut Bars

Ingredients for 9 servings

2 kiwis, mashed
1 tbsp maple syrup
½ tsp vanilla extract
2 cups old-fashioned rolled oats
½ tsp salt
¼ cup chopped peanuts

Directions and Total Time: 5 minutes

Preheat oven to 360 F.

In a bowl, add kiwi, maple syrup, and vanilla and stir. Mix in oats, salt, and peanuts. Pour into a greased baking dish and bake for 25-30 minutes, until crisp. Let completely cool and slice into bars to serve.

Tropical Cheesecake

Ingredients for 4 servings

2/3 cup toasted rolled oats
¼ cup plant butter, melted
3 tbsp pure date sugar
6 oz cashew cream cheese
¼ cup coconut milk
1 lemon, zested and juiced
¼ cup just-boiled water
3 tsp agar agar powder
1 ripe mango, chopped

Directions and Total Time: 20 minutes + cooling time

Process the oats, butter, and date sugar in a blender until smooth.

Pour the mixture into a greased 9-inch springform pan and press the mixture onto the bottom of the pan. Refrigerate for 30 minutes until firm while you make the filling.

In a large bowl, using an electric mixer, whisk the cashew cream cheese until smooth. Beat in the coconut milk, lemon zest, and lemon juice. Mix the boiled water and agar agar powder until dissolved and whisk this mixture into the creamy mix. Fold in the mango.

Remove the cake pan from the fridge and pour in the mango mixture. Shake the pan to ensure a smooth layering on top. Refrigerate further for at least 3 hours. Remove the cheesecake from the fridge, release the cake pan, slice, and serve.

Raisin Oatmeal Biscuits

Ingredients for 8 servings

½ cup plant butter
1 cup date sugar
¼ cup pineapple juice
1 cup whole-grain flour
1 tsp baking powder
½ tsp salt
1 tsp pure vanilla extract
1 cup old-fashioned oats
½ cup vegan chocolate chips
½ cup raisins

Directions and Total Time: 20 minutes

Preheat oven to 370 F. Beat the butter and sugar in a bowl until creamy and fluffy. Pour in the juice and blend. Mix in flour, baking powder, salt, and vanilla. Stir in oats, chocolate chips, and raisins. Spread the dough on a baking sheet and bake for 15 minutes. Let completely cool on a rack.

Coconut & Chocolate Brownies

Ingredients for 4 servings

1 cup whole-grain flour
½ cup unsweetened cocoa powder
1 tsp baking powder
½ tsp salt
1 cup pure date sugar
½ cup canola oil
¾ cup almond milk
1 tsp pure vanilla extract
1 tsp coconut extract
½ cup vegan chocolate chips
½ cup sweetened shredded coconut

Directions and Total Time: 40 minutes

Preheat oven to 360 F. In a bowl, combine the flour, cocoa, baking powder, and salt.

In another bowl, whisk the date sugar and oil until creamy. Add in almond milk, vanilla, and coconut e smooth. Pour into the flour mixture and stir to combine. Fold in the coconut and chocolate chips. Pour t greased baking pan and bake for 35-40 minutes. Let cool before serving.

Cashew & Plum Cheesecake

Ingredients for 4 servings

2/3 cup toasted rolled oats
¼ cup plant butter, melted
3 tbsp pure date sugar

6 oz cashew cream cheese
¼ cup oats milk
¼ cup just-boiled water

3 tsp agar agar powder
4 plums, cored and finely diced
2 tbsp toasted cashew, chopped

Directions and Total Time: 20 minutes + cooling time

Process the oats, butter, and date sugar in a blender until smooth. Pour the mixture into a greased 9-inch springform pan and press the mixture onto the bottom of the pan. Refrigerate for 30 minutes until firm while you make the filling.

In a large bowl, using an electric mixer, whisk the cashew cream cheese until smooth. Beat in the oats milk. Mix the boiled water and agar agar powder until dissolved and whisk this mixture into the creamy mix. Fold in the plums.

Remove the cake pan from the fridge and pour it in the plum mixture. Shake the pan to ensure a smooth layering on top. Refrigerate for at least 3 hours. Take out the cake pan, release the cake, and garnish with the cashew nuts. Serve sliced.

Peanut Chocolate Brownies

Ingredients for 12 servings

1 ¾ cups whole-grain flour
1 tsp baking powder
½ tsp salt
1 tbsp ground nutmeg

½ tsp ground cinnamon
3 tbsp unsweetened cocoa powder
½ cup vegan chocolate chips
½ cup chopped peanuts

¼ cup canola oil
½ cup dark molasses ½ cup water
⅓ cup pure date sugar
2 tsp grated fresh ginger

Directions and Total Time: 40 minutes

Preheat oven to 360 F.

Combine the flour, baking powder, salt, nutmeg, cinnamon, and cocoa in a bowl. Add in chocolate chips and peanuts and stir. Set aside. In another bowl, mix the oil, molasses, water, sugar, and ginger. Pour into the flour mixture and stir to combine. Transfer to a greased baking pan and bake for 30-35 minutes. Let cool before slicing.

Chocolate Campanelle with Hazelnuts

Ingredients for 4 servings

½ cup chopped toasted hazelnuts
¼ cup vegan chocolate pieces

8 oz campanelle pasta
3 tbsp vegan margarine

¼ cup maple syrup

Directions and Total Time: 10 minutes

Pulse the hazelnuts and chocolate pieces in a food processor until crumbly. Set aside.

Place the campanelle pasta in a pot with boiling salted water. Cook for 8-10 minutes until al dente, stirring often. Drain and back to the pot. Stir in almond butter and syrup and stir until the butter is melted. Remove to a plate and serve garnished with the chocolate-hazelnut mixture.

Poppy-Granola Balls with Chocolate

Ingredients for 8 servings

½ cup granola
¼ cup pure date sugar
½ cup golden raisins

½ cup shelled sunflower seeds
¼ cup poppy seeds
1 ½ cups creamy almond butter

2 cups vegan chocolate chips

Directions and Total Time: 25 minutes

Blend the granola, sugar, raisins, sunflower seeds, and poppy seeds in a food processor. Stir in the almond butter and pulse until a smooth dough is formed. Leave in the fridge overnight. Shape small balls out of the mixture. Set aside.

Melt the chocolate in the microwave oven. Dip the balls into the melted chocolate and place on a baking sheet. Chill in the fridge for 30 minutes, until firm. Serve.

2 dates, pitted and chopped
1 tbsp chia seeds

...e zest, coconut milk, dates, and chia seeds. Blitz until smooth. Transfer to a bowl
...p with berries, whipped cream, or toasted coconut and serve.

...colate Granita

_ tbsp fresh mint, minced
¼ cup non-dairy milk
3 tbsp non-dairy chocolate chips
2 tbsp goji berries

Directions and Total Time: 5 minutes

In a food processor, place the almond butter, pear, and mint. Pulse until smooth. Pour in milk, while keep blending. Add in chocolate chips and berries. Transfer to a glass and serve.

Maple Fruit Crumble

Ingredients for 4 servings

3 cups chopped apricots
3 cups chopped mangoes
4 tbsp pure maple syrup
1 cup gluten-free rolled oats
½ cup shredded coconut
2 tbsp coconut oil

Directions and Total Time: 25 minutes

Preheat oven to 360 F.

Place the apricots, mangoes, and 2 tbsp of maple syrup in a round baking dish.

In a food processor, put the oats, coconut, coconut oil, and remaining maple syrup. Blend until combined. Pour over the fruit. Bake for 20-25 minutes. Allow cooling before slicing and serving.

Sherry-Lime Mango Dessert

Ingredients for 4 servings

3 ripe mangoes, cubed
⅓ cup pure date sugar
2 tbsp fresh lime juice
½ cup Sherry wine
Fresh mint sprigs

Directions and Total Time: 15 minutes

Arrange the mango cubes on a baking sheet. Sprinkle with some date and let sit covered for 30 minutes. Sprinkle with lime juice and sherry wine. Refrigerate covered for 1 hour. Remove from the fridge and let sit for a few minutes at room temperature. Serve in glasses topped with mint.

Almond & Chia Bites with Cherries

Ingredients for 2 servings

1 cup cherries, pitted
1 cup shredded coconut
¼ cup chia seeds
¾ cup ground almonds
¼ cup cocoa nibs

Directions and Total Time: 20 minutes

Blend cherries, coconut, chia seeds, almonds, and cocoa nibs in a food processor until crumbly. Shape the mixture into 24 balls and arrange on a lined baking sheet. Let sit in the fridge for 15 minutes.

Glazed Chili Chocolate Cake

Ingredients for 4 servings

1 ¾ cups whole-grain flour
1 cup pure date sugar
¼ cup unsweetened cocoa powder
1 tsp baking soda
½ tsp baking powder
1 ½ tsp ground cinnamon
¼ tsp ground chili
⅓ cup olive oil
1 tbsp apple cider vinegar
1 ½ tsp pure vanilla extract
2 (1-oz) squares vegan chocolate
¼ cup soy milk
½ cup pure date sugar
3 tbsp plant butter
½ tsp pure vanilla extract

Directions and Total Time: 60 minutes

Grind the cashews and 3 tbsp of date sugar in a blender until a fine powder is obtained. Pour in soy milk and blitz until smooth. Add in tofu and vanilla and pulse until creamy. Remove to a bowl and refrigerate covered for 30 minutes.

In a bowl, mix the raspberries, lemon juice, and remaining date sugar. Let sit for 20 minutes. Assemble by alternating into small cups, one layer of raspberries and one layer of cashew cream, ending with the cashew cream. Serve garnished with mint leaves.

Cashew & Cranberry Truffles

Ingredients for 4 servings

2 cups fresh cranberries
2 tbsp pure date syrup
1 tsp vanilla extract
16 oz cashew cream
4 tbsp plant butter
3 tbsp unsweetened cocoa powder
2 tbsp pure date sugar

Directions and Total Time: 15 minutes

Set a silicone egg tray aside. Puree the cranberries, date syrup, and vanilla in a blender until smooth.

Add the cashew cream and plant butter to a medium pot. Heat over medium heat until the mixture is well combined. Turn the heat off. Mix in the cranberry mixture and divide the mixture into the muffin holes. Refrigerate for 40 minutes or until firm. Remove the tray and pop out the truffles.

Meanwhile, mix the cocoa powder and date sugar on a plate. Roll the truffles in the mixture until well dusted and serve.

Coconut Peach Tart

Ingredients for 8 servings

½ cup rolled oats
1 cup cashews
1 cup soft pitted dates
1 cup canned coconut milk
2 large peaches, chopped
½ cup shredded coconut

Directions and Total Time: 10 minutes

In a food processor, pulse the oats, cashews, and dates until a dough-like mixture forms. Press down into a greased baking pan.

Pulse the coconut milk, ½ cup water, peaches, and shredded coconut in the food processor until smooth. Pour this mixture over the crust and spread evenly. Freeze for 30 minutes. Soften 15 minutes before serving. Top with whipped coconut cream and shredded coconut.

Mango Muffins with Chocolate Chips

Ingredients for 12 servings

2 medium mangoes, chopped
1 cup non-dairy milk
2 tbsp almond butter
1 tsp apple cider vinegar
1 tsp pure vanilla extract
1 ¼ cups whole-wheat flour
½ cup rolled oats
¼ cup coconut sugar
1 tsp baking powder
½ tsp baking soda
½ cup unsweetened cocoa powder
¼ cup sesame seeds
A pinch of salt
¼ cup dark chocolate chips

Directions and Total Time: 40 minutes

Preheat oven to 360 F.

In a food processor, put the mangoes, milk, almond butter, vinegar, and vanilla. Blend until smooth.

In a bowl, combine the flour, oats, sugar, baking powder, baking soda, cocoa powder, sesame seeds, salt, and chocolate chips. Pour into the mango mixture and mix. Scoop into greased muffin cups and bake for 20-25 minutes. Let cool completely before removing from the cups.

Easy Maple Rice Pudding

Ingredients for 4 servings

1 cup short-grain brown rice
1 ¾ cups non-dairy milk
4 tbsp pure maple syrup
1 tsp vanilla extract
A pinch of salt
¼ cup dates, pitted and chopped

Directions and Total Time: 30 minutes

In a pot over medium heat, place the rice, milk, 1 ½ cups water, maple, vanilla, and salt. Bring to a boil, then reduce the heat. Cook for 20 minutes, stirring occasionally. Mix in dates and cook another 5 minutes. Serve chilled in cups.

Vanilla Cookies with Poppy Seeds

Ingredients for 3 servings

¾ cup plant butter, softened
½ cup pure date sugar

1 tsp pure vanilla extract
2 tbsp pure maple syrup

2 cups whole-grain flour
¾ cup poppy seeds, lightly toasted

Directions and Total Time: 15 minutes

Beat the butter and sugar in a bowl until creamy and fluffy. Add in vanilla, and maple syrup, blend. Stir in flour and poppy seeds. Wrap the dough in a cylinder and cover it with plastic foil. Let chill in the fridge.

Preheat oven to 330 F. Cut the dough into thin circles and arrange on a baking sheet. Bake for 12 minutes, until light brown. Let completely cool before serving.

Kiwi & Peanut Bars

Ingredients for 9 servings

2 kiwis, mashed
1 tbsp maple syrup

½ tsp vanilla extract
2 cups old-fashioned rolled oats

½ tsp salt
¼ cup chopped peanuts

Directions and Total Time: 5 minutes

Preheat oven to 360 F.

In a bowl, add kiwi, maple syrup, and vanilla and stir. Mix in oats, salt, and peanuts. Pour into a greased baking dish and bake for 25-30 minutes, until crisp. Let completely cool and slice into bars to serve.

Tropical Cheesecake

Ingredients for 4 servings

2/3 cup toasted rolled oats
¼ cup plant butter, melted
3 tbsp pure date sugar

6 oz cashew cream cheese
¼ cup coconut milk
1 lemon, zested and juiced

¼ cup just-boiled water
3 tsp agar agar powder
1 ripe mango, chopped

Directions and Total Time: 20 minutes + cooling time

Process the oats, butter, and date sugar in a blender until smooth.

Pour the mixture into a greased 9-inch springform pan and press the mixture onto the bottom of the pan. Refrigerate for 30 minutes until firm while you make the filling.

In a large bowl, using an electric mixer, whisk the cashew cream cheese until smooth. Beat in the coconut milk, lemon zest, and lemon juice. Mix the boiled water and agar agar powder until dissolved and whisk this mixture into the creamy mix. Fold in the mango.

Remove the cake pan from the fridge and pour in the mango mixture. Shake the pan to ensure a smooth layering on top. Refrigerate further for at least 3 hours. Remove the cheesecake from the fridge, release the cake pan, slice, and serve.

Raisin Oatmeal Biscuits

Ingredients for 8 servings

½ cup plant butter
1 cup date sugar
¼ cup pineapple juice
1 cup whole-grain flour

1 tsp baking powder
½ tsp salt
1 tsp pure vanilla extract
1 cup old-fashioned oats

½ cup vegan chocolate chips
½ cup raisins

Directions and Total Time: 20 minutes

Preheat oven to 370 F. Beat the butter and sugar in a bowl until creamy and fluffy. Pour in the juice and blend. Mix in flour, baking powder, salt, and vanilla. Stir in oats, chocolate chips, and raisins. Spread the dough on a baking sheet and bake for 15 minutes. Let completely cool on a rack.

Coconut & Chocolate Brownies

Ingredients for 4 servings

1 cup whole-grain flour
½ cup unsweetened cocoa powder
1 tsp baking powder
½ tsp salt

1 cup pure date sugar
½ cup canola oil
¾ cup almond milk
1 tsp pure vanilla extract

1 tsp coconut extract
½ cup vegan chocolate chips
½ cup sweetened shredded coconut

Directions and Total Time: 40 minutes

Preheat oven to 360 F. In a bowl, combine the flour, cocoa, baking powder, and salt.

In another bowl, whisk the date sugar and oil until creamy. Add in almond milk, vanilla, and coconut extracts. Mix until smooth. Pour into the flour mixture and stir to combine. Fold in the coconut and chocolate chips. Pour the batter into a greased baking pan and bake for 35-40 minutes. Let cool before serving.

Cashew & Plum Cheesecake

Ingredients for 4 servings

2/3 cup toasted rolled oats	6 oz cashew cream cheese	3 tsp agar agar powder
¼ cup plant butter, melted	¼ cup oats milk	4 plums, cored and finely diced
3 tbsp pure date sugar	¼ cup just-boiled water	2 tbsp toasted cashew, chopped

Directions and Total Time: 20 minutes + cooling time

Process the oats, butter, and date sugar in a blender until smooth. Pour the mixture into a greased 9-inch springform pan and press the mixture onto the bottom of the pan. Refrigerate for 30 minutes until firm while you make the filling.

In a large bowl, using an electric mixer, whisk the cashew cream cheese until smooth. Beat in the oats milk. Mix the boiled water and agar agar powder until dissolved and whisk this mixture into the creamy mix. Fold in the plums.

Remove the cake pan from the fridge and pour it in the plum mixture. Shake the pan to ensure a smooth layering on top. Refrigerate for at least 3 hours. Take out the cake pan, release the cake, and garnish with the cashew nuts. Serve sliced.

Peanut Chocolate Brownies

Ingredients for 12 servings

1 ¾ cups whole-grain flour	½ tsp ground cinnamon	¼ cup canola oil
1 tsp baking powder	3 tbsp unsweetened cocoa powder	½ cup dark molasses ½ cup water
½ tsp salt	½ cup vegan chocolate chips	⅓ cup pure date sugar
1 tbsp ground nutmeg	½ cup chopped peanuts	2 tsp grated fresh ginger

Directions and Total Time: 40 minutes

Preheat oven to 360 F.

Combine the flour, baking powder, salt, nutmeg, cinnamon, and cocoa in a bowl. Add in chocolate chips and peanuts and stir. Set aside. In another bowl, mix the oil, molasses, water, sugar, and ginger. Pour into the flour mixture and stir to combine. Transfer to a greased baking pan and bake for 30-35 minutes. Let cool before slicing.

Chocolate Campanelle with Hazelnuts

Ingredients for 4 servings

½ cup chopped toasted hazelnuts	8 oz campanelle pasta	¼ cup maple syrup
¼ cup vegan chocolate pieces	3 tbsp vegan margarine	

Directions and Total Time: 10 minutes

Pulse the hazelnuts and chocolate pieces in a food processor until crumbly. Set aside.

Place the campanelle pasta in a pot with boiling salted water. Cook for 8-10 minutes until al dente, stirring often. Drain and back to the pot. Stir in almond butter and syrup and stir until the butter is melted. Remove to a plate and serve garnished with the chocolate-hazelnut mixture.

Poppy-Granola Balls with Chocolate

Ingredients for 8 servings

½ cup granola	½ cup shelled sunflower seeds	2 cups vegan chocolate chips
¼ cup pure date sugar	¼ cup poppy seeds	
½ cup golden raisins	1 ½ cups creamy almond butter	

Directions and Total Time: 25 minutes

Blend the granola, sugar, raisins, sunflower seeds, and poppy seeds in a food processor. Stir in the almond butter and pulse until a smooth dough is formed. Leave in the fridge overnight. Shape small balls out of the mixture. Set aside.

Melt the chocolate in the microwave oven. Dip the balls into the melted chocolate and place on a baking sheet. Chill in the fridge for 30 minutes, until firm. Serve.

Coconut Chia Pudding

Ingredients for 4 servings

Zest and juice of 1 orange
1 (14-oz) can coconut milk
2 dates, pitted and chopped
1 tbsp chia seeds

Directions and Total Time: 30 minutes

In a blender, put the orange juice, orange zest, coconut milk, dates, and chia seeds. Blitz until smooth. Transfer to a bowl and put it in the fridge for 20 minutes. Top with berries, whipped cream, or toasted coconut and serve.

Homemade Goji Berry Chocolate Granita

Ingredients for 4 servings

1 pear, chopped
1 tbsp almond butter
2 tbsp fresh mint, minced
¼ cup non-dairy milk
3 tbsp non-dairy chocolate chips
2 tbsp goji berries

Directions and Total Time: 5 minutes

In a food processor, place the almond butter, pear, and mint. Pulse until smooth. Pour in milk, while keep blending. Add in chocolate chips and berries. Transfer to a glass and serve.

Maple Fruit Crumble

Ingredients for 4 servings

3 cups chopped apricots
3 cups chopped mangoes
4 tbsp pure maple syrup
1 cup gluten-free rolled oats
½ cup shredded coconut
2 tbsp coconut oil

Directions and Total Time: 25 minutes

Preheat oven to 360 F.

Place the apricots, mangoes, and 2 tbsp of maple syrup in a round baking dish.

In a food processor, put the oats, coconut, coconut oil, and remaining maple syrup. Blend until combined. Pour over the fruit. Bake for 20-25 minutes. Allow cooling before slicing and serving.

Sherry-Lime Mango Dessert

Ingredients for 4 servings

3 ripe mangoes, cubed
⅓ cup pure date sugar
2 tbsp fresh lime juice
½ cup Sherry wine
Fresh mint sprigs

Directions and Total Time: 15 minutes

Arrange the mango cubes on a baking sheet. Sprinkle with some date and let sit covered for 30 minutes. Sprinkle with lime juice and sherry wine. Refrigerate covered for 1 hour. Remove from the fridge and let sit for a few minutes at room temperature. Serve in glasses topped with mint.

Almond & Chia Bites with Cherries

Ingredients for 2 servings

1 cup cherries, pitted
1 cup shredded coconut
¼ cup chia seeds
¾ cup ground almonds
¼ cup cocoa nibs

Directions and Total Time: 20 minutes

Blend cherries, coconut, chia seeds, almonds, and cocoa nibs in a food processor until crumbly. Shape the mixture into 24 balls and arrange on a lined baking sheet. Let sit in the fridge for 15 minutes.

Glazed Chili Chocolate Cake

Ingredients for 4 servings

1 ¾ cups whole-grain flour
1 cup pure date sugar
¼ cup unsweetened cocoa powder
1 tsp baking soda
½ tsp baking powder
1 ½ tsp ground cinnamon
¼ tsp ground chili
⅓ cup olive oil
1 tbsp apple cider vinegar
1 ½ tsp pure vanilla extract
2 (1-oz) squares vegan chocolate
¼ cup soy milk
½ cup pure date sugar
3 tbsp plant butter
½ tsp pure vanilla extract

Mango Chocolate Fudge

Ingredients for 3 servings

1 mango	¾ cup vegan chocolate chips	4 cups pure date sugar

Directions and Total Time: 10 minutes + chilling time

In a food processor, blend the mango until smooth.

Microwave the chocolate until melted. Add in the pureed mango and date sugar and stir to combine. Spread on a lined with waxed paper baking pan and chill in the fridge for 2 hours. Once chilled, take out the fudge and lay on a cutting board. Discard the waxed paper. Slice into small pieces and serve.

Coconut & Chocolate Macaroons

Ingredients for 4 servings

1 cup shredded coconut	1 tbsp vanilla extract	¼ cup maple syrup
2 tbsp cocoa powder	⅔ cup coconut milk	A pinch of salt

Directions and Total Time: 25 minutes

Preheat oven to 360 F.

In a pot, place the shredded coconut, cocoa powder, vanilla extract, coconut milk, maple syrup, and salt. Cook until a firm dough is formed. Shape balls out of the mixture. Arrange the balls on a lined with parchment paper baking sheet. Bake for 15 minutes. Allow cooling before serving.

Melon Chocolate Pudding

Ingredients for 4 servings

1 cup cubed melon	2 tbsp unsweetened cocoa powder	½ ripe avocado
4 tbsp non-dairy milk	2 tbsp pure date sugar	

Directions and Total Time: 25 minutes

Blitz the milk, cocoa powder, sugar, and avocado in a blender until smooth. Mash the melon with a fork in a bowl. Mix in the cocoa mixture and serve.

Sicilian Papaya Sorbet

Ingredients for 4 servings

8 cups papaya chunks	2 limes, juiced and zested	½ cup pure date sugar

Directions and Total Time: 5 minutes freezing time

Blend the papaya, lime juice, and sugar in a food processor until smooth. Transfer the mixture to a glass dish. Freeze for 2 hours. Take out from the freezer and scrape the top ice layer with a fork. Back to the freezer for 1 hour. Repeat the process a few more times, until all the ice is scraped up. Serve frozen garnished with lime zest strips.

Hazelnut Topped Coconut Caramelized Bananas

Ingredients for 4 servings

2 bananas, peeled, halved crosswise and then lengthwise

2 tbsp coconut oil	2 tbsp spiced apple cider
2 tbsp coconut sugar	Chopped hazelnuts for topping

Directions and Total Time: 15 minutes

In a skillet over medium heat, melt the coconut oil. Place in bananas, cook for 2 minutes. Turn them, cook for another 2 minutes. Pour the sugar and cider around the bananas, cook for 2-3 minutes, until thickens and caramelize. Serve into bowls topped with remaining liquid and hazelnuts.

Apple & Cashew Quiche

Ingredients for 6 servings

5 apples, peeled and cut into slices	1 tsp ground cinnamon	½ cup finely chopped cashew
½ cup pure maple syrup	½ cup whole-grain flour	⅔ cup pure date sugar
1 tbsp fresh orange juice	½ cup old-fashioned oats	½ cup plant butter, softened

Directions and Total Time: 45 minutes

Preheat oven to 360 F.

In a bowl, mix the flour, sugar, baking soda, baking powder, cinnamon, and chili.

In another bowl, whisk the oil, vinegar, vanilla, and 1 cup cold water. Pour into the flour mixture, stir to combine. Pour the batter into a greased baking pan. Bake for 30 minutes. Let cool for 10-15 minutes. Take out the cake inverted onto a wire rack and allow to completely cool.

Place the chocolate and soy milk in a pot. Cook until the chocolate is melted. Add in sugar, cook for 5 minutes. Turn the heat off and mix in butter and vanilla. Cover the cake with the glaze. Refrigerate until the glaze set. Serve.

Vanilla Cranberry & Almond Balls

Ingredients for 12 servings

2 tbsp almond butter	¼ cup sesame seeds, toasted	Zest of 1 orange
2 tbsp maple syrup	1 tbsp chia seeds	1 tbsp dried cranberries
¾ cup cooked millet	½ tsp almond extract	¼ cup ground almonds

Directions and Total Time: 25 minutes

Whisk the almond butter and syrup in a bowl until creamy. Mix in millet, sesame seeds, chia seeds, almond extract, orange zest, cranberries, and almonds. Shape the mixture into balls and arrange on a parchment paper-lined baking sheet. Let chill in the fridge for 15 minutes.

Pressure Cooker Apple Cupcakes

Ingredients for 4 servings

1 cup canned applesauce	6 tbsp maple syrup + for sprinkling	½ tsp apple pie spice
1 cup non-dairy milk	¼ cup spelt flour	A pinch of salt

Directions and Total Time: 25 minutes

In a bowl, combine the applesauce, milk, maple syrup, flour, apple pie spice, and salt. Scoop into 4 heat-proof ramekins. Drizzle with more syrup.

Pour 1 cup of water in the IP and fit in a trivet. Place the ramekins on the trivet. Lock lid in place; set the time to 6 minutes on High. Once ready, perform a quick pressure release. Unlock the lid and let cool for a few minutes; take out the ramekins. Allow cooling for 10 minutes and serve.

Roasted Apples Stuffed with Pecans & Dates

Ingredients for 4 servings

4 apples, cored, halved lengthwise	4 dates, pitted and chopped	1 tbsp pure maple syrup
½ cup finely chopped pecans	1 tbsp plant butter	¼ tsp ground cinnamon

Directions and Total Time: 40 minutes

Preheat oven to 360 F.

Mix the pecans, dates, butter, maple syrup, and cinnamon in a bowl. Arrange the apple on a greased baking pan and fill them with the pecan mixture. Pour 1 tbsp of water in the baking pan. Bake for 30-40 minutes, until soft and lightly browned. Serve immediately.

Caribbean Pudding

Ingredients for 4 servings

3 kiwis, divided	1 tbsp cornstarch	1 tbsp turmeric
1 (13.5-oz) can coconut milk	1 tsp vanilla extract	Ground cinnamon
¼ cup organic cane sugar	2 pinches of salt	

Directions and Total Time: 10 minutes + chilling time

In a blender, place the 2 kiwis, coconut milk, sugar, cornstarch, vanilla, and salt. Blitz until smooth. Stir in turmeric. Pour into a pot. Bring to a boil, lower the heat and simmer for 3 minutes, until pudding consistency is achieved. Remove to a bowl and let cool. Refrigerate covered overnight to set.

Before serving, cut the remaining kiwi into slices. In small glasses, put a layer of pudding, a layer of kiwi slices, a layer of pudding, and finish with kiwi slices. Serve sprinkled with cinnamon.

Directions and Total Time: 55 minutes

Preheat oven to 360 F. Place apples in a greased baking pan. Stir in maple syrup and orange juice. Sprinkle with ½ tsp of cinnamon. In a bowl, combine the flour, oats, cashew, sugar, and remaining cinnamon. Blend in the butter until the mixture crumbs. Pour over the apples and bake for 45 minutes.

Tofu & Almond Pancakes

Ingredients for 10 servings

1 ⅓ cups almond milk
1 cup almond flour
⅓ cup firm tofu, crumbled
3 tbsp plant butter, melted
2 tbsp pure date sugar
1 ½ tsp pure vanilla extract
½ tsp baking powder
⅛ tsp salt

Directions and Total Time: 15 minutes

Blitz almond milk, tofu, butter, sugar, vanilla, baking powder, and salt in a blender until smooth. Heat a pan and coat with oil. Scoop a ladle of batter at the center and spread all over. Cook for 3-4 minutes until golden, turning once. Transfer to a plate and repeat the process until no batter is left. Serve.

Almond Berry Cream

Ingredients for 4 servings

3 (15-oz) cans almond milk
3 tbsp maple syrup
½ tsp almond extract
1 cup blueberries
1 cup raspberries
1 cup strawberries, sliced

Directions and Total Time: 10 minutes

Place almond milk in the fridge overnight. Open the can and reserve the liquid. In a bowl, mix almond solids, maple syrup, and almond extract. Share berries into 4 bowls. Serve topped with almond cream.

Blueberry Lime Granizado

Ingredients for 1 serving

½ cup pure date sugar
2 cups blueberries
2 tsp fresh lemon juice

Directions and Total Time: 15 minutes

Place the sugar and ½ cup water in a pot. Cook for 3 minutes on low heat until the sugar is dissolved. Remove to a heatproof bowl and chill for 2 hours in the fridge. Blitz the blueberries and lemon juice in a blender until smooth. Add in cooled sugar and pulse until smooth. Place in an ice cream maker and follow the directions. Once ready, serve immediately or freeze another 1-2 hours for a firm texture.

Coconut Bars with Chocolate Chips

Ingredients for 16 servings

¼ cup coconut oil
1 cups shredded coconut
¼ cup pure date sugar
2 tbsp agave syrup
1 cup vegan chocolate chips

Directions and Total Time: 45 minutes

Grease a dish with coconut oil. Set aside. In a bowl, mix the coconut, sugar, agave syrup, and coconut oil. Spread the mixture onto the dish, pressing down. Place the chocolate chips in a heatproof bowl and microwave for 1 minute. Stir and heat 30 seconds more until the chocolate is melted. Pour over the coconut and let harden for 20 minutes. Chop into 16 bars. Store in a container for up to 1 week.

Lemon Blackberry Cake

Ingredients for 4 servings

4 peaches, peeled and sliced
2 cups fresh blackberries
1 tbsp cornstarch
¾ cup pure date sugar
2 tsp fresh lemon juice
1 tsp ground cinnamon
½ cup whole-grain flour
½ cup old-fashioned oats
3 tbsp plant butter

Directions and Total Time: 45 minutes

Preheat oven to 370 F. In a bowl, mix the peaches, blackberries, cornstarch, ¼ cup of sugar, lemon juice, and ½ tsp of cinnamon. Pour the batter into the pan. Set aside. In a bowl, stir the flour, oats, butter, remaining cup of sugar, and remaining cinnamon. Blend until crumbly. Drizzle the topping over the fruit. Bake for 30-40 minutes, until browned. Serve.

Cinnamon Tropical Cobbler

Ingredients for 6 servings

3 apples, shredded	2 tbsp cornstarch	1 ½ tsp baking powder
2 ripe pineapples, chopped	1 tsp ground cinnamon	¼ tsp salt
2 tsp lemon juice	½ tsp ground allspice	2 tbsp peanut butter, softened
½ cup + 2 tbsp pure date sugar	1 cup whole-grain flour	½ cup soy milk

Directions and Total Time: 45 minutes

Preheat oven to 390 F. Arrange apples and pineapples on a greased baking pan. Drizzle with lemon juice, cornstarch, cinnamon, and allspice. In a bowl, combine flour, sugar, baking powder, and salt. Stir in the peanut butter with a fork until the batter resembles crumbs. Mix in soy milk. Spread the mixture over the fruit and bake for 30 minutes.

Balsamic-Glazed Caramelized Quinces

Ingredients for 4 servings

1 cup balsamic vinegar	¼ tsp grated nutmeg	¼ cup coconut oil
¼ cup + 3 tbsp pure date sugar	A pinch of salt	2 quinces, cored and cut into slices

Directions and Total Time: 20 minutes

Heat a saucepan over medium heat and add in the balsamic vinegar, ¼ cup of date sugar, nutmeg, and salt. Cook for 10-15 minutes, stirring occasionally until the liquid has reduced by half.

Melt the coconut oil in a skillet over medium heat and in place in the quinces; cook for 5 minutes until golden. Stir in 3 tbsp of date sugar and cook for another 5 minutes until caramelized. Serve in a plate drizzled with the balsamic glaze.

Pumpkin Brownie

Ingredients for 4 servings

3 oz dairy-free dark chocolate	½ cup pumpkin puree	⅓ cup whole-wheat flour
1 tbsp coconut oil	2 tbsp pure date sugar	½ tsp baking powder

Directions and Total Time: 20 minutes

Microwave chocolate and coconut oil for 90 seconds. Mix in pumpkin purée and sugar. Stir in flour, baking powder, and pinch of salt. Pour the batter into ramekins. Arrange on a baking dish and pour in 2 cups of water. Bake for 20 minutes at 360 F. Let cool for a few minutes. Serve topped with raspberries.

Coconut & Date Truffles with Walnuts

Ingredients for 8 servings

1 cup pitted dates	extra for coating	1 tsp vanilla extract
1 cup walnuts	½ cup shredded coconut	¼ tsp salt
½ cup sweetened cocoa powder, plus	¼ cup pure maple syrup	

Directions and Total Time: 15 minutes

Blend the dates, walnuts, cocoa powder, maple syrup, vanilla extract, and salt in a food processor until smooth. Let chill in the fridge for 1 hour. Shape the mixture into balls and roll up the truffles in cocoa powder. Serve chilled.

Pumpkin & Mango Lemon Cake

Ingredients for 8 servings

1 ½ cups whole-grain flour	½ tsp baking powder	⅓ cup canola oil
¾ cup pure date sugar	½ tsp ground cinnamon	2 tsp grated lemon zest
¼ cup yellow cornmeal	½ tsp ground allspice	2 tbsp water
1 tsp baking soda	½ tsp ground ginger	1 mango, chopped
½ tsp salt	1 cup pumpkin puree	

Directions and Total Time: 60 minutes

Preheat oven to 360 F.

In a bowl, mix flour, sugar, cornmeal, baking soda, salt, baking powder, cinnamon, allspice, and ginger. In another bowl, whisk pumpkin puree, oil, lemon zest, and water, until blend. Add in the mango. Pour the flour mixture into the pumpkin mixture and toss to coat. Pour the batter into a greased baking pan and bake for 45-50 minutes. Let cool before slicing.

RECIPE INDEX

1. Acorn Squash Stuffed with Beans & Spinach 84
2. African Zucchini Salad 52
3. Alfredo Rice with Green Beans 97
4. Almond Berry Cream 141
5. Almond & Chia Bites with Cherries 138
6. Almond & Chickpea Patties 102
7. Almond & Coconut Granola with Cherries 26
8. Almond Flour English Muffins 14
9. Almond Oatmeal Porridge 23
10. Almond & Raisin Granola 22
11. Almond Yogurt with Berries & Walnuts 22
12. Amazing Tofu Burgers 81
13. Amazing Yellow Smoothie 27
14. American-Style Tempeh Bake with Garden Peas 75
15. Apple & Arugula Salad with Walnuts 61
16. Apple & Cashew Quiche 140
17. Apple Chocolate Smoothie 28
18. Apple-Date Couscous with Macadamia Nuts 24
19. Apple & Kale Salad with Raspberry Vinaigrette 62
20. Apple & Spinach Salad with Nuts & Cranberries 64
21. Apple & Spinach Salad with Walnut Crunch 61
22. Artichoke & Potato Salad 58
23. Artichoke & Tomato Tart with Peanuts 105
24. Arugula Coconut Soup 33
25. Arugula & Hummus Pitas 124
26. Asian Quinoa Sauté 90
27. Asian-Style Bean Soup 31
28. Asian Veggie Stew 50
29. Asparagus & Mushrooms with Mashed Potatoes   93
30. Asparagus with Creamy Puree 70
31. Aunt's Apricot Tarte Tatin 128
32. Authentic Guacamole 124
33. Avocado Coconut Pie 67
34. Avocado Salad with Sesame Seeds 59
35. Avocado Truffles with Chocolate Coating 130
36. Awesome Barley Jambalaya 87
37. Baked Apples Filled with Nuts 129
38. Baked Brussels Sprouts with Cranberries 118
39. Baked Cheesy Spaghetti Squash 68
40. Baked Mustard Beans 87
41. Baked Potato & Black-Eyed Pea Salad 60
42. Baked Potatoes & Asparagus & Pine Nuts 103
43. Baked Spicy Eggplant 112
44. Baked Tofu with Roasted Peppers 72
45. Balsamic Artichoke Hearts 104
46. Balsamic-Glazed Caramelized Quinces 142
47. Balsamic Lentil Salad 54
48. Balsamic Roasted Red Pepper & Pecan Crostini ... 123
49. Balsamic Veggie & Rice Stew 49
50. Banana French Toast with Strawberry Syrup 20
51. Banana-Strawberry Smoothie 29
52. Basil Beet Pasta 101
53. Basil Bell Pepper & Mushroom Medley 102
54. Basil Coconut Soup 40
55. Basil Pesto Seitan Panini 74
56. Basil & Tofu Stuffed Portobello Mushrooms 81
57. Bean & Brown Rice with Artichokes 95
58. Bean & Couscous Salad 53
59. Bean & Farro Salad 52
60. Bean Gyros 81
61. Bean & Pecan Sandwiches 90
62. Bean & Pecan Stuffed Mushrooms 103
63. Bean & Roasted Parsnip Salad 62
64. Bean & Spinach Casserole 80
65. Beet & Carrot Stir-Fry 116
66. Beet & Cucumber Salad with Balsamic Dressing 59
67. Beet Slaw with Apples 62
68. Beet Tofu Salad 51
69. Bell Pepper & Mushroom Soup 34
70. Bell Pepper & Quinoa Salad 63
71. Bell Pepper & Seitan Balls 114
72. Bell Pepper & Spinach with Walnuts 106
73. Bell Peppers Stuffed with Spinach & Tofu 123
74. Bell Pepper & Tempeh Balls with Asparagus 79
75. Berries, Nuts & Cream Bowl 126
76. Berry Cupcakes with Cashew Cheese Icing 132
77. Berry Hazelnut Trifle 130
78. Berry Macedonia with Mint 133
79. Berry Quinoa Bowl 29
80. Black Bean Burgers with BBQ Sauce 73
81. Blackberry Waffles 24
82. Black-Eyed Pea Oat Bake 89
83. Black-Eyed Pea Soup 34
84. Black-Eyed Peas with Sun-Dried Tomatoes 96
85. Black Olive & Chickpea Lunch 80
86. Blueberry Chia Pudding 16
87. Blueberry Lime Granizado 141
88. Blueberry Muesli Breakfast 22
89. Breakfast Naan Bread 15
90. Broccoli Fennel Soup 31
91. Broccoli Hash Browns 13
92. Broccoli & Mango Rice Salad 60
93. Broccoli Stuffed Cremini Mushrooms 82
94. Brown Rice & Bean Chili 43
95. Brussels Sprouts & Tofu Soup 36
96. Buckwheat Pilaf with Pine Nuts 94
97. Bulgur & Bean Bowls with Tortilla Chips 109
98. Bulgur & Kale Salad 56
99. Buttered Carrot Noodles with Kale 110
100. Butternut Squash Coconut Cream Soup 37
101. Butternut Squash Soup 45
102. Cabbage & Bean Stir-Fry 84
103. Cabbage & Red Bean Chili 46
104. Cacao Nut Bites 126

#	Entry	Page
105.	Caprese Casserole	74
106.	Cardamom Coconut Fat Bombs	130
107.	Caribbean Lentil Stew	48
108.	Caribbean Pudding	139
109.	Carrot & Black Bean Chili	85
110.	Carrot & Cabbage Salad with Avocado & Capers	55
111.	Carrot & Mushroom Broth	47
112.	Carrot Nori Rolls	116
113.	Carrot Salad with Cherries & Pecans	62
114.	Carrot-Strawberry Smoothie	27
115.	Cashew Buttered Quesadillas with Leafy Greens	70
116.	Cashew Cheese Pimiento Biscuits	20
117.	Cashew & Cranberry Truffles	135
118.	Cashew Cream Cheese	12
119.	Cashew & Plum Cheesecake	137
120.	Cashew & Raisin Salad with & Haricots Verts	57
121.	Cauliflower Dill Soup	31
122.	Cauliflower Soup with Leeks	35
123.	Cayenne Kale	108
124.	Cayenne Pumpkin Soup	34
125.	Celery Buckwheat Croquettes	92
126.	Celery Butternut Squash Soup	40
127.	Celery & Potato Rice Soup	44
128.	Celery & Potato Soup	30
129.	Cheddar Grits with Soy Chorizo	17
130.	Cheesy Cauliflower Casserole	65
131.	Cherry & Pistachio Bulgur	94
132.	Cherry & Quinoa Tacos	84
133.	Chicago-Style Vegetable Stew	49
134.	Chickpea & Bean Patties	80
135.	Chickpea & Celery Salad	55
136.	Chickpea & Faro Entrée	64
137.	Chickpea & Pecan Balls	121
138.	Chickpea & Quinoa Salad with Capers	61
139.	Chickpea & Vegetable Soup	36
140.	Chili Bean & Brown Rice Tortillas	70
141.	Chili Broccoli & Beans with Almonds	105
142.	Chili Cannellini Bean Stew	50
143.	Chili Gazpacho	46
144.	Chili Roasted Hazelnuts	123
145.	Chimichurri Fusili with Navy Beans	93
146.	Chinese Fried Rice	92
147.	Chinese-Style Cabbage Salad	59
148.	Chipotle Kidney Bean Chili	85
149.	Choco-Berry Smoothie	29
150.	Chocolate Bars with Walnuts	115
151.	Chocolate Campanelle with Hazelnuts	137
152.	Chocolate & Carrot Bread with Raisins	19
153.	Chocolate Fudge with Nuts	131
154.	Chocolate-Mango Quinoa Bowl	23
155.	Chocolate & Peanut Butter Cookies	131
156.	Chocolate Peppermint Mousse	129
157.	Christmas Potato Salad	62
158.	Cilantro Chickpea & Corn Salad	60
159.	Cilantro Okra	98
160.	Cinnamon-Brandy Acorn Squash	108
161.	Cinnamon Buckwheat with Almonds	26
162.	Cinnamon Faux Rice Pudding	130
163.	Cinnamon-Maple Popcorn	116
164.	Cinnamon Pumpkin Pie	133
165.	Cinnamon Tropical Cobbler	142
166.	Citrus Asparagus	99
167.	Citrus-Parsley Mushrooms	125
168.	Classic French Toasts	14
169.	Classic Minestrone Soup	42
170.	Classic Walnut Waffles with Maple Syrup	24
171.	Coconut Artichoke Soup with Almonds	42
172.	Coconut Bars with Chocolate Chips	141
173.	Coconut Blueberry Muffins	25
174.	Coconut Chia Pudding	19
175.	Coconut Chia Pudding	138
176.	Coconut Chocolate Barks	132
177.	Coconut & Chocolate Brownies	136
178.	Coconut & Chocolate Cake	133
179.	Coconut & Chocolate Macaroons	140
180.	Coconut Chocolate Truffles	134
181.	Coconut Cream Pumpkin Soup	30
182.	Coconut & Date Truffles with Walnuts	142
183.	Coconut Fruit Smoothie	28
184.	Coconut Mushroom Soup	37
185.	Coconut Oat Bread	21
186.	Coconut & Parsley Wraps	122
187.	Coconut Peach Tart	135
188.	Coconut Porridge with Strawberries	13
189.	Coconut & Raspberry Pancakes	16
190.	Coconut & Tofu Soup	41
191.	Cold Vegetable Soup	43
192.	Coleslaw & Spinach Salad with Grapefruit	58
193.	Colorful Quinoa Salad	58
194.	Corn & Bean Quesadillas	64
195.	Couscous & Lentil Curry	108
196.	Couscous & Quinoa Burgers	89
197.	Cowboy Salad	63
198.	Cranberry Oat Cookies	28
199.	Cream Soup of Zucchini with Walnuts	34
200.	Creamy Bell Pepper Goulash	107
201.	Creamy Brussels Sprouts Bake	73
202.	Creamy Sesame Bread	15
203.	Crispy Corn Cakes	18
204.	Crispy Mushroom Wontons	121
205.	Crispy Squash Nacho Chips	118
206.	Cuban-Style Millet	91
207.	Cucumber & Carrot Pizza with Pesto	88
208.	Cucumber, Lettuce & Tomato Salad	56
209.	Cucumber & Pear Rice Salad	64
210.	Cucumber Stuffed Tomatoes	124
211.	Cumin Red & White Cabbage with Apples	101
212.	Curried Indian Rolls	87

213.	Curried Tofu with Buttery Cabbage	66	267.	Habanero Pinto Beans with Bell Pepper Pot	88
214.	Curry Bean with Artichokes	95	268.	Hazelnut Snack	120
215.	Curry Cauli Rice with Mushrooms	111	269.	Hazelnut Topped Coconut Caramelized Bananas	140
216.	Curry Mango-Tofu Pitas	120	270.	Hearty Smoothie	27
217.	Daikon Salad with Caramelized Onion	54	271.	Herbed Vegetable Traybake	114
218.	Daikon & Sweet Potato Soup	36	272.	Herby Quinoa with Walnuts	83
219.	Date Caramelized Vegetables	100	273.	Holiday Pecan Tart	132
220.	Delicious Matcha Smoothie	29	274.	Homemade Goji Berry Chocolate Granita	138
221.	Dijon Faro & Walnut Salad	87	275.	Homemade Kitchari	90
222.	Dijon Potato & Carrot Salad	63	276.	Homemade Ramen Soup	34
223.	Dijon Potato Salad	61	277.	Homemade Seedy Bars	120
224.	Dijon Roasted Asparagus	115	278.	Homemade Succotash Stew	48
225.	Dilly Potatoes	105	279.	Hot Bean & Corn Soup	39
226.	Dinner Rice & Lentils	97	280.	Hot Bean Salad	88
227.	Easy Garbanzo Soup	41	281.	Hot Coconut Beans with Vegetables	86
228.	Easy Maple Rice Pudding	135	282.	Hot Crunchy Nuts	116
229.	Easy Pineapple & Jicama Salad	60	283.	Hot Lentil Soup with Zucchini	42
230.	Eggplant Fries with Chili Aioli & Beet Salad	69	284.	Hot Lentil Tacos with Guacamole	86
231.	Eggplant & Hummus Pizza	98	285.	Hot Paprika Lentils	84
232.	Eggplant with Tofu	109	286.	Hot Seitan with Rice	79
233.	Endive Slaw with Olives	95	287.	Italian Bean Soup	36
234.	Energy Chia-Peach Smoothie	27	288.	Italian Holiday Stuffing	94
235.	Fall Medley Stew	50	289.	Italian Potato & Swiss Chard Au Gratin	103
236.	Fantastic Green Salad	61	290.	Italian Vegetable Relish	58
237.	Faro & Black Bean Loaf	91	291.	Jalapeño Quinoa Bowl with Lima Beans	74
238.	Fennel & Corn Chowder	47	292.	Japanese-Style Tofu with Haricots Vert	99
239.	Fennel & Parsnip Bisque	47	293.	Kale & Hummus Pinwheels	123
240.	Festive Nicoise Salad Potato Salad	63	294.	Kale Mushroom Galette	70
241.	Four-Seed Crackers	118	295.	Kale & Mushroom Pierogis	68
242.	French Mushroom Tarts	121	296.	Kale Pizza with Grilled Zucchini	81
243.	French Vegetable Byaldi	104	297.	Kale & Potato Stew	47
244.	Fresh Peach Smoothie	29	298.	Kentucky Cauliflower with Mashed Parsnips	110
245.	Fried Broccoli Salad with Tempeh & Cranberries	54	299.	Kiwi & Peanut Bars	136
246.	Garbanzo Quesadillas with Salsa	122	300.	Korean-Style Buckwheat	102
247.	Garlicky Broccoli Soup	39	301.	Korean-Style Millet	97
248.	Garlic Roasted Carrots	98	302.	Layered Raspberry & Tofu Cups	134
249.	Garlic Veggie Bisque	41	303.	Leek & Mushroom Stroganoff	108
250.	Ginger Broccoli Soup	35	304.	Lemon-Almond Waffles	14
251.	Ginger Squash Soup	41	305.	Lemon Blackberry Cake	141
252.	Gingery Pea & Potato Skillet	82	306.	Lemon-Maple Glazed Carrots	119
253.	Glazed Chili Chocolate Cake	138	307.	Lemon Potato Salad with Kalamata Olives	59
254.	Greek Salad	51	308.	Lemony Arugula with Pine Nuts	107
255.	Green Avocado Carbonara	67	309.	Lemony Chickpeas with Kale	97
256.	Green Bean & Rice Soup	45	310.	Lemony Ditalini Salad with Chickpeas	64
257.	Green Beans & Grilled Tempeh	78	311.	Lemony Green Bean Risotto	85
258.	Green Bean & Zucchini Velouté	46	312.	Lemony Quinoa Muffins	23
259.	Green Onion Corn & Bean Soup	40	313.	Lentil Stuffed Avocados	109
260.	Green Pea & Lemon Couscous	93	314.	Lentil & Sweet Potato Tortillas	108
261.	Green Salsa	125	315.	Lettuce & Tomato Salad with Quinoa	57
262.	Grilled Tofu Mayo Sandwiches	111	316.	Lime Avocado Ice Cream	127
263.	Grilled Vegetables with Romesco Dip	126	317.	Lime Lentil Soup	35
264.	Grilled Zucchini with Spinach Avocado Pesto	68	318.	Lime Pumpkin Soup	43
265.	Guacamole with Daikon	117	319.	Louisiana-Style Sweet Potato Chips	114
266.	Habanero Bean Soup with Brown Rice	40	320.	Macedonia Salad with Coconut & Pecans	130

#	Title	Page
321.	Mango Chocolate Fudge	140
322.	Mango Muffins with Chocolate Chips	135
323.	Mango Rice Pudding	28
324.	Mango Rice Salad with Lime Dressing	51
325.	Maple Banana Oats	25
326.	Maple Blueberry Smoothie	27
327.	Maple Fruit Crumble	138
328.	Maple-Glazed Butternut Squash	117
329.	Maple Green Cabbage Hash	101
330.	Maple-Pumpkin Cookies	121
331.	Mashed Broccoli with Roasted Garlic	112
332.	Matcha-Infused Tofu Rice	92
333.	Mediterranean Chickpeas with Vegetables	85
334.	Mediterranean Pasta Salad	56
335.	Mediterranean Soup	39
336.	Mediterranean Tahini Beans	116
337.	Mediterranean Vegetable Stew	50
338.	Medley of Mushroom Soup	31
339.	Melon Chocolate Pudding	140
340.	Melon & Cucumber Gazpacho	105
341.	Mexican Bean Salad	55
342.	Mexican-Style Soy Chorizo & Rice Bowls	77
343.	Mexican Tofu Scramble	13
344.	Mexican Tortilla Soup	32
345.	Middle Eastern Onion Phyllo	124
346.	Millet Salad with Olives & Cherries	54
347.	Mint Ice Cream	129
348.	Minty Berry Cocktail	125
349.	Minty Eggplant Salad	57
350.	Miso Green Cabbage	98
351.	Mixed Berry Yogurt Ice Pops	131
352.	Mixed Seed Crackers	111
353.	Mixed Seeds Bread	15
354.	Mixed Vegetables with Basil	112
355.	Mom´s Caesar Salad	60
356.	Morning Green Smoothie	28
357.	Morning Naan Bread with Mango Jam	18
358.	Morning Pecan & Pear Farro	24
359.	Moroccan Bean Stew	49
360.	Mushroom & Bean Stew	49
361.	Mushroom Broccoli Faux Risotto	111
362.	Mushroom, Chickpea & Eggplant Stew	48
363.	Mushroom Crepes	19
364.	Mushroom Curry Pie	66
365.	Mushroom Curry Soup	39
366.	Mushroom Fried Rice	94
367.	Mushroom & Green Bean Biryani	67
368.	Mushroom Lettuce Wraps	69
369.	Mushroom Rice Soup	43
370.	Mushroom & Spinach Chickpea Omelet	16
371.	Mushroom & Tofu Soup	37
372.	Mustard Green & Potato Soup	38
373.	Mustard Mac & Cheese	126
374.	Mustard Tofu-Avocado Wraps	117
375.	Mustard Tofu & Cauliflower	109
376.	No-Bread Avocado Sandwich	13
377.	Noodle Soup	42
378.	Nutty Date Cake	132
379.	Oat & Chickpea Burgers with Avocado Dip	79
380.	Oatmeal Cookies with Hazelnuts	134
381.	One-Pot Red Lentils with Mushrooms	91
382.	Onion Rings & Kale Dip	113
383.	Orange-Bran Cups with Dates	24
384.	Orange-Carrot Muffins with Cherries	23
385.	Orange-Glazed Raspberry Muffins	20
386.	Orange Granola with Hazelnuts	21
387.	Orange & Kale Salad	52
388.	Orange Kale Stir-Fry	105
389.	Oregano Chickpeas	92
390.	Oriental Bulgur & White Beans	91
391.	Paprika Baked Beans	124
392.	Paprika Cauliflower Tacos	96
393.	Paprika Fava Bean Patties	89
394.	Paprika Hummus with Mushrooms	123
395.	Paprika Roasted Nuts	112
396.	Paprika Tofu & Zucchini Skewers	115
397.	Parmesan Baby Potatoes	117
398.	Parmesan Broccoli Tots	114
399.	Parsley Bean & Olives Salad	88
400.	Parsley Carrots & Parsnips	99
401.	Parsley Faro & Bean Casserole	106
402.	Parsley Pumpkin Noodles	110
403.	Parsley Veggie Broth	11
404.	Party Matcha & Hazelnut Cheesecake	134
405.	Pasta Primavera with Cherry Tomatoes	83
406.	Pasta & Tomato Soup	38
407.	Pea & Basil Fettuccine	78
408.	Peanut Chocolate Brownies	137
409.	Peanut Quinoa & Chickpea Pilaf	102
410.	Pearl Barley & Vegetable Stew	47
411.	Pecan & Pumpkin Seed Oat Jars	22
412.	Pecan Tempeh Cakes	119
413.	Pepita Cheese Tomato Chips	118
414.	Peppered Pinto Beans	96
415.	Pesto Bread Twists	14
416.	Pesto Mushroom Pizza	77
417.	Picante Green Rice	90
418.	Pistachios & Chocolate Popsicles	134
419.	Plant-Based Cashew Cheese	11
420.	Plant-Based Cheddar Broccoli Gratin	78
421.	Plant-Based Cheddar Cheese	12
422.	Plant-Based Mozzarella Cheese	12
423.	Plant-Based Parmesan Cheese	12
424.	Pomegranate Bell Peppers & Eggplants	107
425.	Pomodoro Cream Soup	37
426.	Poppy-Granola Balls with Chocolate	137
427.	Potato & Cauliflower Hash Browns	16
428.	Potato & Green Bean Salad	57

#	Recipe	Page
429.	Potato Soup with Kale	38
430.	Power Green Smoothie	27
431.	Pressure Cooker Apple Cupcakes	139
432.	Pressure Cooker Celery & Spinach Chickpeas	95
433.	Pressure Cooker Green Lentils	94
434.	Pressure Cooker Green Onion & Potato Soup	33
435.	Primavera Lettuce Rolls	125
436.	Pumpkin Brownie	142
437.	Pumpkin Cake with Pistachios	17
438.	Pumpkin & Garbanzo Chili with Kale	45
439.	Pumpkin & Mango Lemon Cake	142
440.	Pumpkin Soup with Apples	38
441.	Quick Fresh Salad	55
442.	Quinoa a la Puttanesca	84
443.	Quinoa & Chickpea Pot	93
444.	Quinoa & Veggie Burgers	72
445.	Radicchio & Cabbage Coleslaw	59
446.	Radish & Cabbage Ginger Salad	58
447.	Radish & Tomato Salad	55
448.	Raisin Oatmeal Biscuits	136
449.	Raisin & Orzo Stuffed Tomatoes	99
450.	Raisin & Pine Nut Zucchini Rolls	102
451.	Raspberries Turmeric Panna Cotta	129
452.	Raspberry Almond Smoothie	26
453.	Rice, Lentil & Spinach Pilaf	88
454.	Rice Noodle Soup with Beans	35
455.	Rice Wine Mushroom Soup	32
456.	Rice with Green Lentil & Celery	83
457.	Roasted Apples Stuffed with Pecans & Dates	139
458.	Roasted Basil & Tomato Soup	33
459.	Roasted Butternut Squash with Chimichurri	73
460.	Roasted Mushrooms and Green Beans Salad	53
461.	Roasted Sweet Potato Porridge	104
462.	Roman Balsamic Tomato Bruschetta	119
463.	Rosemary Baked Potatoes with Cherry Tomatoes	99
464.	Rosemary Tomato Soup with Parmesan Croutons	45
465.	Rosemary White Bean Soup	37
466.	Rotini & Tomato Soup	44
467.	Saucy Seitan with Sesame Seeds	82
468.	Sautéed Veggies with Rice	104
469.	Savory Pasta Salad with Cannellini Beans	51
470.	Savory Seitan & Bell Pepper Rice	93
471.	Savoy Cabbage Rolls with Tofu & Buckwheat	76
472.	Scallion Sweet Potatoes with Chili Corn Salad	78
473.	Scrambled Tofu with Bell Pepper	17
474.	Scrambled Tofu with Swiss Chard	25
475.	Seitan Cakes with Broccoli Mash	71
476.	Seitan Cauliflower Gratin	75
477.	Seitan & Lentil Chili	86
478.	Seitan & Spinach Salad a la Puttanesca	53
479.	Sesame Cabbage Sauté	113
480.	Sesame Kale Slaw	97
481.	Sesame Roasted Broccoli with Brown Rice	100
482.	Sesame Tempeh Sauté	106
483.	Shallot Lentil Soup with Walnuts	43
484.	Sherry Eggplants with Cherry Tomatoes	101
485.	Sherry-Lime Mango Dessert	138
486.	Sherry Shallot Beans	92
487.	Sicilian Papaya Sorbet	140
488.	Sicilian Spaghetti Squash	106
489.	Simple Apple Muffins	22
490.	Simple Pear Oatmeal	29
491.	Simple Pesto Millet	96
492.	Simple Vegetable Broth	11
493.	Smoked Tempeh with Broccoli Fritters	65
494.	Southern Apple Cobbler with Raspberries	128
495.	Southern Bean Salad	86
496.	Soy Chorizo & Avocado Tacos	120
497.	Soy Chorizo Stuffed Cabbage Rolls	113
498.	Spaghetti Squash in Tahini Sauce	100
499.	Spanish Gazpacho	46
500.	Special Butternut Squash Chili	85
501.	Spicy Apple Pancakes	26
502.	Spicy Bean Soup	32
503.	Spicy Broccoli in Pecan Pesto	109
504.	Spicy Cheese with Tofu Balls	71
505.	Spicy Nut Burgers	120
506.	Spicy Pistachio Dip	112
507.	Spicy Potato Soup	44
508.	Spicy Quinoa Bowl with Black Beans	21
509.	Spicy Steamed Broccoli	97
510.	Spicy Vegetable Paella	103
511.	Spicy Veggie Steaks with Green Salad	65
512.	Spinach & Chickpea Pizza with Avocado	83
513.	Spinach Chips with Guacamole Hummus	110
514.	Spinach & Kale Soup with Fried Collards	30
515.	Spinach & Potato Soup	32
516.	Spinach, Rice & Bean Soup	35
517.	Spinach Salad with Blackberries & Pecans	62
518.	Spinach Soup with Gnocchi	44
519.	Squash Salad	51
520.	Squash & Zucchini Stir-Fry	100
521.	Steamed Broccoli with Hazelnuts	98
522.	Strawberries Stuffed with Banana Cream	115
523.	Strawberry & Pecan Breakfast	20
524.	Stuffed Zucchini Rolls with Tempeh & Tofu	78
525.	Sudanese Veggie Stew	48
526.	Summer Banana Pudding	129
527.	Sunday Soup	38
528.	Sweet African Soup	44
529.	Sweet and Spicy Brussel Sprout Stir-Fry	73
530.	Sweet Kiwi Oatmeal Bars	26
531.	Sweet Orange Crepes	21
532.	Sweet Potatoes with Curry Glaze	100
533.	Swiss Chard & Pecan Stuffed Mushrooms	125
534.	Tamari Lentil Dip	122
535.	Tangerine Banana Toast	25
536.	Tangy Bean Tomato Soup	32

#	Recipe	Page
537.	Tangy Nutty Brussel Sprout Salad	52
538.	Tarragon Potato Chips	122
539.	Tempeh Coconut Curry Bake	76
540.	Tempeh Garam Masala Bake	74
541.	Tempeh & Vegetable Stir-Fry	82
542.	Thyme Black Bean Loaf with Artichokes	107
543.	Thyme Pumpkin Stir-Fry	25
544.	Tofu & Almond Pancakes	141
545.	Tofu Cabbage Stir-Fry	65
546.	Tofu Eggplant Pizza	101
547.	Tofu Goulash Soup	30
548.	Tofu Loaf with Nuts	77
549.	Tofu Mayonnaise	12
550.	Tofu Skewers with Salsa Verde & Squash Mash	69
551.	Tofu & Spinach Lasagna with Red Sauce	66
552.	Tofu Stuffed Peppers	118
553.	Tofu & Tomato Sandwiches	117
554.	Tomato & Alfredo Fettuccine	77
555.	Tomato Artichoke Pizza	75
556.	Tomato & Avocado Lettuce Salad	53
557.	Tomato Bean & Bulgur Salad	63
558.	Tomatoes Stuffed with Chickpeas & Quinoa	114
559.	Tomato Lentil Stew	48
560.	Traditional Cilantro Pilaf	91
561.	Traditional Lebanese Salad	55
562.	Tropical Cheesecake	136
563.	Tropical French Toasts	19
564.	Tropical Salad	56
565.	Tropical Smoothie Bowl	28
566.	Turmeric Bean Soup	33
567.	Turnip & Parsnip Broth	11
568.	Turnip & Rutabaga Soup	42
569.	Vanilla Berry Tarts	131
570.	Vanilla Brownies	127
571.	Vanilla Cookies with Poppy Seeds	136
572.	Vanilla Cranberry & Almond Balls	139
573.	Vanilla Crepes with Berry Cream Compote Topping	18
574.	Vanilla White Chocolate Pudding	128
575.	Vegan Cheesecake with Blueberries	127
576.	Vegan Cordon Bleu Casserole	76
577.	Vegan Mushroom Pizza	68
578.	Vegetable & Black Bean Soup	40
579.	Vegetable Chili	46
580.	Vegetable & Hummus Pizza	80
581.	Vegetable & Rice Soup	36
582.	Vegetable & Rice Vermicelli Lettuce Rolls	122
583.	Vegetable Soup with Vermicelli	39
584.	Vegetarian Quinoa Curry	96
585.	Veggie Paella with Lentils	95
586.	Veggie Panini	17
587.	Walnut Chocolate Squares	127
588.	Walnut Lentil Burgers	89
589.	Walnut & Tempeh Ball	119
590.	Warm Collard Salad	52
591.	Warm Green Bean & Potato Salad	54
592.	Watercress & Mushroom Spaghetti	82
593.	White Chocolate Fudge	130
594.	White Pizza with Mixed Mushrooms	71
595.	White Salad with Walnut Pesto	86
596.	Yummy Vegetarian Burritos	119
597.	Zesty Rice Bowls with Tempeh	76
598.	Zoodle Bolognese	72
599.	Zucchini & Bell Pepper Salad with Beans	56
600.	Zucchini Boats with Vegan Cheese	72

Made in the USA
Coppell, TX
02 November 2020